Babies

Dr Christopher Green

Babies

A parent's guide to enjoying baby's first year

Illustrations by Roger Roberts

SIMON &
SCHUSTER

London · New York · Sydney · Toronto

Author's note

It is an unfortunate fact that the English language has no polite and neutral term to refer to both boys and girls at the same time. I have, therefore, alternated using 'he' and 'she' by chapter. Please interpret this to suit your own little one.

First published in Australia in 1988 by
Simon & Schuster Australia Pty Ltd
Suite 2, Lower Ground Floor, 14–16 Suakin Street, Pymble NSW 2073

First revised edition published in 1996
Second edition published in 2001
This updated and revised edition first published in Great Britain
by Simon & Schuster UK Ltd, 2010
A CBS COMPANY

Text © Christopher Green
Illustrations © Roger Roberts, Simon & Schuster Australia

1 3 5 7 9 10 8 6 4 2

Simon & Schuster UK Ltd
1st Floor
222 Gray's Inn Road
London WC1X 8HB

www.simonandschuster.co.uk

Simon & Schuster Australia
Sydney

Internal Design by Squirt Creative
Illustrations by Roger Roberts
Additional illustrations by Margaret Hastie

A CIP catalogue record for this book
is available from the British Library.

ISBN: 978-1-84737-779-1

Printed in the UK by CPI Mackays, Chatham ME5 8TD

Contents

Acknowledgements

My first thank you is to my late wife, Dr Hilary Green, without whose inspiration, support and encouragement none of my books would have been created. Sadly Hilary never saw the completed new edition of this book, but through it her ideas will be remembered.

Thanks also to the gifted editors who have brought colour to my writing: Michael Morton-Evans and Belinda Castles.

I also very much appreciate the help of the following:

Vanessa Hill (Aus)
Professor Irene Green (UK)
Dr Morag Reid (UK)
Professor Michael Green (UK)
Sue Solvyns (Aus)
Judi Green (Aus)
Gaye Faunders (Aus)
Dr Henry Kilham (Aus)
Sue Williams (Aus)
Janis Mendoza (Aus)
Dr Joe Waks (Aus)
Dr Huntley Dunne (Aus)
Lorraine Partington (Aus)

About the author

I was born in Belfast in peaceful times and spent a happy childhood there. I have to admit that I wasn't particularly keen on school. I felt that it interfered with my life, in particular my love of climbing mountains and sailing. But I battled through and made it to university where I studied medicine, specialising in paediatrics. As a young doctor I practised in Canada and volunteered in Malawi. Working in a 40-bed hospital in Africa I discovered the reality of life and death. Along with my wife, Dr Hilary Green, we helped as best we could, performing emergency caesareans, administering the only form of anaesthetic available—an ether mask. At night, when the electricity was off, we used lanterns and because ether is so flammable we had to do without anaesthetics until dawn. Hardly any drugs were available in general, and the enormity of disease and sickness was overwhelming.

I went on to carry out postgraduate studies at the Sydney Children's Hospital, working towards being a specialist with seriously ill children. That was my area of interest and how I wanted to distinguish myself. However, within a year in Sydney I had accidentally stumbled into the area of child development, in particular finding practical solutions to behavioural problems. I realised I could make a real difference in an area no-one seemed to be doing much about. Such are the chance happenings that decide the course of our lives.

Returning as a consultant and lecturer to the Royal Belfast Hospital for Sick Children, I published a paper promoting the use of nebulisers for severe asthma, a treatment at that time successfully used in Australia but not the UK, though it is now widely accepted. More significantly for my later career I published a paper on toddler behaviour which drew wide attention.

After three years, and with heavy hearts, we left the security of a close extended family in Belfast with our two toddlers. It was a painful yet exciting time and it was difficult to know whether it was the right decision as I moved my family across the world to be Head of the Child Development Unit at the Sydney Children's Hospital.

Over the next twenty years I spent every day working with children and their parents, who taught me almost everything I know. I also ran parents groups, which snowballed into lectures, radio appearances and eventually television. I did a lot of talking and enjoyed it immensely! And people seemed to like what I was saying. It was suggested that I write a book and to date I have written four books with twenty editions in over twelve languages. After leaving our home in Ireland, Sydney was kind to us. Our family loved the outdoor life, my boys were quickly addicted to surfing, and I was busy with lectures in the UK, the US, New Zealand and Australia.

But this busy, happy life came to an abrupt halt in 1999 with a near-death medical emergency—a stroke resulting from surgery that didn't go to plan. I recovered with a clear head but without the ability to speak. As my speech began to return, the enforced change of pace made me realise what was most important in life and in the care of children. However, this newfound perspective was severely tested by the shatteringly early death of my wife Hilary after 30 years of marriage.

Again I was forced into recovery mode and I'm happy to tell you that there have been good times since the bad. I have recently been awarded an AOM in the Queen's Birthday Honours list for services to children's medicine and I married my new wife, Judi. We love the sea and escape when we can, to sleep in on our little yacht in a quiet bay. There is now even more time to reflect on what is important. And my writing has once more been there to help.

This book comes from a gentler author than the busy doctor of old. The secret to successful childcare is what we all know in our hearts: children need our attention and our appreciation, to be noticed and listened to. That never changes. This book is not intended as a manual. It is a reminder to everyone to witness the wonder of small children because it is so fleeting and so very precious.

Introduction

It is 22 years since the first edition of *Babies* was published. It is amazing how much the world has changed in that time. In 1988, Ronald Reagan was President of the USA and none of us knew what the internet was. Now we have Barack Obama, Google and a new century. The world seems like a very different place to the one in which I sat down to write my first book about the everyday miracle we know as babies.

I've changed a lot too since that day. There have been many years of working with small children on a daily basis, but just as importantly as a lifetime of caring for babies and their families has been an event in my personal life which turned everything upside down. Several years ago I was struck by a serious illness. The road to recovery has been long and hard, but I have emerged with a deeper interest in the miracle of life that I had perhaps come to take for granted. You see before you a gentler Dr Green who is less concerned with 'taming' small children than appreciating the wonder they bring to our lives. What I hope you will find in this book is friendly advice that's been tried and tested with thousands of babies. It comes from a point of view that has mellowed with the years and with experience of life.

The world may have changed, and me along with it, but surprising as it may seem, babies ultimately remain the same. A bit bigger perhaps, but still the same little bundle of baffling behaviour and joy. And parents bring along the same fears, frustrations and uncertainties to the job, along with their astonishment that this little person they have created is so perfect. (Often this sense of wonder is strongest when their child is fast asleep and for the moment incapable of reducing them to a nervous wreck!)

All the parents I've met want to know pretty much the same thing. Is this normal? Is it time to worry? And time and again parents and professionals come up against the same eternal truths:

- New babies cry more than you expect.
- New babies wake more at night than you expect.
- New parents are more uncertain than they ever have been before.
- New parents are more tired than they could have imagined possible.

Add to these the shock of birth, the scrambled hormones and emotions, the gap between expectations and reality and it's no wonder that along with the joy of new life comes a feeling at times of being overwhelmed.

In this edition of *Babies* I have kept in mind that amid the deluge of expertise available these days, new mums and dads can feel swamped. A great deal of the information out there may be this year's fad, soon to be replaced by next year's big thing, and so on. It can be hard to hear useful advice when your head is full of the clamour of experts and media pundits.

This book draws upon 30 years of working day to day as a paediatrician with a special interest in small children and their families, and aims to provide an up-to-date and commonsense foundation for peaceful parenting. My own experience of being the father of a colicky baby taught me very quickly how easy it is to feel like a failure. Sometimes what we all need is a gentle voice to remind us to give things a little time and the baby a little cuddle and ask ourselves if the problem in front of us is as insurmountable as it seems. The best way forward is to understand, nurture and enjoy your baby and each other whenever possible.

I must admit that many of the practical ideas in this book are not mine, but those of the many, many parents I have worked with over the decades. As you read the book you may chuckle as you recognise yourself, your husband, your mother-in-law or your baby behaving as irrationally as we all do. Parents need a sense of humour to survive. If you can stand back and laugh at what you and your children get up to then children can be a lot of fun.

The new *Babies* is about living with a very brief miracle. The part of your life when your children are small passes too quickly to spend it worrying needlessly. Just when you're coming to terms with the tiny person that has barged into your world, along comes toddlerdom and a whole new set of trials, tribulations and triumphs. Relax. Enjoy the ride. It will be quick, exhilarating and frequently delightful. This is what the new Greener way of caring for children is all about.

Dr Christopher Green

Planning for a
new life

We used to talk about the 'change of life child'. I believe that every first baby is a change of life child. After the birth, you will never be quite the same person again. And though it may be hard to believe when you peer into the mirror to find a sleep-deprived stranger looking back at you, this change is for the better. This book is about change, attitudes and expectations and steering your way through them all to enjoy these years of wonder.

Charting the course

It takes at least a year's planning to sail around the world. The sailor who means to survive and succeed takes the time to plot a course that will as far as possible avoid pirates and tornadoes but allow for squally days and difficult tides. When we plan a family, it's easy to drift along unprepared or at the other extreme frighten ourselves rigid with the fear of failure.

Let's for a moment take an idealistic approach and assume that there is time to plot our course a few months before we embark. This book is a map and a guide. It aims to help you sail into new waters happily and survive the odd day of drenched exhaustion.

If the mooring ropes have slipped away and you have set sail on this journey of a lifetime, you may wish to join us in Chapter Two, in which Baby is ready to join us, and the adventure really begins. Otherwise, let's take a little time to prepare.

Time to commit

When we talk about the word 'commit', committing murder may spring to mind. The difference here is that the sentence for committing to children is life, not fifteen years or so!

Jokes aside, this time before the baby arrives is a time for you to make a shared commitment to your partner. Everyone will be happy to share the joy and wonderment of a new baby, but we mustn't forget the messy bits of childhood, the sleepless nights, the sickness and the worries about every facet of being responsible for a small, helpless person.

And those caring for Baby should ideally make a commitment to themselves to be as healthy as possible. We're talking about the long haul. You're going to need a body that will see you through. It needs to be nourished with healthy food, a bit of activity, at most only moderate alcohol intake and avoidance of smoking and other harmful substances.

A healthy environment also requires stability. In a home with children the best path is usually the most peaceful path. Dramatic confrontations should be rare. (Toddlers may have their own ideas about this but we do not need to join in the fun). Your family, whether it's made up of Mum and Dad or an array of aunties, grandparents and second cousins, needs to share a commitment to a stable and loving environment.

You don't need to be Dr Phil to know that children thrive when their families are happy and united. This provides the foundation for emotionally intact adults. If there are problems at home that go beyond the usual wear and tear of family life they need to be resolved peacefully. This may require new skills and at times superhuman effort. We can all agree that the effort is worth it, when we see happy and secure children growing into happy and secure adults.

Apples don't fall too far from the tree

As we wait for the baby to grow, many of us spend a lot of time dreaming about a perfect little child with lovely habits and manners. I am sure that you will do your best to create a model citizen, but it is interesting to note the degree to which our own traits and temperaments are passed onto our children.

If you are both tall, clearly there is a good chance that the baby will grow up to be tall as well. The same goes for temperament. You and your partner's little ticks and habits may decide whether your children will be easy, exciting or difficult.

In my work with hard-to-handle children I often saw a tired mum who would ask me: How did we end up with such a non-stop, busy, difficult child? Then Dad barges in twitching, rocking in his seat and bursting with the need to get on with life outside the four walls of my office. You don't need a geneticist to tell you what's going on here.

If you are both blessed with even tempers and tend to breeze through life without a backward glance, you may well be the lucky parents of an 'easy' baby, toddler, schoolchild and adult. If one of the parents has a short fuse and is never quite settled, there's a good chance of a more 'interesting' journey.

I only touch on this fascinating topic briefly here, and I am not suggesting a lengthy period of abstinence or contraception while you hunt down the perfect genetic material to pass on, but when we are shaping our expectations of parenthood, it is as well to remember that the apple never falls too far from the tree.

The best start

The science of reproduction is an interesting subject but Nature has a way of ignoring our best-laid plans. You can plan to the very day when to stop the pill in order to have a spring baby, but it's a lucky fluke if you can really plan what happens next. You may not be able to decide when the baby is coming, but you can prepare yourself for a healthy start.

If you know you want to conceive in the next year, ideally you would plan at least three to six months out from possible conception. You would have a preconception consultation with your doctor, a longer-than-usual appointment that will involve a fairly detailed discussion about your health and family background as well as various tests.

You should expect questions about medications, including herbal preparations, smoking, alcohol and recreational drugs. It's a good idea for Dad to get checked out as well but obviously Mum is going to bear the brunt of the medical scrutiny. Your doctor will want to know whether you are up to date with Pap smears and will test you for immunity for diseases such as rubella. If there is not enough immunity to rubella a vaccination can be offered, but be quite sure you are not pregnant and strict contraception must be used for at least another month afterwards as the vaccination presents a risk to an existing foetus. The risk from rubella is serious though, so if there's time, it is worth protecting yourself and your baby with the immunisation.

Then it's time to explore the family tree. Your doctor will want to know whether there are any inheritable conditions where there may be an increased family susceptibility like diabetes or neural tube defects. And lastly you need to discuss whether you are expecting public or private health care for your pregnancy and birth. Be aware that there are waiting periods for private cover if you are not currently a member of a fund.

The mother-in-waiting now needs to do a little health house-keeping.

- Take 0.5 mg of folic acid in a supplement each day, if possible for three months before conception and the first three months of pregnancy.
- Reduce coffee intake to two cups a day at most.
- Alcohol consumption should be very moderate or avoided altogether.
- X-rays are to be avoided.
- Be careful around fish. There are some, like swordfish and tuna, that have been found to have risky levels of mercury.
- Avoid unpasteurised cheese, paté and smoked salmon, and salads, cold meats and sandwiches that have been sitting under a deli counter because of the danger of listeriosis. Always aim for fresh, unfiddled-with foods.
- Don't overheat your body in spas and saunas.
- Sensible exercise is a good idea and so in general is sex!

And now you're seaworthy ...

What are the odds?

Once you are ready to make a baby you would probably love to conceive instantaneously, but in the interests of sanity it's not a bad idea at this stage to be aware of the statistics of successful conception.

For under 35s:
- After one month, twenty per cent of couples having regular sex may expect to conceive.
- After six months, 60 per cent will conceive.
- After a year the figure is around 85 per cent.

For this age group, it's advisable to wait a year before talking to your doctor about any kind of intervention. When the mother is over 35 we would get onto it a little sooner. In this case it's worth a chat with your doctor after six months of trying.

Stacking the odds in your favour

Making babies is supposed to be so natural that it just happens, but Nature often needs a little nudge. Here are a few ideas that may help put you over the line.

Timing is everything
- The clock starts on the first day of a woman's period.
- Fourteen days later the egg is ready.
- This egg will survive for about one day.
- The sperm will survive for about two to four days.
- So around this time, about halfway through a woman's menstrual cycle, is when Dad is called to action.

It looks easy, but Nature is not a machine. Most eggs arrive around the fourteenth day, but some arrive sooner, some later, and even in the same woman there are variations.

In the old days we used to graph temperature to try to predict the egg's release. Now there's a much more accurate method. You can buy a kit from the pharmacy that will test urine or saliva and tell you with 99 per cent certainty the two days within which ovulation will occur.

Why not try ...?
- Good health can make a difference: cut out smoking and alcohol, eat good food and be active.

- Why not try the old wives' tale that says the man should do away with his tight 'Jocks' in order to drop the temperature of the relevant equipment. This seems to have worked a treat for generations of kilt-wearing Scots!

Lastly, one of the most important things you can do is relax. That's a hard thing to do when you want something more than anything else, and you're worrying about split-second timing and when to race home from work for an important meeting with your husband. But when reproduction becomes a duty rather than a joy it can hinder rather than help the situation.

Life goes on in the meantime and it is too precious to waste worrying. Try not to push too hard, the odds are good that Baby will come along soon enough.

How did I get here?

While we're coasting along, waiting for Baby to make an appearance, it is worth stopping to think about the mind-boggling statistics of reproduction. Truly, the odds of you being *you* are infinitesimal.

Each woman has the capacity to make one million eggs, or each ovary is capable of carrying 500,000 eggs.

Obviously only a small proportion of these will be used, just one or two a month, while the next cab off the rank beeps its horn to get going. Overall, a woman will probably release about 400 eggs in her lifetime.

Meanwhile, a man will produce many trillions of sperm. On one sexual encounter he will release about 80 million. (Yes—80 *million*.) You wonder why it can take awhile to conceive with that many tadpoles swimming around, but it's a difficult journey and only the strongest survive.

Actually, it's staggering to think how you ever came to be here in the first place. All the people in the world, all those eggs and sperm, and here you are. There's no-one else like you. And there'll be no-one else like your baby either. Life *is* a miracle.

Is this it?

The first you know of pregnancy is usually a missed period, but women often say that they feel different too. There may be queasiness or a tingling sensation in the breasts. Nowadays most women bypass the doctor at this stage and buy a test from the pharmacy. These are very accurate, but many do a second test, just to be sure it's really happening.

Then it's time to talk to your doctor, discuss the kind of care you'll be having if you haven't already and make sure you're on top of what you need to do to keep healthy. Then you'll begin scheduling tests, in particular the scans.

SCANS

When I was a medical student I was strongly influenced by a very wise obstetrician who had the uncanny knack of knowing how a baby was doing with the very few tests that were then available. He taught me a lot about obstetrics, but there has been a massive change in the technology since those days, particularly in the use of scans. Nowadays a skilled obstetrician has the support of amazing technology, giving you access to a huge amount of information before the baby ever emerges from the womb.

Ultrasound is a technology that works like a depth sounder used by deep-sea fishermen to find the biggest shoals of fish. The fisherman transmits a sound down from the boat which bounces off the ocean floor and is picked up by a receiver on the boat. This tells the distance from the boat to the bottom of the ocean. The sound waves also bounce off any fish in the line of fire, though the fish are completely unaware that anything has happened. Exactly the same thing applies to your baby. The sound waves bouncing off the baby give us a large amount of information in a painless, safe and evermore detailed manner.

The ten-to-thirteen week scan

This gives early, basic information, showing whether the mother's dates are correct and whether major systems are developing normally. This scan also measures nuchal translucency, which is then correlated with other data to give an adjusted risk of chromosomal defects. If the risks are above an acceptable score more invasive tests will be suggested. It's possible to get false readings which can lead to weeks of needless worry, but don't let that put you off. The ultimate aim of all these tests is a healthy baby and decent quality of life for the parents.

I am a strong believer that every test suggested should be taken, the results considered very seriously and advice acted upon. What you decide now has a permanent bearing on the lives of three people.

The eighteen-to-22 week scan

This will be a memorable day. It is the day on which you will be introduced to the little person who is inside of you, and who may have given you several months of heartburn.

As Mum and Dad are shown legs, feet, brain, heart, they are given a wonderful journey around the baby they are waiting for. Many mums say that they felt that this was the moment they began to bond. One told me that later, when she met her baby in person, she recognised her nose from the scan pictures.

The scan will show a lot, including a little heart giving life. At this check, you will often be able to see whether it's a boy or girl, but the sonographer won't tell you if you don't want them to. You'll often see Baby flipping around like a mad thing, even before you've felt any movement, and occasionally the scan can show you the wonderful moment in which a thumb finds a mouth. Suddenly there's something to show for the nausea and tiredness. Baby is really in there!

After this scan, we're halfway there.

SPEED BUMPS—THE COMMON CONCERNS OF PREGNANCY

In Victorian novels ladies 'with child' seemed to do an awful lot of swooning, fainting and being taken weak. We're a bit more realistic now about what goes on: overwhelming tiredness, tender breasts and a stomach that may well reject anything that goes near it. In the 21st century, most first-time mums are trying to hold down a busy job and their breakfast all at the same time!

Nausea—'morning' sickness

This seems to get going in earnest at about the sixth week of pregnancy and for many mums has gone by the tenth to twelfth week. Everyone is affected differently. Some just feel a little fragile, while others are turned inside out with morning, noon and night sickness. For a few unfortunate mums, this goes on solidly for nine long months, turning a time of happiness into an endurance test.

The treatment of morning sickness is much the same as for sea sickness, but without the tablets. As you roll your way across the Pacific on that big white cruise ship, you soon learn to nibble and to avoid strong-tasting and fatty foods.

If you feel delicate:
- Keep a packet of dried fruit or a few biscuits or crackers with you throughout the day.
- Toast and black tea have stood the test of time and been the saviour of generations of pregnant mums.
- Ginger settles things down for many—ginger tea, ginger biscuits, ginger beer—whatever helps.
- Get Dad involved, he can bring you some food before you get out of bed—that first moment when you try to get out of bed with an empty stomach is often the worst.
- If nausea is extremely severe an obstetrician may discuss the use of antiemetics.

Beware of major cooking projects in the first months as the smells of cooking can cause a very sudden upset in the stability of the stomach. A microwave can be very handy. Not only is it quick, but it keeps its smells to itself until the food is ready.

Talk to other mums and get their best tips. Remember that it will probably be over by the twelfth week.

Tiredness

This is a major complaint and many women will say that they felt utterly washed out even before they realised they were pregnant. This is presumably due to the sudden change in the delicate balance of the body's hormones. The good news is that for most women this will settle down after a few months.

There are no medals for pretending you're full of energy. Don't be afraid to put your feet up, grab a snooze or go to bed early whenever possible.

Back discomfort

In the final months of pregnancy there often comes back discomfort. It's not generally an acute pain, just an inability to get comfortable whatever position you try in a chair or in bed. That's why you often see well-advanced mums clutching their little back pillows.

Because of the change in the centre of gravity some mums develop a curve in their back with tummy out and shoulders drawn back that leads to discomfort in the lower spine. The physiotherapist at the antenatal class will demonstrate exercises to try or offer advice on how to hold a better posture.

Heartburn

Over-relaxed muscles of the gut and increased abdominal pressures let acid food regurgitate out of the stomach. There are a few ways to reduce or avoid the discomfort of heartburn. Try not to overfill the stomach, avoid stooping by bending your knees to lift and even place the head of the bed on bricks to work with gravity. A good antacid can be used to neutralise things. These won't harm the baby but if in doubt check with your pharmacist or doctor.

Let's cut the gloom
We could sit here all day talking about restless legs, sleep disturbance, uncomfortable breasts and all the rest, but while none of this is much fun, it will be over soon. Some mothers get through the unpleasant bits by reminding themselves of the amazing fact that they are making a human being. Some are lucky enough to get off scot-free. So let's move swiftly on, safe in the knowledge that all this will be forgiven and forgotten once we meet the little person who's caused all this trouble.

ANTENATAL CARE—THE WAITING GAME

The first thing to get used to when you discover that you are pregnant is waiting. It's not just the nine-month wait for the baby. You wait to be seen at the doctor's, you queue to have tests, you wait to see the results. Then you queue to book the next appointment.

Antenatal clinics have much in common with airports. It's not the length of the flight that wastes your day, it's all the hanging around at the terminal. Of course you don't have to check in an hour before take-off, but unfortunately clinics rarely run to timetable. Just when you thought you were home and hosed, off runs your obstetrician to the labour ward and you're left (along with a lot of other people) for the rest of the day. Take a good book and be mentally prepared for a wait, then if it runs to time you will be pleasantly surprised.

The antenatal class
These classes are run by maternity units in public and private hospitals and some health centres. I see these as essential for the first baby and many find it helpful to return for the second as a useful refresher.

All the wonderful things you learn here about pregnancy, birth and the baby are no longer thought of as 'secret women's business'.

It's recognised that this is life-changing stuff for Dad too. If he's been buried under work and hasn't had a chance to think about what's approaching, now is the time for him to get on board. The more fully all involved understand the phenomenon of birth, the more deeply they will cherish the experience and the less bewildering they will find it. Some of the bigger hospitals even have information sessions for grandparents!

The classes will provide commentary on what your body is going through now and what's on the road ahead. There'll be talks, videos and practical demonstrations. You'll find out how to strengthen the body for delivery and how to succeed at breast-feeding, options on pain reduction, breathing to assist the delivery, what partners can do to help and information on the early days of caring for your baby. There will also be a visit to a delivery suite. This might not seem very important but getting familiar with the space now will reduce stress on the day. You'll also be given plenty of information about when to call the birthing unit and when to just pile in the car and get going.

The classes are often lighthearted and casual though the subject matter may be all you've thought about for months. There is often a lot of laughter in an antenatal class as couples swap stories and remedies and share the nerves that come before the Big Day.

Nesting

You might think nesting is for the birds but humans nest too. Call it whatever you like as you dream of the perfect yellow for Baby's room and browse catalogues from the baby stores, but humans instinctively prepare themselves for the arrival of a baby.

Nesting starts in the middle months of pregnancy and may intensify as the countdown begins. In these months the expectant mother will often be elated, energetic and glowing. So this is a time of planning, renovation and painting (take care with nasty solvents—Dad can clean the brushes) and buying, borrowing or begging all the gear. Nesting is also a time to take stock and tidy up. All this preparation is like painting the set for opening night.

Some are superstitious about planning or buying so much as a nappy ahead of the moment when they actually feel their baby in their arms. That's OK, but it might be useful to have a bit of a window-shop or browse on eBay for a last-minute spree. When the baby comes you'll be too busy to decide what sort of stroller you want. And failing all else, the baby capsule needs to be in the car by the time you leave hospital.

At our place the Greens were major renovators and nesters. We wanted everything just right when we came home from hospital with a new family member. The bright shiny new paint did not impress the baby. All he wanted was warmth, a good supply of milk and lots of love. But for tired parents, it was a nice environment to be in and a comfort in the sleepless nights ahead.

BIRTHING OPTIONS

When Baby is just a tiny bump it seems like birthing options are a long way off but it's often necessary to book as far ahead as possible or choices become limited.

The options are:
- public maternity hospital unit where you'll see the midwives—this may be shared care with your GP
- private maternity hospital unit
- birth centre (public)
- home birth

Hospital
Giving birth in a large hospital gives you the extra security of readily available specialist obstetricians, anaesthetists, paediatricians, a neonatal intensive care unit, blood bank and testing laboratory.

Not all hospitals are the same. Your local country hospital's public ward may be a more homely experience than staying in the private ward of a big city hospital. But private is generally quieter and if nothing else the food is better!

The choice is a bit like deciding whether to fly long haul in economy or business. It is still long and tedious and the only real concern is a safe arrival.

Birth centre

This is a relatively new concept and is the closest thing to a home birth experience that you'll find in a hospital environment. It's the best of both worlds: access to the security of the hospital and a quieter, cosier room that may make you feel more relaxed. It's close to the main birthing unit so if there are any problems, such as not progressing, you can be moved easily. These centres are increasingly popular so think about this option early if it appeals to you.

Home birth

This option appeals to many because you are not subject to the regimentation of a hospital regime and many find their home environment a source of comfort. Sometimes those on their second pregnancy may decide they're ready to give birth at home.

Whichever birth it is if you take this option your obstetrician will screen you carefully to ensure that yours is a low-risk pregnancy. The birth will be screened by a specialist midwife who will provide support, guidance and reassurance.

There is always the chance for families who plan a home birth that their doctor may decide at a late stage that they need to be in hospital. Others may have to be rushed to hospital as events unfold. Families who feel strongly about home birth may suffer disappointment if it turns out this way.

In my early years as a paediatrician I spent countless days and nights in the delivery room and special care unit. I know that about five per cent of babies are slow to start breathing and for that reason if no other I favour hospitals. My view is that whatever option you choose the main goal must always be a safe outcome for mother and infant. The birth may not turn out quite as planned, but as long as everyone's safe, this is only the start of the road. It's what happens next that really matters. We have the whole of childhood to look forward to.

THE FINAL COUNTDOWN

As the day approaches when we will meet the little person who will mean so much to us, the first-time mum will have trouble seeing past that hurdle called birth. It's easy to believe as you anticipate the birth that once it's out of the way, all the stress and worry will be at an end. The second-time mum knows that birth will be over quickly and the real concern is how she will cope with the tiredness and demands of looking after a baby as well as a jealous toddler.

Perhaps what experience teaches us is that we can never know in advance exactly how things will be: the birth, the baby, even ourselves. It's easy to waste a lot of energy worrying about the wrong things. We don't know what will happen. That's why it's an adventure.

Ready or not, it's time to set sail …

Birth—the story really begins

A s the 40-week wait grinds to an end, this is where our story really begins. By now the memory of a slim figure and a walk without a waddle will be but a distant one. The trip to hospital is close and all thoughts will now start to focus on that one major event—giving birth. There will, of course, be a few nagging worries. How will I know when it's time to go to hospital? Will the birth be painful? Will I be sore afterwards? Will I cope with the baby? Who will look after the other children? Will my husband starve to death? What will my home look like when I get back? Will someone have remembered to take the garbage out? Will the dog be weak with malnutrition? What overgrowth of fungus will be in the fridge? All these questions and more will begin to niggle at you. The secret is to think ahead, plan ahead and be prepared!

THE PREPARATIONS

A packed bag

First you should pack that little bag of life's necessities which you will take to the hospital. You're not packing for a world tour, so keep the contents simple. A couple of pairs of pyjamas, a dressing gown, toiletries and a couple of books—these are the sorts of things you will need. Visitors can always bring what you forget and anyway most hospitals have shops these days and are very keen to accept your money! For those with toddlers, remember to keep the bag well out of reach. Helpful little hands may repack it with personal treasures. The discovery of a much-chewed teddy bear instead of your pyjamas is only likely to add to the confusion of your sudden arrival in the labour ward. As the day draws closer, make sure the labour unit is handy, that you have reliable transport and that you have the booking papers.

Other children

If you have other children, plans must be made for them to be looked after when you go. Grandparents are often the best people to look after the children, but if they are not available, anyone the child knows well and feels happy with will do. Children should be told what is about to happen, whether they fully understand the finer details or not. You should be quite open in your talk of babies right from the earliest days. If you don't include children in conversations about the baby, they will pick up the change in the air and feel anxious. They can understand being told about a new brother or sister, and about crying babies and pooey nappies. Lots of preparation will help smooth out any problems of jealousy and gives the best chance of producing an enthusiastic little helper.

Malnutrition and husbands

If you are married to a non-cooking male, you had better run a crash course in tin-opening, egg-boiling and bacon-frying, or leave a few frozen offerings in the freezer. If you return home to discover these haven't been touched and the family ate take-away every night, don't worry. This reduction in catering output need only be temporary. As your strength returns, so will a more impressive menu. But be reassured, however much your husband complains, nothing is going to drop off due to malnutrition!

Baby names

It may seem a little premature at this stage, but it does help to consider a few children's names before the event. When you first hold the little one and your eyes meet, how much nicer to have a name on your lips than to have to say 'it'. On the subject of names, let me just offer a couple of tips. It is generally unwise to resurrect one from an old boyfriend or girlfriend. I realise that for those parents who led a particularly active life before marriage, this may reduce the available repertoire quite dramatically. Nevertheless it is better to choose elsewhere. Beware of old family names. Your great uncle may have been very kind to you in his will, but there's no need to lumber your son with his old-fashioned name. Be careful of the names from current TV soap operas. Thirty years on, your favourite TV character's name may seem a bit dated. Also I would plead against those way-out labels favoured in trendier quarters.

Some children will be severely handicapped by the name attached to them by their parents. Imagine being called after the heart-throb of the day and turning out to be a short, fat, awkward boy with glasses, or being christened Innocence when at eighteen you're out on the town every night. Research has actually shown that children with way-out names more frequently end up in psychiatric clinics, though I suspect that it may be not so much the name as living with the strange people who thought of it in the first place. Life is tough enough without lumbering children with any extra burdens.

Current favourites include: Jack, William, Joshua, Thomas, Oliver, James and Ethan for boys, and Mia, Chloe, Isabella, Charlotte, Emily, Olivia and Sophie for girls, but next year, who knows? (Names sourced from McCrindle Research.)

THE START

In the final days of pregnancy the baby's head moves down into the pelvis. For some first-time mums this happens late, while others feel the pressure so low down that at any moment they expect to see a little face smiling up from below.

The uterus is in a state of constant movement throughout pregnancy which can feel like weak, poorly co-ordinated contractions. When these become strong and regular, this is the real thing. At antenatal classes you will have been told when to ring for advice and when to come in, but if you are in any doubt don't worry yourself—worry someone else! Make the phone call.

Sometimes the baby seems quite content to stay put and the expected day of birth comes and goes without so much as a murmur. If this goes on too long the obstetrician may decide to bring on labour artificially. He can either use an instrument to break the waters or the drug Syntocinon can be dripped slowly into a vein. Both these methods are very common and very safe. Some mothers feel robbed if they cannot go through all the stages of labour naturally, while others don't give a fig for Nature and if things can be easier and more predictable, they are glad to get going. The goal is a happy, healthy baby.

At the beginning of labour it is normal to have a small show of blood, but if it's any more than a tiny bit, you must shout for help at once. The baby has spent nine months floating in a water-filled bag and when this breaks the action begins. This can happen at any time, usually in hospital, sometimes quietly at home in bed or occasionally in the supermarket. But for most mums there is no bleeding, no great flood, no panic, just regular labour pains—and your antenatal class will have given you a good idea of when it's time to go.

Before leaving home try and have a quick shower in the comfort of your own bathroom. Tell your children that you are going to the hospital and then take off, bag in hand. Unless things are extremely advanced, drive slowly. Some fathers seem to conceive in a rush and try and end the event with equal speed. Driving from home to hospital like a Grand Prix competitor is unnecessarily dramatic and is likely to cause more problems than it will solve.

The hospital admission

Hospital can be a pretty daunting place but you will have already been there for the antenatal class, so you will know where to go and will feel comfortable in the environment. When you first present yourself at the front desk the person who greets you can set the seal on your mood. You'll meet the usual range of personalities in the birthing unit. Most are there because they love babies and the miracle of birth. Don't let the odd grumpy one put you off. Luckily most receptionists have that knack of receiving you like royalty. They make you feel like a most important person, and of course, that's what you are.

Once the admission papers have all been filled in, it's off to the labour ward or birthing centre. Here the contractions will be timed, the baby's heart checked, your blood pressure taken and an examination given to see how the birth canal is opening. From now on it's a waiting game.

THE BIRTH

Labour is often a long, slow affair. There will be plenty of time for lying down later, but in the early stages it is best to walk around. Your birth partner and your MP3 player will get you off to a good start.

As things progress, relief from pain is freely available either from injected drugs, a self-administered gas mixture or an epidural anaesthetic which numbs all feeling in the lower half of your body. Some believe in less medical interference and more natural childbirth. When all's said and done, it's your body. If you want pain relief, just ask.

Various birth positions are also on offer. Guided by your midwife, you can try whatever seems most comfortable: flat on your back with knees bent or on your side as favoured by our Victorian

great-grandmothers.You can also squat, use a birthing chair or choose any other position you like.You can even give birth in water. This is for you, your midwife and your obstetrician to work out.

Episiotomy is where a cut is made to ease the passage of the baby's head through the last stretches of the birth canal. This used to be common practice and then lost some popularity. It is now on the return as refusal to cut in a planned position seems to slow delivery and increase the risk of accidental tearing of the tail which is to be avoided.

Fathers at birth

As a medical student performing my first deliveries it was a rare occurrence to see a father in the labour wards. They usually stayed at work until the phone call came and then headed for the hospital, probably via the pub. Those who asked to be present were looked upon as some sort of pushy pervert. Everyone seemed to forget that fathers knew their wives quite well and were in fact a 50 per cent shareholder in the baby. But life has changed in an important way—partners are now considered crucial for support, comfort and sharing in the wonder of the experience.

Many first-time dads feel apprehensive about the birth. They may not like hospitals or any thought of blood or pain. They may be the type who faint at a glimpse of 'House' or go into convulsions at the mere thought of the dentist's chair. But be reassured, very few ever seem to get upset or make a goose of themselves when it comes to the real thing.

Sometimes first-time fathers think they can sit and conduct a deep and meaningful conversation with their wife, philosophising about art, culture, politics—or last week's football game—as the baby quietly slips out. The reality is that when the pains start

The first hours

When the baby finally arrives after so much anticipation, he is given to an amazed, tired and exhilarated Mum for a cuddle and a bit of closeness and warmth. Now you see this wonderful little person up close. The umbilical cord is clamped, often by the father. He splutters, breathes and a small voice lets out its first cry. The midwife will take the baby onto the resuscitation table to apply suction to the nose and throat. He might need a little bit of oxygen to get him going. About five per cent of all babies are slow to start breathing. In the maternity hospital, expert care and oxygen are always close at hand, so you will have the support that you need.

On the table he is kept warm and checked to assure you that all the fingers, toes and other bits and pieces are fine. Then back to Mum where he belongs. Once all the busyness of birth is over, it is the time for parents and babies to have some time alone to marvel over each other. Mum holds the tiny baby close. You kiss his cheek or head, feel the little fingers, smell the wonderful scent of the newborn baby. You've witnessed a miracle. Now is a special time: the beginning of your lives together.

coming, regular conversation becomes very one-sided. It is presence and support that is needed, not an armchair debate. Dad is the cheerleader, there to urge the home team on to even greater efforts as they push hard in the last quarter.

Going it alone

What you have before you now began when two cells met, joined and attached themselves to the inside of Mum's womb. In those early days the rapid growth quickly became specialised: one part of growth is about creating systems like the heart, the individual parts of the body and even the personality. The other aspect of growth is the development of the placenta into a life-giving system that enables nutrients and oxygen to travel along the umbilical cord giving life to the developing foetus.

As early as five weeks after conception there is heart activity and blood circulation. The heart pumps blood around the body via the umbilical vessels to the placenta, which then provides oxygen and nutrients for the developing baby. These tubes also remove waste products at the same time.

Now, at birth, we witness a miracle: the change in the heart and circulation of a baby. Before delivery the plumbing is all attached to the umbilical cord with various shunts and holes in the heart to keep the flow moving. It's not unlike an astronaut out for a space walk all wired up and connected to a life-support system. At birth the umbilical cord is cut, separating baby from the supply system. In just a minute the holes are blocked, the shunts closed and blood rushes to the lungs. With one independent breath Baby has left behind the mother ship and is now ready to live life on the outside.

The hospital—the staff—the routine

It may seem as though some midwives want to run a maternity ward like the army. The day begins at an ungodly hour with the baby at your bedside and a vacuum cleaner roaring in your ear like a 747. Staff whirr around you, temperatures are taken, babies fed, beds straightened, and whenever you visit the nursing room, there seems to be yet another change of staff. As the day progresses, feeds have to be given, physiotherapists see if you are moving properly, wounds are examined, babies are checked out and the obstetrician will make a high-speed visitation, whizzing in and out with soothing words like a nun on roller skates. But really, this is the hospital's rhythm, not yours. Hospitals are busy places that operate on extreme levels of organisation, but the only rhythm you need to pay attention to is the one of feeding and rest that you and your baby need.

If you have any queries or doubts about your recovery from birth or caring for your baby, ask your midwife or obstetrician on one of their visits. They often seem to be in a rush, but if you have your questions ready ahead of time, you should be able to find out what you need to know. If you don't understand what's being said, ask for an explanation. After all, it's your body and baby we are talking about.

Another important consideration is mealtimes. Some hospitals produce excellent food, while others take exactly the same ingredients and produce a meal that would make even the healthy feel sick and the sick feel sicker. But you are only in hospital for a couple of days and though the food may be unexciting, it will be nutritionally sound. If you need a little spoiling get your visitors to smuggle in some take-away food from outside. This alleviates the monotony of hospital diet and reintroduces your tastebuds to that lost ingredient—flavour. In between mealtimes keep nibbling away at the fruit bowl. You don't need this to stop scurvy, but it's refreshing and will help get the sluggish bowel into a state of movement.

Visiting rules have been greatly eased over recent years. Most hospitals provide a general visiting time but Dad gets special treatment so that the three most important people can have time together in peace. Also your other children should be brought in and introduced to the newborn as soon as possible.

The two-day crash course (if you're lucky!)

As will be obvious, this is a hospital, not a spa resort, and there's some hard work ahead. Just as the dust is settling after the birth and you're ready for a good rest, there's the first feed to manage. This will be a memorable occasion—you may only produce 7 ml but you've proved you can do it.

Don't be disheartened if your first experiences of breast-feeding seem a bit alien. No-one expects you and your baby to do it perfectly on the first day. Remember the baby starts off with good stores of nutrition from the umbilical cord and only needs a little nourishment at the beginning. There are breast-feeding classes and lactation consultants available at hospital and beyond. Help is at hand to get you off on the right foot and your confidence will soon soar. The midwives will also supervise you as you bath, change and settle the baby safely to sleep in the correct position.

What about Mum?

Gone now are the pre-birth days and waddling like a duck. Now the postnatal mum is moving like a saddle-sore member of the cast from a TV Western. Some manage to move with relative elegance, while others feel they have given birth to a rhinoceros, horns and all! However, with gentle exercise and bathing such discomfort soon goes. With help and advice from the midwives the wounds will heal and the pain will disappear. The physiotherapist will help you move more comfortably in spite of your slack ligaments. She will talk about strengthening your back and pelvic floor, and demonstrate recovery exercises for your stressed body. As you recover and learn how to care for a baby, you will be supported and encouraged in a way that builds your confidence.

Advice

You probably found as soon as you announced your pregnancy that advice is not something that's ever in short supply around caring for babies. That's because most people over a certain age have had a crack at it with varying degrees of success, and their successes have often been hard won, so they want to tell you about them.

The internet is also a major and valuable source of advice for today's parents. A word of warning. Anyone can offer advice on the internet and if you try and take it all on you'll be left confused and stressed. Look for the websites of the major childcare and health organisations, or those recommended by your hospital or clinic, and you shouldn't go too far wrong.

The best advice about advice is that there are many loving, sensible ways to bring up a baby, and you must latch onto the advice that feels right for you and your style. No baby is the same and no mum and dad are the same. Raising a child is a long process of figuring out what is right for you and your family and that starts here.

Feeling the way

The days immediately after birth are a time of confusion to your body and brain. All those hormones produced by the placenta reduce sharply after birth leaving muscles, ligaments and many body functions in an unsettled state. Emotions are also very mixed, with elation, uncertainty, discomfort, tiredness, lack of confidence and even some tears all vying with each other. Throughout these ups and downs there is a feeling of wonder. Mum looks at her tiny baby and just cannot believe it. She might think: How did we create such a perfect baby and how will he manage in this imperfect world? Others might begin to worry about whether they are as happy and bonded as the experts say they should be.

There are a lot of opinions floating around about what is *supposed* to happen. Bonding may be immediate or take some time. In real life, bonding may take place at the first scan, just after birth or some time later. It does not work to a schedule, but it will come. Remember, love is something which develops over a long period and lasting relationships are rarely made in minutes. Don't try too hard. Nature will take care of things, just as it always has. (See Chapter Seven.)

It is usual for a new mother to feel very clingy towards her newborns. She is like a mother lion ready to snap at any threat to her cubs. It's natural to get upset when a crowd of visitors plays pass the parcel with the little one. If you don't want the baby lifted up and passed around, it's your decision and you should let everyone know how you feel. But Dad needs equal access. If you think he's not as good at the job as you, then make sure he gets all the practice he needs. He needs to bond too and to learn how to care for his baby. Start well now and everyone will feel involved from the very beginning.

It's time to go home

It's been a long journey already, but the biggest adventure lies ahead. It may seem bewildering to step out into the world with a very small child in your care, but you are not alone. Apart from experienced family and friends, there are a number of professionals you can call about anything to do with the care of babies and their health, and of course your own. The hospital and your early childhood centre will load you up with information about resources.

So, it's time. You step out of the hospital door with your little bundle, wondering just who this little person is. And that's the subject of the next chapter.

Going to hospital—what to bring

- Medical papers for admission.
- Parking money.
- Several pairs of pyjamas. These are good because they open down the front for breast-feeding.
- Bed jacket, shawl or cardigan to keep shoulders warm when sitting up in bed.
- Comfortable slippers.
- Comfortable pillow if you have a favourite.
- Lip balm.
- Dressing gown for wandering around the ward.
- Nursing bras.
- Nursing pads may be needed.
- Sanitary pads are usually provided, but check if you are going to a small hospital.
- Glasses, it can be easy to forget these in the rush.
- Toilette requirements—toothbrush, toothpaste, nice soap, face washer, shampoo, hairbrush.
- Mobile phone and charger.

- Make-up and perfume—to help you feel more like a person than a patient.
- Some way of relaxing—a good book, MP3 player, knitting, crochet, *Babies*.
- A purse with a little money and a photo of your other children.
- Camera—make sure it's charged.
- Snacks and water.

Leave ready for husband to bring

- If you like you could take a small packet of spare nappies, but the hospital will generally provide these.
- Some clothes—probably a little stretch suit and singlet—for Baby to come home in.
- Baby blanket.
- Baby capsule. Make sure it's installed and ready and you've had a practice run at the fastenings.

PS—Don't panic, most hospitals have a shop to buy what you forget.

Getting to know
your newborn

Y ou're home. Here is Baby in your house which you've lovingly prepared for her arrival. She's so small, so delicate, you think, and then: I know so little about babies! How can I ever handle such a fragile little mite who can scream so loudly?

Well, don't despair, help is there. First of all, despite initial impressions, babies are remarkably resilient. They would need to be when you think of all the traumas they endured in the obstacle course of birth. Of course there will be an awful lot of learning ahead, but if you use commonsense, relax and trust your natural instincts, it all comes together. All you need is a little basic information about what is normal and what to expect and then, with a charge of confidence, you can get going.

The first impression

The newborn usually has a small, ruddy, red body, bluish hands and feet, and a head which seems quite out of proportion to the rest of her. She lies with arms and legs flexed up, which is scarcely surprising when you think that for the past nine months she has been all curled up in Mum's tum. In such cramped living conditions there was never enough space to have a good stretch, and certainly insufficient for a daily aerobics work-out.

Apart from jumping at loud noises there is no obvious impression of hearing and her eyes drift round in what at first appears to be a purposeless way. Don't be fooled, she sees and hears far more than you realise, being remarkably aware of both your face and voice. In the early weeks she seems to sleep most of the time, completely unperturbed by light or noise.

A little baby can cough and sneeze, and often does. Her mouth and eyelids may move in sleep as though she is dreaming of some particularly interesting moment of a past existence (for all we know, she is). She will often give a sudden startle in her sleep for a reason which is best known to herself.

She will cry at birth and regularly thereafter. It is a little voice which can come out with amazing intensity. To first-time parents all cries will sound the same, but after a few weeks the subtle differences between boredom, pain and hunger cries become strikingly apparent.

The dimensions

There are several questions friends ask immediately after every birth. How are Mother and Baby? What is the sex? And what about the weight?

Between 38 and 41 weeks most babies decide they've had enough and deign to appear in this world. But despite many babies having identical gestation periods they somehow manage to come out with a variety of different shapes and sizes.

Weight

The average birth weight is 3.3 kg (7½ lb). In the final months of pregnancy the baby is all tanked up with fluids and kilojoules like a camel preparing to cross the Sahara. These nutrients will fuel her for her strenuous journey into the outside world and keep her going through the first days when breast-feeding gives comfort, but few kilojoules.

These reserves of fuel and fluid are gradually burned up and this explains why the first days are a time of weight loss rather than gain. As a rule of thumb, it is said that a baby can lose up to ten per cent of birth weight in the first few days only to have it all regained by at latest the tenth day. Once the weight starts to increase it will probably increase by just under 30 g (1 oz) a day for the next four months. This will vary from baby to baby and week to week, so don't become obsessed with each gram of gain. It is health, not the weighing machine we are really interested in. As a student I was taught to allow for the weight gain being just under the ounce or 30 g per day by calculating on the basis of an ounce a day and none on Sundays. This had absolutely no religious significance, but was just a nice Irish rule of thumb, which added up to 6 oz or 180 g per week, which is the average figure. If other signs are OK, like regular wet nappies and good health, let your visiting midwife do the sums. She'll let you know whether the weight gain is fine.

If your baby is of near average birth weight then this will have almost doubled by four months, and trebled by a year. The actual size at birth bears only a small relationship to the child's weight at twelve months, and almost none whatsoever to her adult weight. It does however exhibit quite a strong family pattern with most brothers and sisters tending to be of roughly the same birth weight. It seems likely that if your first one called for a mighty push, then the chances are the next will be much the same.

Of course there are medical reasons for some babies being born either very small or particularly large. Mums with high blood pressure, or who have placenta problems, tend towards small babies, while mums with uncontrolled diabetes may produce larger ones.

Though 3.3 kg (7½ lb) is the average weight, ten per cent of normal babies will be 4 kg (9 lb) and a further ten per cent as little as 2.5 kg (6 lb). Right from birth, boys tend to be slightly heavier and longer than girls, the difference being on average 100 g (3.5 oz) in weight and 1 cm (0.4 in) in length.

Length

The average baby at birth has already grown about 50 cm all in the nine months from conception. I find this quite mind-boggling. Just imagine a spotty adolescent growing that fast during her puberty growth spurt—you'd be lengthening her blue denims by a centimetre twice a week!

It's also fascinating to realise that at birth a baby has already gained roughly one-third of her ultimate adult height. By two and a half years she has reached almost half her final elevation, and close to her eighth birthday, she will have reached the three-quarter mark.

Head size

The head circumference of the average full-term baby is 35 cm with a variation of plus or minus 2 cm. Obviously if the head is extremely large, small or changes size unexpectedly, this could be a cause for concern, but slight differences are of little importance.

A big head does not mean a big intelligence. Often it contains just the same amount of cleverness but simply less well packed. Heads are like computers. The size of the case that covers all those silicon chips bears no relationship to the complexity of the works.

Please take these figures of dimensions as only a very rough guide. Don't go rushing off to put your baby on the kitchen scales or run a tape measure round her and then worry yourself unduly. Each child is an individual and as such some won't match the textbook tables. There are many children who never measure up to average but they are still very normal.

Approximate heights (cm) of children 1-5 years						
	Average		Tall average (upper 10 %)		Short average (lower 10 %)	
	Girls	Boys	Girls	Boys	Girls	Boys
Birth	51	51	52.5	53	47	48
3 months	60	62	63	64	56	57
6 months	66	68	69	71	62	64
9 months	71	73	74	76	67	69
1 year	74	76	79	82	69	71
2 years	85	87	91	95	79	80
3 years	94	95	101	104	87	88
4 years	101	102	109	111	94	95
5 years	107	109	116	118	99	101
Adult	163.5	177	171	185	156	168

Approximate weights (kg) of children 1-5 years						
	Average		Heavy average (upper 10 %)		Light average (lower 10 %)	
	Girls	Boys	Girls	Boys	Girls	Boys
Birth	3.2	3.3	3.7	4	2.5	2.5
3 months	5.4	6.0	6.5	7	4.5	5
6 months	7.2	7.8	8.5	9	6	6.5
9 months	8.6	9.2	10	10.5	6.5	8
1 year	9.5	10.5	12	13	7.5	8.5
2 years	12	13	15.5	16	10	10.5
3 years	14	15	18	19	11.5	12
4 years	16	17	21	21.5	13	13.5
5 years	18.5	19	24.5	24.5	14.5	15
Adult	56.5	69	72.5	87	47	57.5

Note: ★Recent studies show that there is generally a small difference in weight between breast-fed and bottle-fed babies and this should be taken into account when reading tables.

The head

Since it is the baby's top that spearheads her descent into the world, it should come as no surprise to find that the head of this spear has become a pointed tip. This change of shape can occur because the baby's skull at this stage is moveable, being made up of a number of bones held together by a kind of flexible fibrous tape.

At birth, as pressure is placed on the skull, the bones overlap and take on a temporary realignment. They mould into a shape rather like an egg which greatly eases the slide through the birth canal. After birth it takes a day or two for the normal shape to return, so don't despair, you've not given birth to an egg-head!

★See 'Effects of infant feeding practice on weight gain from birth to 3 years', LJ Griffiths et al: http://adc.bmj.com/cgi/content/abstract/94/8/577

Birth may be quite traumatic for Mother, but make no mistake, it's no picnic for Baby either. If you had to spend at least twelve hours standing on your head trying to get out of a confined space, and your reward was a suction pipe poked up your nose, you'd be crying when you got to the other end too.

Where the birth pressure has been on the top of the head a circle of spongy, fluid-filled skin marks the spot for a few days. There is no cause for alarm, this mark is only skin deep and doesn't mean that the baby has been injured in any way. If it has been a breech birth with the baby being round the wrong way, the swelling can be on a very different part. Sometimes the nose gets a bit squashed and it is not unusual for a few bruises to show, particularly where instruments were necessary. But don't worry, bumps, bruises and swellings on the outside rarely have any bearing on the state of the important bits on the inside.

There is one spot at the top of the skull where the bones don't quite join. This leaves a little gap known as the 'soft spot', or more correctly as the anterior fontanelle. Don't be frightened of this. It is present in all babies. It is not delicate, painful or dangerous to touch. The brain beneath it is well protected by a tough fibrous covering. By six months it will have almost closed over and certainly all traces will have long gone by two years.

The newborn's head is large and her neck strength almost non-existent. Be careful when you lift your baby up in the early months, as she cannot support her own head at this stage. For the short time that it takes to develop good head control, it's best to be a supporting parent.

The skin

When you are first handed your newborn she will not have the clean, sparkling appearance you expect. At birth, when the moisture has been dried off, the skin is often seen to be coated in a creamy, greasy paste called vernix. This disappears with the first bath. But then you may notice the little one is covered in a fur of fine hair. No, she has not regressed to the Stone Age. This is quite normal and will all drop out in the first month.

As for the baby's head of hair, there is a great variation in the luxuriance of growth. Some children are born with a great black mop, while most tend towards a 'bald is beautiful' style. If both parents are blonde or red-haired, don't panic when you see a jet-black mat. This colour bears little relationship to the final tint.

The skin of a newborn baby is amazingly red. The reason for this is that at birth the baby's red blood count will probably be 25 per cent greater than Mother's. This explains why your baby has such a ruddy hue and you look so pale in comparison.

We saw in the previous chapter how the plumbing changes when the umbilical is cut just after birth. Under the circumstances it's not surprising that the heart takes some time to come to terms with the new order of things and while this is happening the flow of blood to the skin and extremities can be rather variable. Dusky hands, feet and mottled skin at this stage are very usual.

Until birth the skin has been immersed in fluid and, like that of a fish, it never gets a chance to dry out. Now out on dry land, it is destined to be sat in dirty nappies, clothed in uncomfortable fabrics which have often been washed in a washing powder that doesn't suit Baby's skin. Whereas most skins cope remarkably well with all this, some get rashes, dry out and need a bit of nurturing.

Baby's little fingers can often have remarkably long nails, which are fairly lethal when it comes to scratching. They should be trimmed early on before the face gets damaged—something that will prob-ably happen the very day you have made an appointment with the photographer.

Vision and hearing

The newborn spends so much time asleep that her eyes are generally only open for intermittent viewing. When awake her eyes will look around in a seemingly purposeless way, giving no impression of vision. In fact the smallest babies can see, but it takes some patience to prove this. Hold the baby on your knee, well supported and facing you. Get your head in line with her eyes and then move ever so slowly from one side to the other. You will see those little eyes following your face with a jerky, but definitely following, movement.

There is a clear colour in Baby's eyes at birth, usually blue, but like the hair this often changes as the baby grows older. So don't count on it to continue. Your blue-eyed little boy may not end up so blue-eyed after all.

When I was a medical student it was fashionable to believe that babies showed no response to normal sound. If you talk soothingly to an upset baby, the crying itself may not cease but its intensity and rhythm usually alters. This shows a definite response to a gentle voice. It has also been shown that as you talk to babies, their arms and legs often move with a body-language rhythm which keeps time with your voice. So babies hear plenty at birth. It just takes us to tune in to recognise their response. These days hearing is checked before you leave hospital and if there is the slightest worry then an absolutely definitive hearing test is performed.

The mouth

Little babies prefer to be a nose breather and not to use their mouths to breathe through. In the early days this opening is reserved for feeding, burping and crying. Consequently if their nose gets blocked and they have to mouth-breathe they become extremely unhappy. This we all discover when our little ones have their first cold.

Reflexes

Newborn babies exhibit a number of primitive reflexes which make you wonder if they haven't been here before in another life. In the first weeks babies have a walking reflex which, on a superficial glance, seems brilliant beyond their age. Hold them upright over a table, tilt them slightly forward and press the soles of the feet firmly down against the surface and off they go in a sort of walk. Unfortunately this does not last. It disappears in three or four weeks and then takes another nine months before the real thing returns.

The feeding reflex is designed as a life preserver. Here you have a baby so delicate and immature, yet if a teat so much as touches the cheek she turns immediately to latch on like a limpet. All a baby needs is to be close to food and feeding will be assured. Sucking is of course another very basic reflex dating back to the earliest days of formation. As with all these reflexes this disappears as the baby matures.

Another lifesaver is the reflex which helps a baby to breathe when the nose is obstructed. If Baby is lying face down on a mattress and airways are obstructed, Samson-like she will muster amazing strength and lift her head to turn it to one side. This is quite amazing when you consider that at this stage the head cannot normally be lifted voluntarily at all. Just take my word for this one. It's truly amazing, but certainly not to be tried out by experimenting parents—it's not 100 per cent reliable.

The grasp reflex is another interesting one. Babies at birth cannot open or close their hands voluntarily. However, if an object is pressed across the palm the hand will clasp around it. This grasp reflex effectively blocks any useful hand function until at about the age of three months it passes and leaves the hand free to work at will.

There's one other reflex that you will probably see your doctor demonstrate when she examines your baby. With the child lying on her back, the head is lifted slightly and let drop suddenly several centimetres into the examiner's hand. This is known as the Moro reflex. The baby is startled in the Moro reflex and her arms and legs will straighten out and then return to the resting flexed position. This reflex disappears at about three months, but while present it reassures us that the baby is moving all limbs in an equal and normal way.

The umbilical stump

This once great lifeline which nourished the baby for nine months is now left to wither and drop off. The cord contains two arteries and a vein which means that in the first days this has the potential to bleed. At birth it is closed off firmly using a special plastic clip, the design of which ensures that once shut on the cord the arteries and vein are locked, immoveable and don't leak. The redundant remnant will remain for between five to nine days getting progressively drier until eventually it drops off. Since we have a strange situation where a piece of dying material is attached to a living body, there must be a kind of no-man's-land where they join. This explains why the stump tends to ooze and remain raw for some time, as it is unsure which way to go.

At bath time the body is cleaned with water and dried. We used to apply a little bit of methylated spirits to the stump but that's no longer recommended. Little hernias that bulge from the umbilicus are amazingly common and in most cases disappear.

The foreskin

The foreskin was put there to protect the delicate and sensitive tip of the penis. During the first few years the skin is still attached to the underlying structures and is not ready to be pulled back. Only after about the fourth birthday will it start to move easily and it should never be forced back before that stage. Thereafter you can start gently retracting it during bath time and it can then become part of the daily wash.

The stomach and bowels

Before birth the gut is in a state of rest and remains unused until introduced to food. It is one of the great miracles that such an untried piece of equipment can be useless one day and the next it is providing valuable nutrition. Digestion is a bit haphazard in the early weeks—after all, it's a bit much to expect a perfect performance from the first trial run.

Babies are born with a good load of spare food on board, bringing with them their own haversack of rations into the world. This allows them to cope with the gradual introduction of a decent diet. As a rough rule of thumb they should be offered about one-third of their ideal daily intake on day one. This should be gradually increased until they are given the full amount by the end of the first week.

When Baby takes the first feed it may well be returned along with a good deal of mucus which was in the stomach at birth. This is a very common occurrence and though things may be unstable for a short while they usually settle down quickly.

At birth the gut contains nothing more than some debris and fluid which the baby has swallowed before delivery. All of this has to pass through before you will see anything that resembles a proper bowel motion. The first motion is usually passed within twelve hours of birth and almost always sometime during the first day. It comes out as a sticky, greeny-black substance which looks foul but has no smell. This is called meconium. By the third day most of this will have passed and partly processed milk products start to appear.

As the gut is trying to come to terms with its new-found function it is not surprising that, initially, motions are poorly digested and pretty loose. Occasionally these motions will be green and watery, giving a false impression of a gut infection. Sometimes the situation is quite explosive with some babies reported to have up to twenty dirty nappies a day while the digestive processes come into balance. Breast-fed babies tend to have a mustard-yellow stool, whereas bottle-fed babies have stools which are pale brown and of a more solid consistency.

It all takes time for equilibrium to set in, so as long as intake is adequate and health appears to be blooming, don't get too worked up about this area of waste disposal.

Conclusion

Now you've used your owner's manual to get to know and understand the wonderful design of your new baby, she's almost ready for her test flight. There are just a few things that sometimes need a little bit of fine tuning before we can really take off ...

4

Common concerns— what to expect

For the new mother, it takes quite a long time before she can relax and know instinctively which are the 'normal, unimportant worries' and which are the genuine problems that need expert help.

This chapter looks at a lot of the common little blemishes and concerns in the hope that many of those unnecessary fears can be diminished. As a doctor, I consider it a big part of my job to help you get a feel for when it's time to worry. Worrying about real problems is a natural part of life, worrying about non-problems is a futile waste of emotional energy. Of course, if you're not sure about a health issue, always be on the safe side and see your doctor.

Head bruising at birth

When you think of the amount of squeezing that babies have to undergo at birth it's little wonder that sometimes they emerge a little bruised and out of shape. At birth the head is rather like a football which has been moulded into an odd shape as it squeezed through the narrow opening. However, within a day the malleable skull bones will slip back into their normal position. Depending on how difficult the delivery was and other factors such as whether or not forceps or vacuum extraction were used, there may be bruising which will last a few days. These little blemishes are only very superficial, and the important bits inside are well protected and unharmed. If your baby is otherwise alert, bright and healthy you can relax.

Scalp swellings at birth

At the moment of birth it is the skin on the crown of the head that forces the baby's exit, so it is hardly surprising that this can become somewhat the worse for wear. Most newborn babies have a soggy swelling over the part of the head that did the pushing. In medical jargon, this is called the caput succedaneum. The name sounds a lot more important than the condition, which will disappear within a couple of days and has no significance other than to remind you which end of the baby came out first.

Cephalhaematoma

This is the medical term that describes a fluid-filled swelling on the baby's head. This is more noticeable and long-lasting than the caput succedaneum. During delivery, one of the little blood vessels that lies on the outside of the skull bones ruptures due to the twisting forces of birth. When it bleeds the blood is trapped between the bone and its strong outside covering, which leaves a prominent fluid-filled lump. This occurs in about one per cent of all babies and lasts anywhere from one month to six months. As the fluid gradually reabsorbs, a rim of bone material can temporarily circle the swelling. This can give the impression that there is a crater in the bone which in fact is not so. The skull is intact, as is all that lies under it. A cephalhaematoma is nothing to worry about. It is quite benign and will go away in due course without any medical interference. Meanwhile the baby will remain perfectly happy and quite unaware of it.

Skin blemishes

It is upsetting when spots and skin rashes deface our little ones, but such blemishes are normal, benign and of course only skin deep. Let's look at the most common ones.

Milia

In the first few days of life most babies are found to have little yellow pin-head spots mostly around the bridge of the nose. These are caused by inexperienced skin glands unplugging themselves and getting their act together. Almost all babies have these in the early days and (like your child) they are 100 per cent innocent. They are of no concern, need no treatment and disappear within one week.

Heat rash

This is a term used to describe a vague, though nevertheless common, condition. By heat rash I refer to those tiny, flat, red pin-head spots that appear without warning and often join to make big red patches. Heat is always blamed, but even that is uncertain. Most occur on the face, creases of the neck and the trunk. They often seem worse in places where the clothes are tight. They come and go without rhyme or reason, the child being completely symptom-free and oblivious to their presence.

Please don't get into a knot worrying about measles, malnutrition or some obscure allergy. If your baby is happy, healthy and these little blemishes come and go, then relax and ignore them. Keep your baby's clothes light, don't let him overheat, and allow only breathable fabrics close to the skin.

Dry skin

Though it is common to say that something is 'as soft as a baby's bottom', some babies do have hides on them that are tough, dry and scaly. Dry skin is often hereditary and sometimes is associated with eczema. Whatever the cause, it takes a bit of extra care to keep these little ones comfortable.

For a start, please be sparing with all the washing and scrubbing clean. Avoid those adult soaps that rob the skin of what little natural oil it possesses. After a bath, skin lotion or cream will leave the skin soft. At our hospital we favoured glycerine and sorbolene cream but there are numerous other types. Have a chat with your chemist and get a large container of quality skin cream.

Cradle cap—scurfy scalp

Babies don't get dandruff. That's a condition which is reserved for teenagers, adults and those boring people on the TV hair-care commercials. Babies, however, do get dry, scaly scalps. If your baby has such a scalp you can either leave it alone altogether, or massage it occasionally with a little oil. In the end the condition will eventually clear itself up whichever way you go. Cradle cap is an extension of this condition which results from the natural oils in the scalp cementing the dry, scaly layers into a brown cap. This does not look too pretty, but it is perfectly harmless. To remove the crusts, massage the top of the head with warm oil (olive or baby oil). Leave it for a couple of hours or overnight and then gently comb the scalp. Continue the process until it's clear. Your chemist can recommend a special product for cradle cap if the oils do not prove to be effective.

Cheek rashes

Some babies are born with the rose-petal cheeks of a blushing film star, while others' continually look rough and chapped. The appearance of the skin depends partly on its genetic toughness and partly on what the baby has been lying on. It stands to reason that a delicate cheek which has been lying on a sheet soggy from dribbling, the dampness of breath and the occasional regurgitation is bound to be affected. It's best to ensure that Baby's sheet is good and soft, and it is important to keep the skin as dry, clean and softened as possible. Here again the glycerine and sorbolene-type creams are of great use.

If the cheeks are chapped, just make certain that this is not due to the little one rolling around on the carpet. Those floor coverings are made tough to withstand heavy footwork and are none too gentle on a child's delicate complexion. Children with eczema are particularly vulnerable. Cheeks, arms and legs can all become irritated if they come into contact with wool or acrylic.

Skin marks

Skin marks come in a variety of colours and configurations, which is probably why they have been given names that sound like they might be species of butterfly. The most common ones are known as the storkbeak mark, the strawberry mark and the Mongolian blue spot.

Storkbeak mark

About half the babies I see have a little red mark on the back of their necks. Their mothers look at me in amazement when I tell them that it is a storkbeak mark and begin to wonder if I'm not from the school of thought that believes babies are found under a gooseberry bush. Nevertheless that's what it's properly called and the mark is due to prominent blood capillaries in the skin. Often the same baby will have little red marks on an eyelid or the forehead as well. Not to worry, these marks are all benign and usually very temporary.

Strawberry mark

This is less common, but when large it can be unsightly and greatly distress the parents. The mark is produced by a benign growth of the large blood vessels in the skin. There is absolutely no sign of its presence at birth, but within a few weeks a small spot will appear which will gradually grow larger, redder and raised above the surface. This increases over the first six months then slowly starts its decline. By the time the child is five years old it will be pretty small and will have gone before the age of ten.

At their peak, strawberry birthmarks look raised and nasty, and it's hard for parents to believe that such a mark could go away without intervention. Generally speaking there is nothing to do but wait patiently and be reassured that it will go away. If you are worried about it, talk to your doctor. She will advise you that Nature will heal it in its own good time and leave no mark, but if you insist on surgical interference you are guaranteeing a scar.

Mongolian blue spot

I was once threatened with legal action by a father who firmly believed that his baby son had been beaten by one of our nurses. It was true that the boy had indeed got large blue marks at the base of his spine and on his buttocks. What the legal profession were not to realise was that this sort of marking is extremely common in newborn babies of southern European, African, Polynesian and Asian descent. These marks have been christened 'Mongolian blue spots' and are present at birth.

Once again there is absolutely nothing to worry about with these. The marks are benign and have no significance whatsoever. Most fade in the first year.

Teeth

It is generally in about the sixth month that the first little pearl pops through, causing about the same level of parental excitement as would finding the genuine object in your pub-lunch oysters. Early teething does not, I'm afraid, indicate advanced development or super-intelligence. If it did all sorts of snappy animals would be telling the human race what to do. Some babies do have teeth at birth; fortunately for the case of breast-feeding, it is rare.

Although teeth usually arrive at six months some first teeth will take up to a year to show. When teeth do appear treat them with care, as there will be no replacements for another six years. I am a believer in the safety and protective effect of fluoridated water. If you are concerned that there may not be proper fluoridation in your water, just ask your dentist.

When it comes to giving sweet drinks, be sensible. Flavoured milks, blackcurrant health drinks and other very sweet cordials are best avoided. Constant irrigation of developing teeth by sugars leads to decay of the front teeth and unsightly brown stumps.

With cleaning, you can't actually scrub round a baby's gums properly until he's about a year old, so I suggest that before then you give him a soft toothbrush to suck so that he can get used to having it in his mouth. Don't bother to use toothpaste at this stage. If you do, just a speck of low-fluoride children's toothpaste is sufficient, not the extravagant fat worm you see on fresh-breath advertisements.

Teething

The process of teething usually starts at six months and can seem to go on until the age of twenty. It can be intermittently unpleasant for all involved, but it shouldn't be a source of anxiety. I know that it is fashionable to blame every cold, cough and cry on teething, but you can't do this for twenty years. Teething can certainly cause some pain in the gums, which in turn can increase salivation and dribbling. It may make your little one more grizzly and sleepless, may change feeding routines and may also affect the bowel exhaust products, none of which is much fun. On the other hand, teething does not cause vomiting, diarrhoea, fits, fevers or bronchitis. The main result of teething is teeth!

Most medicos discourage any treatment of teething, but I believe a little paracetamol, a teething ring or your chemist's favourite gum-rub gel never go amiss.

Mouth problems

Tongue tie

True tongue tie can happen but it must be as rare as the proverbial hen's teeth. The average baby's tongue is strapped to the floor of the mouth. 'Look, the baby's tongue-tied!' cry the relatives. Not so, this is quite a normal state of affairs. As the jaw and mouth grow, any apparent problem disappears. Babies can feed, babble and cry very nicely, thank you, without ever protruding their tongues. It is exceptionally rare for tongue tie to cause genuine speech or feeding problems except in very rare instances. When your toddler won't eat his vegetables, the problem is one of behaviour not tongue tie. Nor is speech held back by a tight tongue. In general as long as the ears can hear and the brain wishes to speak, the tongue will do its job.

Oral thrush

This is extremely common in babies and usually causes no symptoms at all. When you look in the mouth there will be little white patches on the cheeks and tongue. At first sight these may look just like milk curds but you'll quickly know that they aren't as they stay put and bleed if you try to remove them.

Thrush is an infection caused by the Candida albicans fungus. It may have been introduced from the birth canal during delivery or later from a contaminated teat, bottle, hand or from chewing an object. No matter how hard you try, total sterility is an impossibility, and candida is pretty common, even in the most impeccably cared-for child.

Treatment for thrush is simple and usually involves the anti-candida antibiotic, Nystatin. You apply drops of this suspension to the mouth after feeds. It is clean, easy to take and very effective. Though not used these days, your granny probably used gentian violet. She painted it on the white areas, which were cured safely and efficiently. But when the purple dripped out the corner of the mouth, it was not unlike Dracula around feeding time.

Though thrush is usually symptom-free, it can occasionally be painful, cause irritability and feeding problems.

Sucking pads and blisters

During the first weeks, little pads or blisters can often be seen on Baby's lips. These are a reaction to the newly discovered delight of sucking. As the lips toughen up the blisters will disappear of their own accord and no treatment is necessary.

Eye problems

The main eye worries in newborn babies are blocked tear ducts, squints and sticky eyes.

Blocked tear ducts

Many babies will have no tears to shed for the first few weeks of life. Mind you, this won't stop them crying. They'll be just as noisy but it will be a sort of dry run for later. Once tears are on tap it is quite common to find a baby with one or both of his tear-draining ducts blocked. The result of this is that his eyes look wet and the tears overflow down his cheeks. Usually a blocked duct will clear itself normally within six months, but you can help it along with a bit of gentle massage, as well as making sure the eye is kept clean. As the dampness and the blockage can encourage infection, antibiotic ointment will be needed if this occurs.

If, after six months, the tear duct still hasn't cleared of its own accord then an eye specialist can re-open the offending channel. This is done under a general anaesthetic in day surgery, and is usually both simple and successful.

Squints

Most babies have two straight eyes which work in tandem as they are supposed to. Some however are born with squints, their eyes intermittently or permanently out of phase. The main reason for a child to squint is that the tiny muscles which control eye movement have been formed either too long or too short. When this is mild, exercise and use of the eyes can bring a cure. In toddlers, glasses and/or patches may be appropriate. If the squint is more pronounced, however, then a relatively simple surgical readjustment is needed.

It's hard to know when to start worrying about a squinting baby. If the problem is only intermittent and tends only to occur when Baby is tired, then there may not be much to worry about. On the other hand, if one eye has a permanent turn then expert help should be sought right away.

An important concern with squinting is the possibility of loss of vision or blindness in one eye. Try and look at this for a moment from the brain's point of view. The brain is receiving two separate pictures which gives double vision. This, the brain reckons, is a pretty uncomfortable situation so it solves the problem by switching off the weaker eye and once more there is single vision. If this continues for many months, the brain loses the power to re-engage the eye and eventually it will never see again.

That is why it is important that an eye specialist should look at a permanent squint as soon as is practicable and determine which is the weaker eye, so that he can either improve its vision with lenses or put a temporary patch over the stronger eye to make the weaker one do more work and build it up that way.

If you have any doubts please seek expert help as soon as possible. Eye specialists can test vision and refraction in extremely small babies and can give patches and glasses to children from a fairly early age.

Sticky eye

This is an extremely common condition in newborn babies. It looks a bit like an infection of the eyes but is usually just an irritation from some of the fluids and debris encountered at birth. The only treatment required is regular bathing of the eyes with sterile water and cotton wool. Infection can occur, usually a little later on, and this leaves the eye with red lids and a sticky crust that is generally worst in the mornings. If you have concerns, consult your family doctor, who may prescribe special antibiotic drops or ointment which resolves the infection.

Breast enlargement (neonatal mastitis)

At birth, Mother's blood is running high on hormones which are designed to kick-start the breasts into action as efficient milk producers for Baby. The placenta protects Baby from most of this abnormal activity but quite often a little will leak through and can cause breast enlargement (neonatal mastitis) in both boy and girl babies. Sometimes small beads of fluid may even appear from the baby's breasts, commonly called 'witch's milk'. It's nothing to worry about, just a natural response to a natural process. Around about day four it will hit its peak and will wane after that. Sometimes enlargement continues for some months and it is often lop-sided. The whole thing is only temporary, needs no treatment and even less concern.

Jaundice

This occurs in all babies to some extent and is caused by an increase in the bile products carried in the blood. These products come from the breakdown of old red blood cells which are then processed by the liver and put out into the gut.

At birth most babies have about a 25 per cent overload of red blood cells. These were required to maintain health in the low-oxygen environment of the womb but are no longer needed once Baby has hit the great outdoors. As the red cells reduce they put a lot of pressure on the processing ability of the baby's immature, inefficient liver. The result is that the unprocessed bile builds up in the blood and the baby turns a little yellow.

There's no need for panic. A simple blood test will determine the exact levels and if they are too high, then treatment, usually in the form of shining a bright light on the skin, will be given. Clever midwives have for years known that exposing jaundiced babies to sunlight reduced the levels. The light breaks down some of the bile in the skin and reduces the load on the liver. So a little jaundice is usual for all babies, while a lot requires monitoring and treatment.

Circumcision

In this crazy world there are many things we accept as correct just because they have been done for years. But hold it! Just because something is done, doesn't necessarily mean that it's right.

Circumcision of boy babies has been one of these accepted things, but it needs to be questioned by all free-thinking parents. In the last twenty years parents have moved away from this, but still some request it to be done.

Of course, there are those who consider circumcision necessary as part of their religious faith and it is not for me to question or criticise this. However, when it is demanded for spurious social reasons—that's different.

Many parents tell me that it's more hygienic. This was certainly true when living in a desert tribe 2000 years ago. Now that we have showers, baths and running water, however, this just doesn't wash (unless the family don't believe in washing either). Then others tell me, 'His father has been done and he will feel different.' What utter rubbish! In an 80-year life span there is but a brief passing interest in your dad's anatomical deformities.

Surely we don't always have to have sons like their fathers. If my nose was broken in my football-playing days, I would never want my boys to look the same as their dad.

I find it hard to come to terms with the concept of inflicting needless pain on any child, just to satisfy tradition or parental hang-ups.

Let's stop and think for a minute. If you were to deliberately and unnecessarily cut off any other bit of your baby you would find yourself before the courts, charged with child abuse and probably lose custody of your child. Remember, circumcision carries risks such as bleeding, infection and occasionally even death. It is certainly a crazy world we inhabit.

OK, you have spotted it—I am not a supporter of unthinking baby circumcision. The message is: if you don't have a religious reason to dismantle God's handiwork, then I would prefer that you leave it alone.

Umbilical hernia

It is very common to see a bit of Baby poking out through the navel. This is a hernia. It may look a little strange but it is a harmless condition that will usually go away of its own accord. Most have disappeared before Baby's first birthday, and the ones which hang around longer are generally gone well before he is six. Only very occasionally is it necessary to consult a surgeon. By and large there's nothing you can do to speed things up. These hernias do not obstruct or cause problems. Leave them alone and let Nature do its work.

Groin hernia (inguinal hernia)

Hernias in the groin are also relatively common, but must be taken seriously. They are due to a defect of the muscles in the abdominal wall and the danger is that part of the bowel can get through which, if it gets stuck, will lead to an obstruction of the gut and eventually serious strangulation. These hernias do not get better without treatment and need safe and simple surgery to put them right. Hernias are caused by a weakness in the design at birth and are not caused by crying, coughing or exertion.

Clicky hips

The diagnosis of clicky hips is very common and happens when the doctor performing the postnatal check notices that the hip is relatively loose. What he will often find is simply loose ligaments caused by a transfer of the hormones Mum needed to allow her to be flexible enough to give birth. The doctor will decide whether clicky hips are a sign of this harmless condition or whether there is a congenital dislocation of the hip.

Congenital dislocation of the hip may be relatively rare but we still take great pains to spot it, as a missed diagnosis can lead to a life-long limp. If the baby has a dislocated hip it means that the top of the femur (thighbone) is displaced some distance from the socket into which it is meant to fit. Unless the femur head and socket grow in the correct position together it can mean that the two will not fit properly when brought together in the future. This is why your baby's hips will be carefully examined before being allowed to leave hospital. Many newborns will have 'clicky hips' when examined at birth and usually this is of no significance. It's the abnormal 'clunk' of a congenital dislocation that doctors look for and this is taken most seriously. If there is any doubt at this time, a temporary splint will be suggested and then the situation reviewed closely until your orthopaedic specialist is completely happy that the hips are normal.

Bandy legs and funny feet

Despite all the kicking, wriggling and crawling that Baby's legs will do in the first year of life there is little or no weight-bearing or upright work. It is therefore hardly surprising that the legs have a strange alignment and the feet flop about a bit. When they start to stand at the age of one, most babies have bow legs and look like professional jockeys. This is a natural occurrence and has nothing to do with being allowed to stand too early. In the strange course of child development it is usual to move from the bends of one year to a fine set of knock-knees at two and a half years old before finally straightening up with the legs of an Olympic athlete.

Talipes (club foot) is a fixed deformity which will be spotted immediately at birth. The foot has limited movement and is turned in. It may need splinting, physiotherapy and, if severe, possibly surgery may be required to resolve it. This must not be confused with the benign in-turned foot posture seen in many normal babies. Here the foot may rest in an in-turned position, but it can be moved fully in all directions and thus will straighten in time.

Flat feet are also quite usual at this early age and resolve themselves as the muscles and ligaments tone up. That is, unless Mum and Dad have feet like pancakes, in which case the little one may follow suit.

My rule with baby feet is this: if the tone is normal and the foot can be moved fully in all directions, then don't worry. But if you still have any doubts, don't hesitate to ask for an expert opinion.

Sweaty heads

Some babies seem to have particularly leaky skin on their heads. They lie on their pillow surrounded by a humid halo which leaves them looking like some sort of soggy saint. This is both common and normal and has no significance whatsoever.

Blue hue

As we have seen, the newborn has a great overload of red blood cells which take about a month to reach normal levels. All this super-red blood can give Baby a ruddy hue. In these early days the body's regulating mechanisms are pretty immature and often inefficient, meaning the allocation of blood to different parts of the body isn't always as perfect as it should be. When circulation is slow the ruddy, red blood will turn to purple, a condition particularly common in the legs. Occasionally the flow of blood to one whole side of the body may be greater than that to the other, giving a momentary two-tone baby, a condition we know as Harlequin baby. Rest assured that blueness and mottled skin in babies is very common and sorts itself out rapidly after birth.

Hiccough

If there's one thing a newborn baby can excel at it's hiccoughing. This is particularly common directly after feeds and is probably due to the pressure of a full little stomach on the diaphragm. It's quite normal.

Snuffles and rattles

These can sound very alarming, particularly in the still of the night. Then suddenly all goes quiet and you start to worry something has happened. It hasn't. That's just one of the new-found joys of parenthood and one that has no easy answer! Unfortunately babies don't understand that one decent cough or a good blow into a tissue will solve everything. Nose-breathing is important to babies and when the nose gets blocked they get upset and cannot feed properly. All you can do is wipe the nose and firmly resist the temptation to stick cotton buds into it. Sometimes a steamy, warm bath helps clear the passages. If things get really bad then obtain some nose drops from your doctor. These are never too popular and can be hard to administer.

Rattly breathing in healthy babies is very normal—they make all sorts of strange noises from the back of their throat at this early age. I wouldn't worry but if you have any doubts don't hesitate to get it checked out.

Sleep jumps

It is common and very normal for young babies to give sudden jumps in their sleep. These little ones have immature brains, not yet fully adjusted to allowing a smooth slide into slumber. At this age they drop off from fully awake to the deepest of sleep in a matter of minutes. With such speed and immaturity, it's not unreasonable to expect the odd short circuit and jump. This doesn't indicate epilepsy or any other dire condition. It's benign and perfectly normal. In fact, most of us wake with a jump from time to time. If it's OK for us, it's OK for Baby!

The messy baby—gastric reflux

Some babies are notoriously messy. You pick them up for a cuddle and find a mouthful of milk down your front. You can always spot the parents of a messy baby—Mum walks around with an old nappy permanently slung over her shoulder and Dad takes to wearing a cream-coloured business suit!

We are all built with a valve at the top of our stomachs which keeps the contents in place. This enables airmen to fly F1-11s upside down and Russian gymnasts to stand on their heads without creating international embarrassment.

In all little babies this valve is immature and very unreliable. They tend to bring up a mouthful of milk with each puff of escaping wind. For some this return is occasional, but for others it happens so often as to become a real hassle for parents.

The 'messy baby' and the 'gastric reflux baby' are effectively the same. The only difference is the severity and effect of the symptoms. They are both experiencing reflux, which means they have an unreliable valve at the top of the stomach.

Occasionally the baby is so troubled that he fails to gain weight and may even bleed as the stomach acid upsets the oesophagus. It is even possible for reflux to leak into the respiratory system, causing coughing, wheezing and very occasionally, pneumonia.

Sometimes it's thought a baby's reflux has inflamed the oesophagus, leading to uncontrollable crying. Some call this colic but often it's not due to inflammation but some reason we don't understand. If you are concerned about reflux and its symptoms ask your paediatrician to check your baby.

Most messy babies are happy, healthy and thriving. For parents the problem is largely one of laundry. These babies find a spontaneous cure with age, mostly when they walk and stay upright. As well, thicker foods are more likely to stay firmly cemented where they belong. Once sitting and the more upright posture starts then gravity will exert a powerful force to keep things in place.

To summarise, gastric reflux is the leaking of stomach contents up the oesophagus. This is common in babies and is usually harmless and needs no treatment. If your baby is happy, thriving and well, then be reassured. All you need is a good supply of bibs, a towel over your shoulder, an efficient washing machine and patience.

Where the reflux is extreme or very slow to resolve, seek medical advice. If there is poor weight gain, blood flecks in the milk or

---

Advice for those with a messy baby

- If the baby is happy, gaining weight, thriving and bringing up no flecks of blood with the milk—relax and be reassured.
- If the problem is major, shows no sign of resolving or has complications then your doctor may suggest the following:
  - Raise head of the cot on blocks or put a pillow under the mattress.
  - Use Gaviscon, a medicine that floats on top of the stomach contents and makes reflux difficult.
  - Try Mylanta or a drug to reduce acid production—check with your paediatrician about medications.
- Practical suggestions:
  - Keep Baby in a plastic-backed bib except for special out-to-impress occasions.
  - Wind well after food (with a towel over your shoulder).
  - Start solids early rather than late.

great irritability, this must be taken seriously and investigated now! Remember that most babies will have got over reflux before their first birthday and very few will need major intervention by the medical profession.

Bowels

The first real poo will make an appearance between about days two to five after birth. This shows the gut is working and can transmit matter from top to bottom.

As the system is relying on an unsophisticated, untried tube, it takes a little while to get settled. The bowels can shift after every feed or even more frequently, taxing the nappy stores severely.

After this the bowels become much more predictable and later still, with the start of mixed feeding, the motions begin to firm up. Now it is quite normal to find pieces of vegetable that have passed through without even their colour fading, let alone any digestion having occurred.

Constipation is unusual in a breast-fed baby, though it occasionally happens with those fed on the bottle. It can lead to a minor tearing of the tail end, which can cause bleeding or pain on passing. As a first response you would try increasing fluid intake, with cooled, boiled water or even the old remedy of a little diluted prune juice.

As Baby grows into a toddler they are almost on an adult diet with lots of variety. The baby moves from gumming the food they eat to using teeth to chew. Real food keeps everything moving and it also leads to the war of wills that comes with the toddler years, but that's another book!

Normal bowel movements vary greatly with age, diet and expectations. At six months I would be happy if there was movement somewhere between six times a day and once every three days. It would be unusual for a very active bowel to be equally active at night. It is lucky for the nocturnal nappy changers that things are usually quieter at that time.

When you start to panic over the bowels, please lift your eyes above the nappy area and carefully observe the whole child. If he is bright-eyed, gaining weight and full of life, the liquidity of what lands in the nappy is unlikely to be of importance. On the other hand if he looks dull, sick and unhappy, then it's time to call for help.

Conclusion

All parents worry about these imperfections and illnesses. If you're really concerned, you must speak to your doctor—but remember, if your baby is happy and well, then whatever little problem he has is probably quite normal and nothing to worry about.

The homecoming—
a shock to the system

A fter the squeaky-cleanness and the sheltered existence of hospital, your home can often seem quiet, isolated and rather lonely. You float out of hospital on your first solo flight, high on a cloud of euphoria, soon to crash-land in the real world outside. These early weeks are a time of tiredness and confused emotions. The whole balance of life at home is in for a major shake-up. No-one says it is going to be a bed of roses but if approached with commonsense, acceptance of change and a sense of humour the moments of pleasure will accumulate quickly and you will soon find your new job less challenging and more joyful.

A NEW LIFESTYLE

The arrival of your first baby is probably the most major and memorable event in your entire life. By comparison, getting married or buying your first home was a mere hiccough. After this birth you, your lifestyle and the whole way you think will never be quite the same again. Marriage at least has a honeymoon before you hit reality, but parenthood hits with a bang. There are many new features of your changed lifestyle—and they take some getting used to.

Worry
Worry becomes a major part of life. I believe most couples only find the true meaning of this word when they have children. It starts with worries over feeding, weight gain and your competence as a parent. Then you have concerns over toddler behaviour, sickness and schoolwork. Worry over children is a part of life and it never seems to cease. Even when they are grown up and have flown the coop you worry about their jobs, their lifestyle, who they're living with—and then the wheel turns full circle and you start losing sleep over your grandchildren.

Becoming number two instead of number one
The self-centred life is history. Yesterday you were living in ancient times. This was a different existence, BC (Before Children). You were

free to go your own way. Now all waking thoughts are focused on a totally dependent youngster.

Spur-of-the-moment decisions that were possible before are now a thing of the past, and excursions into life outside require planning. Often by the time all the gear is assembled and you've looked at the disturbance to feeding and sleeping routines it hardly seems worth the effort. But it is worth the effort. Don't stick in this rut. Don't chain yourself to the home like some oddball recluse. This is never good for Mum, Dad or Baby's emotional happiness.

It is particularly important to hold on to some outside social life. Most babies are remarkably portable, especially if they are good, settled sleepers, and they can accompany you in the bassinet. Of course it's hard if you have a colicky, poor sleeper who is resistant to any change. These little ones leave you manacled to the home as if a ball and chain were attached to your left foot. But don't give up. This is when good grandparents and real friends will hopefully come to the rescue to let you out.

Party pooping

Childless friends may feel you are a lost cause. As your friends talk to you they wonder if you really went to hospital to have a baby or to have some essential piece of brain removed. Certainly in their eyes you are not the same carefree, fun-loving person they used to know. When invited somewhere exciting you hum and haw like a politician, never prepared to commit yourself as it all depends on sleep, feeding or whatever. You are now a prize party pooper. At midnight, just when things are really starting to rave, you rush off like Cinderella to arrive home before the babysitter puts on an ugly turn. In the past it was all gossip about holidays, parties, music and good times, now life seems stuck in a groove. As you ramble on about the first tooth, baby fashion and the latest baby food, you are surrounded by a sea of yawning faces. Overnight you have become a crashing bore to the childless, but don't worry, one day their turn will also come.

Don't get alarmed. Your real friends will always stay close and as they watch the baby grow they will become quite involved, emotionally as well as in support and help.

THE NEW DAD

When two's company . . .

I often used to witness a phenomenon I thought of as 'the dethroned dad'. While Mum is busy getting used to having Junior around, Dad is being hit with a massive reshuffle of attention in his home life. The focus of attention suddenly swings away onto the new lodger and some dads find their noses firmly out of joint. Often there is jealousy of the strong bond between Mother and Baby, one which is hard to compete with.

This happens less in this new golden age of the hands-on father. Most are over the moon about the new arrival in their home and suffer separation anxiety as they go off to work, happy to receive pictures of what Baby's up to on their phone and computer while they're away. Today's dads are closer to their children—thank goodness!—and this does away with a lot of that 'dethroned' feeling. The answer is always more involvement from Dad, not less.

Delegation issues

Shared care is important right from the word go. Mothers of the newborn protect their young like a bird in the nest, but this clinginess must not go overboard. Often I see mums who are so possessive and unsharing that you would think birth had occurred by immaculate conception without any male help. Father does have equal rights and it is a wise Mother who tries to involve him in all aspects of childcare right from the start. Dad may be slow and clumsy at what he does, but it's better that he share the load than leave you to do everything. Don't criticise and redo his less-than-perfect efforts, just be thankful you have such a willing and caring partner. Remember, CEOs who can't delegate face defection from senior management.

Learned helplessness

This is a very special talent perfected by generations of fathers. This selective childcare is a great skill when it comes to changing a nappy, preparing food and working the night shift. The strange thing is that the more enjoyable tasks are often learned with consummate ease. Usually this learned helplessness can be prevented by getting things off to the right start and working out the ground rules of co-operation and shared responsibility from the very beginning.

Sleep deprivation

Sleep deprivation is no fun for anyone but it does seem to be particularly troublesome to dads. From my observations most can put up with cold food, unwashed clothes and reduced attention, but when deprived of sleep they fall apart. Of course this is not a problem if you have been blessed with a good sleeper, but when darkness is a time of torture then it is so much easier with a team of two involved parents. If Mum is breast-feeding and it's food that Baby is crying for, then obviously Dad won't be able to provide what's required. However, he can offer comfort and deliver the baby to the source of food.

The witching hour

With most young children the lowest spot of the day is that witching hour between 5 and 6 pm in the evening. This is the time when crying, irritability and colic are often at their peak. Mums are frazzled after a very full day and now they attempt valiantly to cook and at the same time calm, feed, wind and walk around pacifying the baby.

This is also the time when most fathers return from work. Instead of a warm cosy greeting, they are met at the door by a screaming baby and an exhausted wife.

This can all come as something of a shock to the husband registering somewhere around ten on the Richter scale. Whether tired or not, dads have to gallop in like the relieving cavalry and take over comfort and care or cook.

The Peter Pan father

The Peter Pan father is fortunately becoming less common. Some fathers simply never accept their new role and remain a sort of pseudo-single. Life goes on unchanged with the club, sport evenings and weekends with the boys. Such husbands may be good providers of money but they provide little else for their wives and children and offer a very poor example for the next generation. These eternal Peter Pans never like to grow up and shoulder adult responsibilities.

Love and cherishing

In the months immediately following birth many mums feel they have lost their identity as an attractive, independent person. Now is the time for Dad to love and boost Mum in her own right and not to fall into the trap of seeing her as an appendage to the baby. Offer love and cherishing, and a good cuddle never goes amiss. Flowers are not just for the birth. They can really brighten up a tired morning. Any excuse is a good one to show a new mother she is loved and appreciated.

THE NEW MUM—DIFFERENT FEELINGS AND EMOTIONS

No-one can ever prepare you for the almighty effect that becoming a mother has on your whole sense of self as well as on your lifestyle. Every new mum experiences many different emotions in the first few months at home.

Tiredness

I realise that this book goes on and on about tiredness but every new mum I have looked after in the last 30 years has suffered from it. Most mums are overwhelmed by tiredness by the end of the day, yet at the same time feel they have achieved virtually nothing. (Well you have. You've got your baby a day older with love and care and in the beginning that's achievement enough.)

Husbands find this hard to understand. I can remember when our first baby was born, coming in every evening to our newly purchased home, expecting to find rooms had been painted and renovation projects completed. In my naive state I could never understand how a now full-time housewife was unable to get on with all this extra work. It only takes dads a few days of looking after a little baby to realise that mothering is a very full-time job, leaving little time for anything else.

Once again, at the risk of appearing a bore, be reassured that there is not a new mother alive who does not sit back in amazement wondering how so little can be achieved when there is apparently so much free time in the day. It took nine months to make this baby and it's going to take at least another three to get the body back into relative equilibrium, and after this between three and nine more before you're firing smoothly on all cylinders again.

Emotional upsets

The early days and weeks after birth are a time for fragile emotions. Tears and confused feelings sneak up like a thief in the night then slip away just as silently. You are not going mad. This is a time of delicate emotions. If you feel a little fragile, hang in there. It will go away in a couple of days. This is so common you can consider it pretty much the norm to feel that way. If you are feeling really battered, turn straight to Chapter Six—The Baby Blues and Postnatal Depression—and get some helpful suggestions.

Isolation

While in that bustling hospital you were surrounded by a safety net of experts always there to support and advise. Now Dad's back at work and home seems very quiet. You are alone and help might seem far away.

The curse of isolation is its ability to magnify and distort. Small, insignificant problems mushroom out of all proportion. It's not that they are big, it's just that when you have no-one to compare notes with you lose all perspective. Lack of friends and family, unsupportive husbands and the baby blues can make the crush of isolation all the more savage. There are many mums who feel cut off and isolated, little realising that they are surrounded by other mothers who feel exactly the same.

Isolation can be a problem in our mobile society as couples move from their close relatives at home to make their own lives. The remedy is to ensure you keep in touch with the real world. Get out there into the fresh air—you'll feel better straightaway. Don't forget the phone either. You can always pick it up and make contact with a friendly voice. And with internet technology even grandma on the other side of the world can be just a click away. She'll love your photos and updates.

Keep in touch with family and friends. Visit the baby clinic regularly and talk to other mums. Generally these days the clinic will put you in touch with a new mothers group—you may make friends for life here with all the babies playing together well into childhood.

These are the sort of friends who know exactly what you're going through and will lighten the load just because they understand.

Identity

The change from working wife to full-time mother does not suit some. One minute you are a respected worker of independent means, the next you are temporarily retired and relying on your husband's salary. This identity crisis affects many first-time mums, especially those who have pursued a busy career before babies.

In the first three months childcare keeps you too busy for much else but thereafter it's worth taking a stand for identity. You must not be a complete slave to your child. The necessity to be a 24-hour-a-day mother is a popular myth, but all mothers are happier and more effective if they make some time for themselves. Babies have rights, but so have their parents and babies do not have to come first all the time. Please do not feel guilty when you sensibly spare a thought for yourself.

What I often heard from my mums was that they missed having a sense of their own identity, that their husbands' lives seemed to have changed so little, while their own revolved purely around the baby's needs. Many mums now are getting really good at making a little time for themselves but some still find the transition difficult, even a shock.

Self-image

After birth self-image is something else that takes a bit of a battering. Let's face it, it's not easy when you've been used to taking care of yourself and your appearance to find you have a wardrobe full of clothes that don't fit and even if they did, wouldn't open easily to breast-feed. Sleepless nights have left black rings under your eyes and a shower in the morning can be something of a triumph.

All mums feel a bit vulnerable at this time and the fantasy of the 'yummy mummy' does no-one any favours. Rest assured: your dark rings, wrinkles and general disarray are what's normal.

Saying that, it's important that you look after yourself and give yourself the occasional treat. Make a little time to have your hair done, or if funds allow, do a little clothes shopping. We all get a bit of a lift from looking our best. There'll be days when it seems like the last thing on a very long list but when you can manage it, a little effort will make you feel like your old self again.

Self-confidence

It is only natural for new parents to lack confidence in their childcare ability. After all, you've never done anything quite like this before. You need to develop a whole new range of skills such as recognising what different cries mean, feeding, comforting and those difficult puzzles such as how to fasten a jumpsuit so that you aren't left with a lone popper at the end.

There's never a shortage of experts to tell you that your baby needs a finely tuned diet of classical music, aromatherapy massage and whatever else the latest trend might be. If you put too much pressure on yourself about what your baby needs there's a good chance all you'll end up with are unrealistic expectations and feelings of utter incompetence. Treat all the childrearing fashions with the healthy scepticism they deserve. Remember, today's cult message soon becomes yesterday's mistake. Remember too that trusting your basic instincts is a good place to start. You'll find when you do, and it all works out, that your confidence will build.

Guilt

Beware of guilt. It is a sneaky enemy which, since Adam and Eve got at the apples, has made countless excellent humans feel miserable. It creeps up on your tired and soggy brain to persuade you that you are incompetent. It is your inadequacy that has caused the nappy rash or the failure of breast-feeding. You feel guilty you do not spend enough time with your baby or are not as well bonded as the expert who wrote the latest book tells you that you should be. You wish to go back to work but ill-founded guilt makes this impossible. You have a crier and after a week of sleepless nights you start resenting what this is doing to your life. But real mothers and fathers shouldn't feel resentment, you think. Then you feel guilty at having such feelings and you're stuck on the merry-go-round of guilt and can't get off.

Well, join the club. There is hardly a mother I know who hasn't been on this trip. Unless it's Wonder Woman or Superman who's reading this book I fear this is just the start of many years of self-doubt and tarnished self-confidence. The amazing thing is that, despite your worries, almost all end up with loving and well-adjusted children.

Don't compare—don't despair

You have been given a unique little human being who's been programmed to have a very individual temperament. Don't compare, don't despair when you find she is not identical to 100 million other babies. Don't analyse every behaviour difference in terms of what you have and have not done. Develop your own style of parenting, the one that suits you. There are many different sorts of babies and many different ways to bring up a little one. Some ways may be slightly better than others but few ways are really wrong.

The very best care you can give is to love, enjoy and have fun with your children and then do what feels right and works for you. If this does not happen to coincide with what other people tell you, then just ignore them.

EASY-CARE LIVING

Making life easy for yourself when you have a new baby is not selfish, it is just good sense. There are no medals for the martyrs to motherhood. Remember tired, tense parents give inferior care, while if you stay on top, so do those around you.

The aim in these early days is easy-care living, where a minimum of effort is used to produce the maximum of effect. Here's roughly how it works.

Cleaning

At this stage in your life no-one expects your home to look like a *Vogue* spread. You have quite enough work on your plate with the newborn to start worrying about the house. It needs to be sanitary not sparkling, so concentrate on the essentials. Time spent with your baby is far more rewarding than time spent with your vacuum cleaner. I know both pick up a lot of dirt, are noisy and need emptying frequently but it's the baby that needs the attention. These first golden days can never be recaptured but the dirt can be rounded up anytime. If your husband, friends or relatives object to untidiness, hand them an apron and direct them to the workplace. Tiredness and guilt about housework must never stop you enjoying time with your baby in these early days.

Food

If small babies can thrive on plain milk, the rest of the family will do equally well on plain food. Don't feel embarrassed to open a tin, or buy some take-out or a ready-cooked chicken. When you cook casseroles, cook in bulk and store a reserve dinner in the freezer. With these, all you need is time to defrost or a quick burst in the

microwave and you have a meal. Encourage your partner's creative abilities by putting him in charge of the kitchen, if he isn't already head chef.

Washing and ironing

When it comes to wet nappies it seems unbelievable just how much water can be manufactured by such a small set of kidneys in one short day. Most families today opt for disposables. If you have made the decision to use cloth nappies rather than disposables then make sure you have plenty of them. Have a large bucket to hide the dirties hygienically and then hit the washer in one large batch.

Encourage the rest of the family to make your life easier. For example, go for easy-care clothes and if a shirt looks halfway reasonable, hang it, don't iron it. If funds permit, the neighbour's high-schooler may like to earn some extra pocket money by helping out with a bit of ironing or cleaning.

Nappy changing

This is going to become one of the more monotonous features of your life for the next 24 months, so you might as well make it easy on yourself.

Prepare the area like a little workshop, with a raised roll-proof table where all lotions, wipes, rubbish bins and buckets are close at hand. Then you can do a speedy change like in the pits at the Grand Prix. It's a good idea to make sure that Dad is fully conversant with nappy changing because his involvement will most certainly be needed. Don't be misled by the view that fathers have some physical or psychological impairment that prevents them from engaging in this activity. An equal share in parenting means he will sometimes have to take on tasks of a pooey nature as well as revelling in the glory of his gorgeous offspring at family gatherings.

Visitors and relatives

Visitors who offer to roll up their sleeves and help are always welcome, and don't be too proud to accept their offers. If they are just hollow utterances they will learn to be more careful what they say next time. Don't be afraid to subcontract out work like a site foreman. While Grandma is running the washing through, a friend could be collecting the shopping, and what a joy are those friends who come bearing a basket of ready-cooked goodies like Red Riding Hood visiting her grandmother.

If your mother, or mother-in-law, is good company and a reasonably tactful diplomat, having her to stay for the first few weeks is an excellent idea. Be aware that even the most saint-like granny can cause some stress to the established equilibrium of your home. Be particularly careful not to share all the responsibility with Nanna so that Dad feels left out and on the opposing team to you when he walks through the door. If he doesn't get on with his mother-in-law before the birth, things are unlikely to alter magically after the event. In this case you'll just have to weigh up the advantages and disadvantages of having a grandmother in the home and be charitable in your behaviour.

Grandparents are often just as elated and involved with the newborn as the parents themselves. The older generation has a fund of excellent help and advice to give but it will fall on deaf ears unless delivered diplomatically. It's jolly hard being a grandparent. You try not to stick your nose in when you see your own children stumbling blindly along into all the same mistakes you made. Good grandparents learn to steer a course of gentle guidance and non-intrusive intervention. Unfortunately at this stage wisdom is not always recognised or welcomed.

Beware of proud, possessive grannies who try to take over the child. Sometimes you might wonder whose baby it is, with Grandma holding on tight like a front-row forward as she hands off all intruders. Some years ago I saw a baby who had two doting Italian grandmothers and bad eczema on the cheeks. Her father was quite convinced the grannies were to blame. 'She has been kissed at least a thousand times a day, since she was born. The skin on her cheeks has never been dry. It's all worn away.'

Getting out

It's all too easy to become housebound with a newborn. All that paraphernalia which goes to make up the average portable nursery seems such an effort to get together that it hardly seems worth it.

A good way round this is to keep a small bag ready-packed with a few nappies and a duplicate set of baby maintenance gear. In this way you can make instant decisions, grab the bag, grab the baby and run for it. Remember to stock the bag up again as soon as you get home or the next time you run for it you might be out of nappies at just the wrong moment.

Outside activity helps everyone's physical and mental state. Try and make a point of getting out somewhere each day, even if it's for a quick walk round the block or to go shopping. With all new mums it's quite natural for them to feel very possessive towards their babies and this makes it hard to leave the child in the hands of even the most competent child minder. But do try. Getting out is a major part of getting yourself together and back to normal again.

When it comes to night-life, this depends on the child. If you have been blessed with a remarkably easy, sound-sleeping baby then you can take the child just about anywhere, anytime, all with few problems. It's not so easy if you have a sensitive screamer who hates any change of routine. If grandparents or a really close friend are prepared to give it a go, then try biting the bullet and leaving Baby for a short time while you get a break in the adult world. If you take an unsettled child out then pick your friends and your venues with care.

Looking after yourself

It is just as important to look after your own wellbeing as it is to look after that of your baby. If you stay on top, so do those who depend on you. If you fall apart they follow you all the way down the slippery slope.

When Baby is asleep, put your feet up, have a cup of tea, a snooze or a relaxing bath. Take it easy and don't worry about all those half-done chores. Don't be afraid to switch the phone to voicemail or put a note on the door while you have a nap. When feeding your baby, sit in a comfortable chair, perhaps one that rocks. When that night shift is cold and long, rug up and have a flask of hot chocolate ready-prepared to pour.

Music can be great therapy enabling your tired body to soar high with the eagles. If you prefer to get away from all the death, destruction and depression on the news, slip on an MP3 player and escape the world for a little while.

Go gently, especially in the first six weeks. There are no prizes for proving how fantastic you are by being back on your feet and up to all your old tricks the day you return from hospital. Don't let anyone, especially your own conscience, make you feel guilty when you think of number one. It is vital that you look after yourself properly— everyone reaps the benefits.

CONCLUSION

With your baby's homecoming you, your lifestyle and the way you think have all undergone massive changes. Patience, flexibility and a sense of humour are needed to survive the shock. It's important that both parents have equal share and equal care of the baby. It's also important that the two of you have some 'together time'. Above all, mothers must look after themselves!

Babies matter but so do their mothers. So don't feel guilty about putting your feet up and ignoring the housework. Family members and visitors are always welcome, as long as they are prepared to pull their weight. Try to get out of the house at least once a day, even if it's only a short canter round the block.

Unessential tasks can wait. Now's the time for getting to know and love your baby.

The baby blues and postnatal depression

W*e all have times when our mood crumbles. It can come with a specific event in our lives but now and then we sink for a while unexpectedly and then bob back up again just as quickly. Depression is different. It's an unremitting low mood that hurts not just sufferers but those around them. In the past it was seen as weak to admit to depression, but now we hear of famous actors, politicians, sports stars and all manner of other brilliant people who live with it. We know now that it can happen to anyone.*

Postnatal depression is really the same as other kinds of depression, but it appears a few weeks to a few months after a woman has given birth. It seems that this is a time when women are much more vulnerable to depression.

There is a difference between postnatal depression and what we know as the baby blues. Both affect mood but the blues last for a few days and are generally to do with a plunge in hormone levels after the birth—it's the downside of that lovely high women feel after the job well done of having a baby. Postnatal depression requires a more hands-on approach.

In this chapter we'll look at the common conditions of baby blues and postnatal depression and see how to help.

THE BABY BLUES

This affects about two-thirds of mums in the first ten days after birth. The peak is probably the third day, though some may be teary right from day one. For most this lasts between 24 and 48 hours, though you may feel a little delicate for up to ten days.

What are the blues? The blues are caused by the massive reduction and reshuffle of hormones that follow delivery and also tiredness and the traumas of birth. The main outward symptom is generally tears and an unexpected feeling of emotional fragility. Little triggers can cause great upsets and the most innocent story on the evening news about a baby being mistreated starts the tears rolling. As you think of your totally dependent baby you wonder why you decided to bring one so perfect into such a cruel world. You are so happy, but still you cry at the drop of a hat.

Be reassured that this feeling is extremely common and very

temporary. It is not a sign of madness, weakness or that you're an inferior parent. Hang in there for a couple of days. It will go just as fast as it came, soon to be a forgotten part of history. All we need is to recognise what's happening and to be reassured that it's normal.

POSTNATAL DEPRESSION

Postnatal depression happens to at least ten per cent of new mums. It's usually in the first two to three months after the birth but it can surface later. It can be mild, moderate or severe. Fortunately the milder end of the spectrum is more common, but it can still be a long journey to the light at the end of the tunnel.

Causes of postnatal depression

The exact cause of postnatal depression is unclear, but as with baby blues it seems to be related to the stresses and hormone changes of birth. This can't be the whole story as it can set in months after birth when your system should have long since settled. There are also reports of adopting mothers and even dads similarly struck down.

Added to the change in the body and mind's chemical balance may be disappointment around expectations to do with the baby. Illness may be a factor or difficulty with breast-feeding. Perhaps the change from the structured life of work to the ups and downs of life alone with a baby plays a part. While being a parent is in the long run a very rewarding job, caring for a small child does not offer the same pattern of reward and encouragement as a satisfying job surrounded by friendly colleagues.

Financial and relationship problems may also weigh into the equation. Genetics are also a factor and a previous incidence of postnatal depression increases the likelihood of another. Lack of support from those close to you can be another source of trouble but most sufferers have a much-wanted baby and live within a close, supportive family network. And of course, lack of sleep doesn't help anyone's sense of wellbeing.

While it's hard to know the exact causes of postnatal depression, sufferers know for certain that it is painful and real.

Symptoms of postnatal depression

No two people experience depression in exactly the same way. And to the outsider, symptoms may be so well hidden that only the most enquiring eye can recognise what is really going on. The following are some of the most common types of feelings and symptoms associated with depression, though the person experiencing the problem may find it difficult to put their feelings into words:

- Numbness/flatness
- Not feeling 'quite right'
- No emotional energy
- Getting through the day on autopilot
- Life as existence rather than a source of enjoyment
- Exhaustion
- Disorganisation
- Difficulty in mustering the optimism to make plans
- Disturbed sleep
- No interest in sex
- Appetite off kilter: suppressed or tendency to binge
- Anxiety, tension, snappiness
- Lack of perspective, little judgement about which issues are serious and which trivial

Postnatal depression has varied symptoms and severities. Occasionally it can be a long, severe and incapacitating illness. However, usually it is just an overdose of those normal 'flat' feelings most mums have to some degree at birth. There is a fine line between where these normal feelings merge with a serious state of depression. Often it depends on the length and the severity of the suffering as well as the resilience of the sufferer.

All of this tends to add up to a feeling that you don't feel the way you're supposed to at this time in your life. You imagined that having a baby would be a source of joy, and there's a painful gap between reality and how you think things should be.

We know that it's common, so you might well ask why it isn't more widely talked about. The reason is that often mums feel such a failure that they keep it to themselves, soldiering on, determined not to let those close to them know how much they hurt.

Often it is not easy to share these feelings as your family may not understand how to deal with the problem. Husbands and children may not realise that you're suffering from depression but they know that something's not right. They may not complain but their way of coping may be to distance themselves.

It's important to remember that for most women, postnatal depression is a brief interruption to the pleasures of motherhood. For a few it lasts longer, sadly leaching the joy from the entire first year. But postnatal depression is not a condition that anybody needs to suffer in silence.

Postnatal psychosis—a rare but serious condition

This is the most extreme form of postnatal depression and occurs in one or two women per 1000. It begins in the early weeks and accelerates quickly. It is a major psychotic disorder which goes beyond depression to a situation in which a mother is frighteningly out of touch with reality. If not taken seriously this condition is a serious risk to mother and baby. Though not common the illness makes headlines as it is sometimes a factor when a baby, child or mother is harmed. Treatment involves close supervision and major drug treatment and often involves a spell in hospital.

Postnatal psychosis will never happen to most women but it shows that birth can trigger dramatic changes in a healthy person's state of mind and so we must pay attention to signs of trouble.

The hidden cost of postnatal depression

I worry a lot about postnatal depression. I worry principally that so many mums suffer in silence and write off this first golden year that should be fun. It seems such a waste of life to be stuck in an emotional desert when things could be so much rosier if help were sought quickly. Another good reason to seek help earlier is for the sake of your family.

No-one can be perfectly cheerful all the time, but subtle harm is done to those living in a home with long-term depression. Babies and children thrive on the spontaneous spark of warm, loving relationships. Depression damps down the emotions. We miss those little cues that babies give us that they are learning something new, that they need our encouragement to have confidence as they grow and develop. A depressed person can become slow to read what a baby needs. The beautifully oiled machinery of communicative relationships becomes clogged and no-one functions as well as they should.

In my days working on 'toddler taming', many children brought to me for bad behaviour didn't actually need taming. They were crying out for close, quality attention. Tantrums are a normal part of development, but some children who behave badly are missing out on something very important.

Partners of sufferers of depression also have a tough time. They find themselves on the other side of a pane of glass from the one they love and they don't understand what has changed.

I want to help mothers with postnatal depression today. I want them to find diagnosis and help quickly. Life is to be lived, not en-dured, for you and the people you love.

You can get through this but you may need help to do it.

Postnatal depression—what to do

Though postnatal depression can sometimes be severe and serious, most of the time it responds to understanding and simple treatment. First you must realise that you are suffering from an extremely common condition which affects more than one out of ten of all mothers. It is not necessary for you to grin and bear it. You may fool your friends but you won't fool yourself.

As the condition closes in, it is all too easy to become immobilised and housebound. If you do you'll soon find it is too much hassle to get yourself up and moving. The less you do the less you will want to do. Isolation itself causes further damage. Too much time spent alone when you feel this way will not do you any favours.

Part of the process of depression is the great lack of enthusiasm to get up and change the status quo. It is always easier to suffer on alone than to do anything that is going to help. This can lead to a long, lonely haul.

Friends and family—please note!

We have been talking about something so common that many who read this will have a loved one who is stuck there right now. Though you are close, usually you have no idea just how upset they are.

If the previous sparkle and enthusiasm for life has gone, this may be all you see. Others may slow down, become disorganised, moody, irritable, have disturbed sleep and lose all interest in sex.

Practical suggestions

- Try not to become isolated from your friends and family. Pick up the phone to a good friend. It'll give you a lift.
- Mixing with other mums at the playgroup may seem difficult but they may be going through similar ups and downs. Your tips and triumphs may buoy them up and vice versa.
- Ask your local baby health sister about a local group for mothers with postnatal depression. It can be an instant pick-up to realise that you are not alone with this.
- Tell your husband how you feel. Your marriage vows said something about loving, cherishing and caring both in sickness and in health and this includes postnatal depression.
- Remember the things that made you happy before you were a mother. Ask for babysitting help for a few hours and play netball or read your book—whatever helps you remember the simple pleasures in life.
- Ask for help. Perhaps you feel most comfortable with your health nurse or doctor. They will advise you and refer you to counsellors if necessary.
- If your doctor suggests medication, keep an open mind. This can be a relatively straightforward way to counter a short-term problem and does not constitute a failure on your part.

Some compensate by becoming active and flitting about like a butterfly. They know that if they never stop to think, they never have time to think how rotten they feel.

Don't be fooled by hollow smiles. Prisoners may laugh and joke in front of the firing squad but this doesn't mean that they are happy! Take time to listen and don't change the subject when the talk turns to feelings. Depressed mums can become terribly isolated. They may be ashamed to admit how they feel. They may not wish to burden those they love with their personal problems and prefer to suffer alone. But their problems must be your problems. As friends and family, do you make time to talk of feelings or is it easier to muddle on, hoping the problem will go away by itself?

A declaration of depression is not a sign of weakness. To admit it is a sign of strength and honesty. It is also a sign of strength to respond with understanding, to manage the ups and downs, celebrating the good days and doing your best on the less rosy ones. Don't give up.

CONCLUSION

Some degree of baby blues affects most new mothers. The blues go as quickly as they come, so give it a couple of days. Postnatal depression is more traumatic and more common than anyone is prepared to admit. This is a reaction to hormones, tiredness and a mammoth change in your life. Talk, time, activity, friends and special groups usually solve the situation. Above all, remember that if you're feeling stuck, you must seek help. There's no point suffering in silence as you become isolated—that gets you nowhere fast. Admitting there is a problem is the first step to getting back on your feet. It is a sure sign of sense and sanity.

- **NHS Choices** www.nhs.uk/conditions/Postnataldepression
- **Mind** (charity for mental health) www.mind.org.uk/help/information_and_advice

Bonding—relax and give it time

T he final contractions are over, the nurse whispers softly, 'It's a beautiful girl'. As the delicate skin of your newborn baby brushes lightly against yours, from somewhere just behind the anaesthetic machine sweet violins start to play.

Congratulations! Now you have bonded, stuck together for all time as if by superglue.

Is it really like that? Well of course it's not. Long-term relationships are not made in minutes. Lasting relationships take time to develop and refine, and the process is very much a two-way street. So what is this thing called 'bonding'?

Bonding refers to that unique relationship which develops between parents and their child. This is a special brand of love. Historically the talk has always been of mother-child bonding. No-one ever seemed to consider Dad very much in this process. Mum was said to hold the key to all emotional development while Dad's role was that of sire and breadwinner. If things went wrong in any way, all the blame was placed unfairly and squarely on one set of shoulders—Mum's! Some cynics refer to this old-fashioned idea as 'mal-de-mer childcare'. Of course it's nothing to do with seasickness, but a tortured use of the French language to suggest bad mothering.

Anyway, this notion is untrue and unhelpful, its only purpose to generate unjust guilt where none should be. Bonding and emotional care are not just for mothers.

Fathers, grandmas, grandpas, uncles, aunts, brothers, sisters and many more also bond and become emotionally involved.

I believe in bonding, but I don't believe in its elevation to a position of compulsory religion. I resent mums being told how they should feel and being made to feel terrible if they don't recognise themselves in the textbooks. I also object to the view that there is a critical period of bonding. This idea states that if you mess it up in the early days, a lifetime of emotional hardship is guaranteed. This is definitely not true. If bonding doesn't happen at birth this does not mean it won't happen at all. It just requires patience and the right environment to let Nature take its course.

How do babies win you over?

Little babies are remarkably responsive at birth when you consider what they have just been through. In the space of a few hours they have been pushed and squeezed, their blood circulation has undergone a major rearrangement, their brains now run on twice the richness of pre-birth blood oxygen, and after living in warm water for nine months they are now air-cooled like the rest of us. To add to the indignation their first view of life is being held upside down with a plastic catheter stuck up a nostril. Yet despite all this the majority of babies enter the world in a state of responsive alertness.

The period just after birth is an important one. The baby is unexpectedly alert, almost as though the grand design allowed this as a time for quiet introductions to get life off to a good start. For an hour or so the eyes are open and the baby stays very awake. This is a time when eye-to-eye contact is very important. Whether part of a grander scheme or just a matter of chance, this is a time for both parents to be with their new child. It is a time to be savoured.

Maybe you felt a connection when you first saw movements at the scan, but now the baby is here, where you can see her properly and touch her skin. Humans have an instinct to bond. For thousands of generations it's how we've survived as a species. You won't be any different, and it starts here.

Ideally, the environment immediately after the birth will allow the process to begin. This is a time for quiet space and time together. A quick photo, a text message sent out so everyone knows Mum and Baby are well, and that's enough of the outside world. This is a special time for you to enjoy the wonder of being a new family.

The instinct is to hold the baby close, for Mum to feel her skin against her own and feel the warmth in her little body. Mum and Dad will marvel over the tiny fingers, the little ears. You will watch the small movements, the breathing, the funny yawns. You will never have seen anything so perfect. There are only beautiful babies in these moments.

The baby-to-mother bond—a two-way street

With all this talk of mothers bonding to their babies we often forget that love has to be a two-way process. Babies must also bond with their mothers. It begins with communication. When we talk of communication we might think of speech, but in the early days it's about body language. Body language is big with babies, but most parents who talk to their little ones have no idea just how much communication is bouncing back. Researchers who have taken video recordings of mothers as they talk to their babies have been surprised at the extent of the two-way process. When you play these tapes back slowly, the baby is often seen to be moving in time with the speech. This response is like me nodding my head to let my patients know I am interested and listening.

As far as bonding goes, the truth is that although mums usually bond to their babies near birth, the baby will take almost another six months to fully return the compliment. In the first months our little ones are blissfully happy in the hands of any warm, loving care-giver. This is usually the mother, although more and more fathers are becoming involved. Between four and six months, babies begin to recognise their main caretaker and will tend to settle more quickly for them. It is generally not until the seventh month that strong attachment comes into the relationship. Suddenly the epoxy sets as hard as nails. The baby, who before then was happy to be handled by just about anyone, now only wants Mum and no-one else will do. Bonding has now been reciprocated. This attachment is usually given to Mum first, with Dad and other close carers being included soon afterwards.

So don't despair, mums, you may have to wait a bit but eventually bonding becomes a two-way process.

Bonding—what's usual

For most mums bonding starts early, to become ever stronger and more mature with close contact and the passage of time. One study★ showed that 41 per cent of mothers said that they first felt for their babies before birth, 24 per cent at the time of birth, 27 per cent in the first week, and the remaining 8 per cent some time later. These, of course, were the first feelings, not the full works. It should be noted that over one-third of the mothers in this study claimed they had no great feelings at birth. For them this was a time of numb indifference. Please don't sit around wondering if you feel as well bonded as some expert says you should. Feelings are to be felt, not analysed. The harder you try the more anxious you become, and this ceases to be a natural process and gets utterly stiff and constipated.

For some, bonding may come with the flash of a thunderbolt, for others it descends unnoticed like the evening dew. Just relax, let Nature take its course—give it time.

Sensible expectations

Some promote the idea of a critical period for human bonding. They believe that immediate closeness and skin contact are imperative and imply that all manner of psychological disasters may befall those who have failed to do it right in these early days. I doubt their claims. For a

---

★Klaus, MH & Kennell, JH, *Developmental-Behavioural Paediatrics*, Saunders, 1983, pp64–80.

start, if early contact is so essential then all adoptions would fail. They don't because adoptive parents have a really strong commitment to their child to make it work. This determination and love more than makes up for anything missed in the early days.

*Klaus and Kennell are well-respected researchers who have done much to make hospital care for mothers and babies a more gentle human affair. In one study they compared a group of mothers who had a small amount of contact with their babies at birth with another group who had unlimited time together. When they followed up the two groups they demonstrated some small improvement in mother-child communication in the maximum contact group, even two years down the track. Impressive as this is, other researchers are not so sure of the relevance of these small differences.

So what are we to believe? For my part the notion that there is a critical period where the whole of life's game is either won or lost is against the teachings of the present. Certainly we must do all in our power to promote good early contact, but let's not go overboard in the process. Extreme views generate unreasonable expectations and anxieties. Lack of early contact may not cause permanent upset to bonding, but the guilt that comes from feeling inadequate most certainly will.

Other factors that influence bonding

It is easy to expect every mother and child to behave and bond in the same way. But each of us is an individual with a unique temperament and way of doing things. Whereas most babies are cute and easy to fall for, there are those who quite definitely are not. They are the ones who are irritable, push you away, seem to cry most of the day or gaze at you with a bored expression as you positively ooze love from every pore in your body. Saints may love all equally, humans are more selective.

Other upsets may also take the gloss off your feelings. There may be the baby blues or postnatal depression, and it's hard to bond when

---

*Klaus, MH & Kennell, JH, *Developmental-Behavioural Paediatrics*, 1992, pp16–26.

your brain is numb, sad and on automatic pilot. The conception may have been unwelcome or the pregnancy really difficult. Labour may have been a harrowing experience and this got you off on the wrong foot. Then there are the hassles of unsupportive partners, financial worries, interfering relatives and inadequate accommodation. All these will play their part in the bonding or non-bonding process. Bonding is not solely to do with close contact and the magic of the moment. Environment, individual differences and family circumstances are also important to some extent.

Special problems—special bonds
Adoption

With adoption there is no nine-month preparation, no skin contact, no breast-feeding. One moment you are a childless couple, the next an unannounced stranger has arrived in your midst. Despite all the theoretical difficulties, adoption usually works very well. It works well because the adopting couple dearly wants the child and pulls out all the stops to make it a success. Of course there is always the chance of stress, but for most couples this closeness and commitment overcomes anything they may have missed in the early days.

Sick and premature babies

Babies born early now have a very good outlook physically and emotionally. The bonding process begins in the midst of uncertainty but as the child grows and develops, bonding grows ever stronger, just as it does with children who have an easier beginning. Your own feelings may be more complicated—perhaps birth came as a surprise and Baby was whisked away for treatment, leaving you empty-handed. The brain can automatically keep its distance from a baby that is so vulnerable. But small babies usually do very well nowadays. Premature nurseries are now places for parents. They are encouraged to visit and are made to feel welcome and at ease.

Modern-day nurseries are not just oases of high technology. They are springs of intense humanity and quality emotional care. All the electronic gadgetry is explained and demystified. Parents can touch, hold little hands, cuddle and help care, and, when the baby gets stronger, have time to become acquainted in a quiet parents' room.

Having a sick or premature baby gets things off to a shaky start, but once the dust has settled the outlook for the long-term emotional future is excellent.

Caesarean section

A few caesarean mums may not be awake to enjoy those first moments of contact but not to worry, it's just a minor hiccough at the start. They will bond and become glued together as firmly as any other mother and child. Most mothers who know that a caesar is on the cards ask their obstetrician that it be done under local anaesthetic (an epidural). Here the lower part of the body is pain-free but they still have the full sensation of eyes to see, brain to wonder and arms to hold and cuddle at birth.

Conclusion—the bonding bus

There's no need to be too scientific about bonding. Don't psycho-analyse yourself and don't sit around waiting for bonding to drop like a brick from heaven. You can't force feelings. And don't let anyone tell you that one slip at the start leads to a lifetime of emotional problems. This simply is not so. You may miss the bonding bus at its first stop, but you can always board later on down the line. Of course it may take a bit longer, but you will still get where you want to go in the end.

Brothers and sisters—adjusting to the new arrival

Y ou don't have to be a toddler tamer to work out that when a newborn barges in on the private kingdom of a resident toddler, the toddler's nose is bound to be put out of joint. Toddlers are interesting little people who generally hit their peak of difficult behaviour between eighteen months and two and a half years of age. If you look at the average spacing between a family's first and second child you'll find that it's just about that length of time.

Toddlers tend to be negative, stubborn and demanding. Even on good days they seek constant attention, wishing to be on centre stage at all times. They are not renowned for deep humanitarian thoughts and actions such as sharing, and, what's more, sense is rarely their strong suit.

Don't despair about your dreams for a happy family. Be reassured that a second or third baby does not have to disturb the sitting tenant. All you need is some forward planning, some consideration of the child's point of view and a lot of cunning.

So let's see how we can get things off to a good start.

Before the birth (telling the toddler)

It's never that easy to be a laid-back supermum when in the throes and throw-ups of early pregnancy. It's at tiring times like these that many people wonder if one child is not the ideal family size! Forty weeks seem like light years in a toddler's time frame, so it's pointless doing any serious talking about babies until towards the end. Once your size has blown out to the point where even an unobservant toddler can spot the difference, then it's certainly time to talk. Don't get too deep and meaningful in your discussions. They don't need to know all the finer points of human reproduction—just simple bits about tummies, brothers and sisters, and a few days in hospital will suffice.

Let them feel the kicking baby and possibly mention a few names you're considering. Talk of dirty nappies and pooing infants is always riveting to toddlers. At this age they see themselves as world experts on such bodily functions. Always emphasise that you are going to need a special little helper if you are ever going to manage.

Sharing love

It's sensible to tell the toddler that of course you will always love him just as much once little brother or sister arrives. Though it's very easy to say, most parents expecting their second child find it hard to believe that they could ever love another as much as the first. Give it a week after the birth and you'll be surprised to find just how easy it is.

Care when in hospital

Don't leave the arrangements for childcare while you are to be in hospital until the last moment. Plan this well in advance. Organise some combination of Dad, Grandma and whoever else makes them feel secure while such a big change is happening.

It's not a bad idea to have a short trial run with the caregiver before the event. This helps acclimatise the child and lets you see that it will all work when you actually have to go to hospital.

Tidying toddler behaviour

The middle months of pregnancy are a good time to tidy up a few toddler management issues. If, for example, they are still sleeping in your bed, now is a good time to serve an eviction order. If you are holding off toilet-training until the summer comes, cut the nonsense and get on with it now. If preschool is about to start, it's best to have it established before, rather than at the time of birth. I'm not suggesting that you engage in some sort of behavioural blitz, but now is a good time to tidy up a few loose ends.

Going to hospital

If all your arrangements for care at home have been well planned you should be able to slip off without a lot of fuss and panic. If it's 3 am and the caretaker is in residence, don't stir Junior—let sleeping toddlers lie. A kiss, a hug, a word or two of love spoken over the slumbering form and then hop it quick. For daylight departures, explain once more what is about to happen, say your goodbyes and make a clean, decisive exit. Don't drag it out, as this winds everyone up and you leave upset and feeling guilty.

The hospital

It's good for toddlers to visit Mum in hospital and be introduced to the source of all the tiredness and turmoil of the last nine months. Hospitals welcome brothers and sisters as long as they don't stampede up and down the corridors, shout noisily, swing on the curtains or turn off ventilators.

Visiting hospital should be a fun family affair and a way of getting things off to a good start. Make sure that the new baby doesn't steal all the thunder. Reserve a large portion of the fuss for your toddler. He's also an important little person and would be the first to admit it. Little ones are sure to want to climb all over Mum in bed and although Florence Nightingale definitely would not have approved of this, her successors will usually turn a blind eye.

The homecoming

The return home is the time when everything should get off to a good start, but often it is handled badly. Mum is tired, clingy and supersensitive to the slightest hint of a toddler terrorist raid on the infant. At the same time toddlers are keen to take up where they left off, and while they are not so greedy as to expect 100 per cent of Mum's attention, they reckon that 95 per cent is a pretty fair proportion.

When you arrive back home let 'the driver' take care of the baggage and the new arrival, which leaves your hands free to greet Junior properly at the door.

A little present organised beforehand might be sound psychology. Your friends and relatives should know (or have been primed) not to walk past the sitting tenant in their haste to drool over the new arrival. If they ride in on their camels bearing gifts and greetings from afar, at least one present should have a toddler's name on it.

Settling in

The experts tell us that all care and attention should be divided equally between our children (at all times). Now that's all very well to say from the relaxed depths of some academic office, not quite so simple, however, when you're up there on the front line. All children do not demand the same care and attention and so the division will never be equal, however hard you try. I think it's best to keep toddlers riding high on a wave of positive attention. Elevate the toddler to the special status of friend, confidante and mother's little helper. Give lots of indirect attention to the toddler as you go about your care of the baby. This side-stream attention may not be ideal, but it will leave most toddlers happy.

For example, when changing nappies, get your helper to bring the tissues, hold the nappy or just keep you entertained with the latest fund of stories from the playgroup. When it comes to feeding, this is a good time to read, play, talk and listen. If you don't plan ahead and set things up to involve the toddler, he will be obliged to gain your attention by less desirable means. When breast-feeding he might demand to latch onto the unoccupied side or create such a scene that you are forced to stop. When everything is delicately balanced in mid-nappy change, he will engage in what sounds like vivisection with the cat and at once he has you hooked. It's best to anticipate these problems and, with a bit of cunning, steer round them.

Toddler regression

It is quite common for toddler behaviour to regress when a new baby arrives. They may want a bottle or to be spoon-fed. They may slip back into baby talk and often toilet-training will take a nosedive. Don't get too analytical about this. Love, time and sensibly shared attention will soon iron out these wrinkles.

Divided care

Try to divide the care wherever possible. At the weekend, for example, while Mum nurses the newborn, Dad can be off having adventures with Big Kid, whether it is shopping, playing in the park or helping Dad in the garden. All this helps to spread the load, gives some individual attention to your older child and lets him feel very important.

Behaviour blow-out

Young children are always at their most difficult when stressed by changes in the equilibrium of their lives. Be more accepting of behaviour irritations at this time. Before you blow your top, be sure that it is the tiresome behaviour that is irritating and not just the low tolerance of your own tired brain. Use the old stand-bys of diversion, pretending to ignore, keeping positive and using time apart as the safety valve when you are losing your cool.

Protective mums

I realise that it is hard for the new mum to sit back while strollers get shoved, dirty digits get poked into orifices and toddlers mountaineer over the sleeping baby. Now is the time to establish that delicate balance between protection and over-protection. The former is of course necessary for survival but, if overdone, leads to rivalry, resentment and cries of favouritism.

Try not to pounce on the toddler every time he comes within a toy's throw of the baby, but rather aim to divert his attention elsewhere. Try to remain as laid-back and philosophical as your sensitivity and commonsense will allow. Remember little ones are a good deal tougher than you think.

The six-month sting

There is another outcome that may sneak up on you unawares. You arrive home with your new baby to find utter peace. Then at about six months, just as you thought it was safe to relax, guerrilla warfare hits you with a bang.

Don't panic, this is an extremely common scenario yet one which will still have a happy ending. You see, when Baby first appeared he lay around doing nothing like a big doll who posed no particular threat to Junior. Then suddenly at six months the doll sits up, starts to gurgle and attracts all the attention. Faced with this unfortunate turn of events the toddler reacts against his change in status and becomes a pest.

All you can do is divert him. Keep him busy and ignore as much of the anti-social behaviour as is reasonable. Divided care, visits to Grandma's, playgroups and lots of positive attention are the best ways to cope.

Bickering, fighting and sibling rivalry are all part of the joys of family life and will go on throughout childhood. As adults we are just as competitive and jealous of those who seem to have more possessions and get greater attention than we do, so why should we be surprised when our junior versions react in a similar way?

Conclusion

A new baby will fascinate most toddlers, but many resent the change it brings to their lifestyle. Toddlers tend to be negative, stubborn, attention-seeking little people who are not too keen to share. So when a new baby arrives, they're not always going to be overjoyed.

Try and give toddlers as much attention as you can and enthuse them to help you look after the new member of the family. Plan ahead, try to be as relaxed as possible and avoid over-protecting the newborn. Keeping your older child permanently happy will not be possible, but you're more likely to keep the peace if you make him feel important.

If you can't give your whole attention, side attention will often do the trick. By this I mean it is possible (and will become natural) to feed, change, bath and comfort a baby while talking to your older child so that he feels valued and loved. He will still have some adjusting to do, but if you can make him feel important and involved from the word go, you'll be off to a good start.

Spacing of children

There is no ideal gap to have between children. The success of any spacing is going to depend mostly on the temperament of the child you have been allotted and how well your energy reserves hold out.

- If you have your children close together, they are usually great mates who gain a lot of fun from each other's company. However, be warned, close children can bicker and fight endlessly. Two children together leading each other on can get into three times the mischief than any child alone could have ever thought up.
- With wide spacing much of the close company is lost, but there are advantages. Mothers enter this later pregnancy better prepared and well rested. An older child is also able to be of some help in looking after his younger brother or sister.
- Personally I like to see a gap of between eighteen months and three years. If less than eighteen months, it is usually too tough on a mother's physical and emotional strength; and if over three, the close companionship that I see as valuable may be lost.
- Life has a way of messing with those who set out to plan their families to almost the exact date of delivery. We can practise birth control with some reliability but conceiving on demand, for many couples, is not quite as predictable. Let's not get too precise. The most important goal for all of us is to have healthy and emotionally happy children, whenever they choose to appear.

The gear for the job

W hen it comes to choosing equipment for your baby, there are a few absolute necessities, some things you might do without but which make life an awful lot easier, and then all those very nice but very extravagant luxuries. What you buy depends on the size of your budget. The upmarket perfectionist may go for the all sparkling new, whereas the realist will gratefully accept anything battered, borrowed or bought on eBay. When you start assembling the equipment you discover an ongoing truth, having children is expensive! My advice is to forget the way something looks, as long as it does the job. Young children are not impressed with labels. In fact they will smear food over them with as much enthusiasm as they would if their gear came from a garage sale. And if your family and friends ask what you need, don't be afraid to say. No-one is afraid to stipulate what they want on their wedding registry, and babies have even more specific requirements than newlyweds.

Let's look at some very basic aspects of day-to-day care and the tools for your new trade.

The baby's room

The current advice from organisations that educate parents and carers about SIDS is to have the baby's cot near your own bed for the first six to twelve months of life. Wherever the cot goes, you will need a dedicated space for changing, organising baby clothes and feeding. One spot where you can find everything is easiest, even if the actual feeding and sleeping happen elsewhere.

In one corner of the room you should erect the nappy change area. Fitted out with all the lotions and potions, this will become a sort of pit-stop area in the racetrack of life where efficient Le Mans–type nappy changes can occur during the day and night. If you happen to have a toddler in the house with a toddler's uncontrollable fiddly fingers, it's best to keep solutions that squeeze out of tubes and ooze out of bottles on a shelf well above her reach. The room should have two kinds of lights: a bright one for seeing clearly what is going on and a dim one near the bed for night-time feeding and checking on Sleeping Beauty. There should also be a comfortable chair to support your tired bones to make the night shift a little less of a hassle.

Sleep and cots

For the first weeks most babies will sleep in a bassinet or a Moses basket beside their parents' bed. This makes it easy for night-time feeding to occur with the minimum of disruption. It also allows a bit of supervision until the parents feel confident enough to be separated from their newborn. And as mentioned above, it's in keeping with safety guidelines.

Sleepwear should be comfortable and easily washable. At birth most prefer to sleep in some type of restrictive wrap. Small babies are generally wrapped firmly for sleep. They will have shown you how to do this at hospital. Before long they will spend most of the night and day in a jumpsuit. These are unisex, useful, easy-care and relatively cheap.

A cot will need to be purchased some months down the track. As you will get at least two years' hard use out of it for each child, you will find that a good cot is a sound investment. A heavy-duty model is often a wise precaution in case your gentle little newborn turns into a tough, active, little rocker.

Check cots comply with current safety standards. Most cots come with a suitable baby mattress which should be fully wet-proofed. Pillows are not suggested for sleep in the first two years. Also keep quilts, lamb's wool, bumpers and soft toys out of the cot for young babies.

Baby wipes

It's hard to think of bringing up babies without a box of tissues at hand. Their advent has been a godsend for keeping little faces, noses and regurgitating bodies clean. Now we have moved one step further in convenience cleaning, with those commercially produced packs of ever-wet wipes. Yes, these are excellent, portable and everybody uses them, but don't forget that good old tap-water is still the cheapest and kindest way to wipe.

The ready-wet tissues contain some additives that can rob delicate skins of their natural oils. They can dry and even irritate. If they suit your child and your wallet and your busy lifestyle, then use them. But if not, pure tap-water or sorbolene and glycerine on a cloth or tissue is still the best bet.

Bathing

Despite the fact that each baby spends the first nine months living underwater, once properly dried out a good many are not that keen on any further immersion. It's probably not so much the water that causes the upset but having their warm clothes removed and with them that swaddled sense of security.

In the early weeks a daily bath is not necessary. If you carefully top-and-tail them this keeps the upper end and the nappy part hygienic and makes daily bathing unnecessary. Bathing at first should be in a special baby bath or a plastic basin and perhaps using a bathing rest. If set on top of a table make sure it is secure and won't tip. You can use an ordinary washbasin or sink if you want, but guard against bashing Baby against the protruding spouts or scalding with an unsuspected drip left hiding in the hot tap. You can test the temperature with your elbow, which is probably the most sensitive part of your body that is conveniently available.

Most babies do well with a soap-free water wash. After all, at this age they don't have quite the same body odours as their sweaty parents

and a light sprinkling of water soon has them smelling like a rose. If you do use soap, make sure that it is a mild baby soap and only use it on bottoms and other heavily soiled areas. Baby oil leaves the skin clean and soft, but be careful when your little one is all oiled up like a sunbather—one wrong move and she may shoot from your grasp like a cork from a champagne bottle.

When it comes to washing the remnants of the umbilical cord use cotton wool with water. The scalp can be cleaned with water, mild baby soap or baby shampoo, depending on the need. It is best, however, to leave the ears alone. There seems to be an irresistible human urge to poke cotton tips into delicate little orifices. It is not necessary and something might get damaged.

Many new parents approach the first baths at home with trepidation. They were shown what to do in hospital by a frighteningly efficient midwife and now they have to submerge this fragile little creature on their own. Here's how to do it. After the first couple of runs you'll be an expert:

- Planning is key: you'll need clean clothes, a new nappy, creams, wipes, a rubbish bin, cotton wool and a soft towel.
- Make sure the room is warm.
- Put the phone on voicemail—this is an intimate time that should not be rushed.
- Remember: never, ever leave a baby alone around water. Hold her tight and don't let her out of your sight.
- Start at the top. Keep her nappy on and her jumpsuit done up to her tummy. Wash her face, neck and head. Use cotton wool for ears and eyes. Dry these bits before moving on.
- Remove nappy. Clean the bottom and wipe.
- Wash body, taking care over the creases and bottom.
- Rinse by pouring water gently over her or dip her in the water if she's happy about it.
- Time for a big snuggle in a soft towel. A little lotion if her skin's dry.
- On go the clean nappy and suit.

Baby clothes

Even if you know the sex of your baby before birth, don't go wild and buy lots of clothes. The sensible thing is to wait and see what clothes you need and when you do start buying, to check the labels to make sure the clothes are the easiest of easy-care. It's fine to have a couple of smart show-off outfits that need handwashing and ironing, but all day-to-day clothing should be of the 'straight into the machine, out, dry and wear' sort.

Different fabrics suit different children. Wool and pretend wool fabrics like acrylic can irritate, particularly babies with a history of eczema. Cotton is about the most comfortable easy-care material when used alone or in a cotton–polyester combination. Little cotton singlets can double as T-shirts in the hot months and as warm under-vests in the winter. The most useful of all baby clothing is the jumpsuit. This has the advantage of being both comfortable and appropriate to wear day or night. Cloth bibs are a must to protect the clothes, particularly if you have a messy baby who does not always keep milk down where it belongs. Knitted bootees are great for gift givers but are an utter nuisance. They are a fiddle to fasten and endless hours of motherhood will be spent crawling around the floor searching for the lost member of the duo.

In the first year shoes are only for show. Not only are they an awful waste of money, they inhibit walking and are about as much use to a human baby as floaties are to a duckling.

Dummies

Babies take immense pleasure from sucking. If the breast is not available then there are many who will happily latch onto the second best option, the dummy. I always used to see dummies as a last resort and had a strong dislike of seeing children anchored by the mouth. But if it gives comfort and peace to a baby that wants to suck, what's the harm? If you have an easy, happy baby, then you don't need a dummy. If you have an unsettled, irritable crier, then pop in a dummy and see what happens. This book is about 'peace in our time'. If dummies make life happier and more peaceful, do it.

Bassinets, baby baskets, slings and backpacks

Small babies are very portable. For the first three months of life a Moses basket or bassinet is all that Baby will need to call home. As well as being her sleeping site, it can also serve as her means of transport. Some models come with a folding base on wheels so that they double as a pram and make for a more portable sleeping platform.

Slings can be used from the earliest weeks and are a method of carrying small babies which is as old as time itself. The simplest sling is in the form of a blanket tied round your neck or waist. Slings and packs suit most children, especially the ones with a grumbling, active temperament who like to be on the move. They give a lovely sense of warmth and closeness while freeing up Mum's arms so that she can get on with other things and in the right sort of sling you can even feed them. The packs are good as they get a little heavier and can be turned around as baby's neck and curiosity strengthen. And they're great for Dads to get a nice walk and cuddle in, doing the groceries, going to a café, giving Mum a little break.

After about six months, when head control starts to strengthen, a framed backpack may be the answer. With these you can walk a fair distance but remember that babies get tired with all the bouncing so save the long hikes for later.

As baby grows, slings and packs may be a little heavy for most of us. Sooner or later we'll have to think about the first set of wheels …

Prams and strollers

The old-fashioned English pram is now a somewhat outdated mode of transport. It is expensive, heavy and usually doesn't fold up, so while it did the job for my mum, it's a no-no on just about all fronts for the modern mother. There's really no great advantage to a pram over the more versatile bassinet on wheels. These may have a less finely tuned form of suspension, but they are so much more portable and can be folded to put in the boot of a car.

At about three months, it's time to purchase a stroller. These are a must for every young child. They are light, fold neatly, are easily

pushed and let your nosey youngster see where she is going in life. You will usually get at least three years of service out of them, which must make them one of the best investments you will make for your baby.

There is an incredible variety these days and some ingenious design has gone into many of them. Some strollers enable Baby to be laid flat or sit up. Many have pump-up wheels like a bicycle for parents who want to do some serious exercise while they're out walking (or running) with their child. These tend to be better on steps as well.

There are also double strollers available, which are useful not just for twins, but if you have a toddler in tow as well. Both can be transported together with the toddler walking for a while and then hopping in beside the baby for a bit of a rest. These have a great payload capacity when it comes to carting children and the shopping.

Choice is made according to budget and needs. Even if you fancy the swish ones you may get a deal on eBay. And think about whether you're going to be hopping on and off the bus, getting up stairs and whether your back is up to lugging a heavy model in and out of the car boot.

Safety capsules and car seats

Car travel is one of the great hazards of our modern-day lives, with injury affecting both adults and children. You must think about car safety right from the very first trip home from the hospital and you must never lower your standards from that moment on.

From birth to nine months it is essential to use a rear-facing restraint. After this they can sit in a forward-facing seat to have a good look around and this seat will last several years. Some seats are designed for both phases, requiring just a flip around as Baby graduates. On the other hand capsules are popular as you can carry her into the café or shops while she's still asleep without having to disturb her. These don't convert into forward-facing seats, so as ever, you need to think about what you're likely to get most use out of.

Most baby books stipulate that you must not use a second-hand seat, even if it is an approved model. Use your commonsense. If you're inheriting a seat check it carefully. There must be no damage to the frame, straps or fastening devices.

Make a firm commitment that each time you go out in the car the journey will not start until all seat belts are fastened. Never let children roam around the car unrestrained and never ever sit a child on your knee in the front seat.

Car doors should be locked, preferably with child safety locks. Don't leave a child unattended in a car and certainly never on a hot day.

Bouncinettes and baby walkers

The bouncinette consists of a metal frame covered in cloth which props the baby up at an angle of 45 degrees and gives her a little bit of bounce. This lets her get up and see the world from a more interesting level. It is useful for feeding and allowing play with toys. It is light and portable, and it can be easily carried from room to room where Baby can be put in and watch Mum as she works. Bouncers are for the floor and not to be used for lifting onto benches or any higher plane. These days there are also a range of baby chairs that similarly allow Baby to watch what's going on.

There is no shortage of movement contraptions for babies. They range from the up-market clockwork cot to the more common jolly jumper. This latter gadget hangs the child from a doorframe like a parachutist suspended on springs. They may be of some benefit to the bored, overactive baby but are unnecessary for the average baby and are generally not recommended. These walkers are dangerous and have caused many accidents.

All child safety organisations strongly oppose the sale and use of baby walkers. So why would I even discuss them? As a children's doctor I had a special interest in helping children who exhibited difficult behaviour. Many of them were perpetually unhappy unless they were able to get up and move about. In the face of having to care for an extremely demanding and irritable infant, I see a place for walkers as a sanity saver. If used, the dangers must be addressed, then the infant carefully supervised and restricted to an area far from steps, fire, flexes and danger.

Toys and mobiles

Little babies need few toys. In the early months it is their own bodies that give them the most enjoyment as first they discover their ten fascinating fingers, followed by ten equally fascinating toes. These are good for chewing and waving about for hours at a time.

Babies are initially very visually interested. Mobiles hung over cots or change tables are a really cheap source of entertainment. By four months, shaking rattles or playing with toys hung from the cot side is fun, and at six months they can take hold of toys, change them from hand to hand and generally pop them in the mouth for a good chew.

Cuddly toys may look sweet but probably appeal more to the

parents than they do to the very young. Nowadays it seems almost compulsory for every child in the Western world to have some sort of shape-insertion game. I don't know if this speeds learning at all, but I do know from painful experience that walking barefoot on the inserts at 3 am brings a parent to full consciousness very quickly.

Don't go overboard with buying toys. What children of this age really need can't be bought. What they need is not toys to play with, but loving parents to play with them.

Conclusion

The tools of your trade will depend very much on what you can afford. If you place safety and usefulness at the top of your list, then you won't go far wrong. Never be ashamed to borrow or use preloved equipment. It makes sound sense.

Think safety

...ays a tendency to believe that accidents happen to other people.
...uldn't possibly happen to us, but of course, as you know, this isn't
...live in a hazardous world and no matter how careful we try to be,
...ways going to be risk. In this chapter let's look at some of the main
areas ... danger for babies and see what can be done to lessen these risks.

HOUSEHOLD DANGERS

For the first five months babies are pretty immobile. Though they can't crawl, they can wriggle, move and fall off things. At about five months they will start to roll around the floor and this is when child-proofing really has to start. The true danger comes when they learn to stand and then nothing that is remotely within their reach is safe. At this age children have no thought as to the consequences of their actions and it is up to us parents to protect them. Trying to educate small babies to such dangers is really an uphill battle.

Some suggestions for home safety
- When your baby starts to walk, tape and pad dangerously sharp corners of furniture.
- Steps should be fitted with a secure safety gate, which should always be kept closed.
- Great care should be taken around windows. Many children have fallen through them. Consider bars and/or catches that prevent them from opening wide and supervise children closely around windows.
- Safety plugs should be fitted into power points.
- All homes should have a life-protecting safety switch/circuit breaker fitted to the main power board.
- Smoke detectors should be checked and a new battery fitted every six months, whether you own or rent.
- Knives and other sharp objects should all be kept well away.
- All fires should be guarded and dangling cords kept out of reach.

- Immobilise some cupboards with locks or tape and hide temptations.
- Adults expect glassware but glass is dangerous with young children around.
- Dangerous household substances like drain cleaner, caustic soda or suchlike are best discarded altogether, but if you must keep them then make sure they are kept under high security.
- Dishwasher detergent is especially caustic, yet often within reach of a crawling child.
- Some products do not immediately ring alarm bells but must also be kept out of reach, like shampoo and fly spray.
- Never leave medicines within reach or in cupboards that a child can climb up to. Always keep them in a place that can be locked. Dispose of old medicines safely.
- Plastic bags or packaging must be safely disposed of or put out of reach.
- Dangling blind cords and any other type of cord are a choking hazard.

With most household accidents involving infants it is the changing speed of mobility that usually fools the parents. From five months to ten months an immobile child suddenly becomes a very active and inquisitive one.

Scalds

I mention scalds specifically since these are a major problem with babies. The main causes are either parents spilling hot drinks on the wriggling baby on their knee or, later on, when cups, jugs and saucepans are pulled down on top of the upright and unthinking explorer.

Some suggestions to avoid scalds
- Try and avoid cooking and nursing your baby at the same time.
- Don't drink hot liquids while you have Baby on your knee.
- Don't leave coffee cups or other hot containers on low tables

or at the edge of tables or benches once your baby has become mobile.

- Don't leave jug or kettle cords dangling over the edge of kitchen benches. Retractable cords are a good idea. Be very careful of iron cords too.
- Always turn the handles of saucepans inwards when they are on the stove.
- Be careful if microwaving a baby's bottle—it can get an awful lot hotter than you think.
- Turn the bath taps firmly off and always run a little cold water last.
- Turn down the thermostat on the hot-water system. You need water to wash, not to sterilise your dishes.
- Keep an extinguisher near the oven.

Baths and water

Although it is the inquisitive toddler who is most at risk when it comes to water, babies also need great care. At this age the greatest danger comes from baths and shallow containers.

Some suggestions to avoid water accidents

- Never leave a baby unattended in the bath. If the phone rings, ignore it or bring the baby with you.
- Never leave a baby unattended in or near a paddling pool.
- Keep the lid firmly on the nappy bucket or keep it out of reach. Buckets can claim lives when babies climb up on them and tumble in.
- Keep toilet lids closed and the door shut.
- Don't trust other young children to supervise the bathing of your baby.
- Always be super-vigilant when near pools or any water. It can take only seconds to drown, and often you don't hear a thing.

Change tables

It's nice to be able to change little babies as they lie still at waist level and you don't have to stoop. However, as the baby becomes more active and starts to roll and wriggle this elevated situation presents some risks.

A few hints for safety on the change table

- Make sure you have all the necessary gear at hand before you change a wriggler.
- Never turn your back on any potential mover.
- Use the floor to change very athletic infants, they can't fall off that!

SAFETY IN CARS

No matter how careful a driver you are, the roads are always a potential danger. You may not make any mistakes, but there is always some other idiot around who might. All you can do is to think safety. This should start right from the time you take your baby home from the hospital. Having set the trend, never compromise with car safety thereafter. Have proper car restraints fitted and establish a rigid law that they be used at all times and that the car never moves until all belts and straps have been securely fastened.

Car safety guidelines

- At birth obtain an approved rear-facing baby-travelling capsule.
- By 9 kg make sure that an approved front-facing car seat has been fitted and is used at all times. When possible this is best attached in the centre of the rear seat.
- Never leave a child in a hot or airless car. And it's rare, but we do hear of cars being stolen with children in them, so keep any time when you're out of the car and the baby is in it to an absolute minimum.
- Don't travel if the driver is drowsy or is liable to get drowsy, and under no circumstances allow any family member to travel in a car with a driver who has had too much to drink. You owe it to your family to be well within the legal alcohol limit when you

take the wheel. You may be able to fool the breathalyser bus, but if you injure your family you'll be fooling no-one.

• Speed is a factor in many accidents. If you have children in the car, travel at sensible speeds. Save lives not seconds!

Sunburn

Babies can easily get too much sun. It is important that right from birth they get shade, sunhats and blockout creams suitable for babies. Lack of care now will ruin the skin and leave them looking like a prune by the age of 30, to say nothing of the danger of skin cancer.

Some rules for your baby outdoors
• Keep him out of direct sun.
• Cover his shoulders and arms and use a hat.
• Overuse suncreams rather than underuse them.
• Never leave a baby in the sun in a car.
• On really hot days try not to travel with your baby.

WHEN PARENTS SNAP

All human beings have their breaking point. For some it's always close at hand, while others seem to be able to take far more punishment before it is reached. There would be very few parents with an irritable, whingeing baby who have not at some time pulled themselves up, very aware of just how close they have been to doing something they might regret. There's no point being pious about this. Let's be sensible when the going gets tough.

When things get difficult
• If you feel you're losing control, quickly load up the stroller and get out of the house. Crying and whingeing never sound quite so bad in the open air and a baby is unlikely to come to any physical harm when in the public gaze.

- If stuck at home and the situation has reached boiling point, put your baby safely into his cot, close the door and go to another room until you have regained control.
- Ring a friend.
- Contact a counselling service.
- Try to get your partner home to bail you out.
- Go to a friend's home.

FIRST AID

All parents should have at least a basic knowledge of first aid including cardio-pulmonary resuscitation (CPR), and every home should carry a first-aid kit with all the usual tweezers, bandaids, bandages, etc.

Remember that poisons information is available 24 hours a day via NHS Direct. If your baby swallows something, ring NHS Direct at once and get advice. And have the number ready on the fridge.

As the child safety organisations say—child safety should be no accident.

- **NHS Direct** 0845 4647

Who is in charge?

Babies and toddlers can be at risk at those times when the usual routine is broken for a party or family gathering. Everyone thinks there are plenty of people to keep an eye on the little ones but no-one is really watching. And in this fun environment children are more likely to do something out of the ordinary. All new parents need to relax and it's lovely to include the kids at gatherings, but as a parent you are captain of the ship. If you are stepping off the bridge then delegate to the next in charge. There must always be someone who knows they are responsible for a child's safety.

Not another nappy!

I t is a well-known scientific fact that what you pour in the top end of your baby is sooner or later going to emerge at the other end. Most parents won't be surprised (or pleased) to hear that every baby soils or soaks about ten nappies (maybe a few less for disposables) every 24 hours and that this will go on day after day for at least the next two years. A quick bit of adding up shows that you are now faced with a massive waste-disposal project where you will change between 7000 and 8000 nappies before drought conditions finally set in.

This is just one of the many joys of parenthood, to be coped with as practically as possible. If you set out to make life easy for yourself you won't regret it. Here are a few tips to start things off:

- *Have a waist-high, no-stoop change table.*
- *Leave wipes, lotions and all gear within easy reach.*
- *Disposable nappies are more convenient.*
- *Have a rubbish bin which can cope with moist waste.*
- *Have nappy buckets with smell-proof lids to catch the discards for cloth nappies.*
- *Use nappy-soak fluids for cloth nappies and try only to wash in batches.*
- *If you can afford it, investigate the option of a nappy service.*

Disposables

When this book was first published, the majority of parents used cloth nappies. This was because disposable nappies at that time were not very absorbent or a good fit. This has completely changed, with more than 80 per cent of parents choosing disposables and more than 99 per cent using them at some time. No doubt this has a lot to do with convenience but it is also due to the improvement in disposable nappies.

Disposables are now made from polyacrylate crystal combined with wood pulp in a waterproof shell. Polyacrylate crystal absorbs moisture, turning it to a gel. This is not harmful and does not irritate the skin. The baby stays much drier, greatly reducing the risk of nappy rash. Occasionally there is an allergic reaction to the material, in which case cloth is the answer. Disposables are available in sizes to suit newborns through to toddlers, and size is selected according to the baby's weight.

There's no green way of disposing of disposables—they go straight in the bin. It's always a good idea to seal them in a plastic bag first, though! In the US it's said that two per cent of garbage is used nappies. There are now more environmentally friendly disposables that are made of biodegradable materials. Some of these may not manage a night shift but many find them suitable for daytime use, and at least it cuts down on waste to a degree.

The traditional towelling square

In the 'good old days' when you were expected to boil all your dirty nappies to kill off all the germs, nappy washing was hard work. Now with washing machines, a good hot mechanical wash will do all the germ killing for you.

If the nappies have been soaking for a while they should ideally get a quick spin first, followed by a rinse and then a hot wash. Any

sort of washing powder will do just as long as the nappy is rinsed out properly. Fabric softeners, which make dry nappies feel much fluffier on little bottoms, rarely irritate babies and are probably worth adding. After they have been washed and dried, leave a few folded and ready to put on.

To cope with the average nine to ten changes a day you are going to need at the very least two dozen towelling nappies. Another dozen would certainly help ease the pressure and keep you in business when wet weather prevents nappies from drying. Don't be too proud to accept a second-hand bundle from a friend whose children have moved on to better things. You can never really have too many so long as you can find a spot for them in your house.

If you are planning to have a large family, be generous with the number of nappies you allow yourself. At the end of your childrearing activities they will probably be worn down to their last threads, but will still make excellent towels to clean up after messy toddlers (and you'll certainly need lots of these!).

Nappy services

There are obvious attractions to flinging a scraped nappy into a sealed container and giving it no further thought until it returns the following week all fluffy, clean and smelling as fresh as the clear spring air. Most large cities have nappy services and it seems that on average they cost about 30 per cent more than the very cheapest disposable nappies but considerably less than the most expensive throwaway models. If you cannot stand dirty nappies and money is not too tight, then why not check in your phone book for your nearest nappy service. You may be surprised to find that it's not as expensive as you thought.

Nappy liners

There are two commonly used sorts of nappy liner, the 'keeps Baby's bottom feeling dry' type and the disposable 'let's not handle the major movements' type. The dry-bottom type is said to pump the wet through into the nappy leaving the child convinced she is dry. This all sounds too good to be true, but it is certainly worth considering in the early months when the nappy situation is pretty fluid. They're not all that expensive, are easily washed and are dry as soon as they hit the clothes line.

The disposable model is just a cheap rectangle of material which lines the nappy and makes cleaning up somewhat less difficult for the delicate. You don't use both together as the disposable square obviously blocks the one-way filter so you will have to opt for one or the other.

In the early months when Baby's skin is delicate and the flow is almost constant, it's probably best to start with the one-way liner. Once weaning starts and bowel movements become more solid then the disposables come into their own. Mind you, I doubt whether your child will know or care if you use neither.

Plastic pants

Grandma cuddles tightly to her little angel. Squelch! Drip! It's like squeezing a lemon! Wet towelling nappies are not much fun when you try to get intimate. They leave you with a wet knee and the baby permanently smells like a hot day at the fish market!

One way to head for hygiene and dryness is to use a pair of plastic pants to cover the wet sponge of a nappy. The only problem with plastic pants is that not only do they protect the clothes but they also trap moisture. Soon the inside humidity is approaching that of the Central Congo Basin and before you know it the sensitive baby has a nasty case of nappy rash. Some children are red and sore within minutes of being encased in plastic. Others seem totally immune and must have bottoms as tough as a hippo's hide.

If your baby's skin is in any way delicate then use plain nappies at home or, better still, disposables. You don't need a degree in medicine to know which children have the tough hides and which are the sensitive ones.

Cloth pants are available to cover wet nappies. These provide reasonable squelch protection, yet spare little bottoms from nappy rash. They are more expensive than plastic, but generally a better buy.

Nappy-soak fluids

Such fluids are by no means a necessity, but they certainly do make life easier. Anything that makes used nappies more pleasant to handle can't be bad and it's nice to think that the cleaning process has started while they're sitting waiting to be washed. If nothing else it helps dispel some of your guilt about that pile glowering at you in the corner of the laundry!

The nappies should be left in the solution for at least six hours, but no longer than 24. Replace the solution daily as the cost is not excessive.

Cleaning fluids

The cheapest, greenest cleaning fluid for a baby's bottom is piped right into your home. It is none other than tap-water and should be used with either a very mild soap or, preferably, no soap at all.

Nappy-change lotions of the commercial variety are much dearer, but are convenient, portable, smell nice and can give some skin protection. They also have the advantage of keeping your own hands soft. Modern pre-wet tissues are convenient and the majority are gentle to delicate skin. Wipes are seen as essential by many and are handy for life on the go, but remember there is a free alternative.

Nappy buckets

Nappy buckets are a necessity. I mean large buckets with lids that keep the sight and smell of soiled nappies well out of the way. They also make life a good deal simpler.

The wet nappies go straight in without a second thought, while the soiled ones need a quick scrape or removal of the nappy liners, and then splash, in they go too. You can even have one bucket for wet ones, and another for the soiled so that the wet nappies can get a separate light wash and the soiled ones can have a hotter going over. But few of us are that organised.

The buckets should be filled with nappy-soak fluid and the nappies should be washed in batches once they have had enough time to soak and you have sufficient numbers to make washing worthwhile.

If you haven't got a bucket, a large, securely tied, polythene bag will suffice.

If you have a baby who is starting to get up on her feet, make sure that bucket lids are firmly in place. Little ones have been known to fall forward and become dangerously stuck or have drowned in these fluid-filled buckets.

Change tables

You can change nappies by lying Baby on a towel on the floor if you want to, but this involves an awful lot of kneeling and stooping. After two years your knees will be nearly worn out from going up and down more times each day than the most devout monk at a monastery.

Your options are: a towel on a normal table, a change mat or a change table. The towel on a table is certainly simple and saves your back to a degree, but there is always the danger of an active baby rolling off onto the floor. These rollers may be best changed on the floor as they can't fall any further.

You can put a special change mat on a bed or table. This is relatively cheap, easily washed and has low sides which gives some protection to the young roller. At the top of the range, you can buy a special change table which is designed at just the right height, has a built-in anti-roll device and folds away when you are finished. Whatever you use, it is much easier for you when kept at waist height.

Fancy fold nappies

I don't intend to go into all the twenty-odd ways there are of folding a nappy. I leave that to the origami teachers. Suffice it to say that there are a number of different ways and everybody will claim that theirs is the most effective. No one way is really any better than another.

If I were you I would start with the universal kite fold as taught to you in hospital. If you begin to feel adventurous later, there are a few other suggestions at the back of this book (see pages 338–41) or try out your friends' favourite folds.

When researching this new edition I came across a number of remarkable designs for nappies. Even more remarkable was the cost!

Wrigglers

Twisters, rollers, wrigglers and kickers are not really a problem in the first six months of nappy change, but after this you can find yourself with your hands full. At one year some are amazingly strong, while the eighteen-monthers can be as difficult to hold down as an Olympic wrestler on the mat.

Don't ever let wriggling and kicking be seen as a game. It may seem like great fun at noon, but at 3 am it has lost all spectator appeal. Don't start something now that will later become a rod to your back.

Before you change a wriggler be sure that all the gear you need is prepared and ready to go. Have the new folded nappy out flat and then with speed and single-minded determination, get in and out quickly.

I have heard of some hard-to-hold babies who are changed tummy down with the nappy arrangement suitably altered. I suppose this enables you to hold the child in something like a half-nelson while the necessary adjustments are made, but it must be no easy matter. The solution to the problems of the athletic wriggler is pre-planning, speed, single-mindedness and never letting it become a game. Diversion on the other hand is a skill best learned now in preparation for the challenges of the toddler years.

Nappy rash

The proper medical term for nappy rash is ammonia dermatitis. This says it all. It's an inflammation of the skin caused by ammonia in the nappy area. In its mildest form, the skin becomes a bit red. When more severe, the skin thickens, wrinkles, cracks and may become ulcerated. Secondary infection, especially with thrush (monilia), is very common.

Freshly passed urine contains no ammonia but lots of urea, which is pretty inert and would not upset even the most delicate of skins. However, once it has sat in the nappy for a while, certain bacteria break it down to ammonia. These busy bacteria are the harmless bugs that live in the normal gut and are always in high supply around the nappy area. There they lurk, just waiting to turn uninteresting inert urea into caustic ammonia.

The whole process is accelerated by warmth and an environment of high humidity. Put a pair of plastic pants over a wet nappy and this raises the humidity and holds in the heat by its blockage of evaporation. Now the bugs whistle away, overjoyed at such an ideal working environment. Change to a dry nappy, rinse the bottom or leave it all exposed to air and they are out of work. Obviously the longer they have to act, the more of the urea will be broken down. Also, the longer the ammonia is in contact with the skin, the more damage it is likely to do.

Understanding this process explains why a newly wet nappy will smell fresh like the morning dew, but leave it for five hours with the bugs and it will pong like a sunbathing fish.

Each baby is born with an individual sensitivity to nappy rash. Some become red within an hour, while others are unmarked after a long night of sodden sleep. It is often the 'good' baby who suffers most. She will sleep quietly all night. If she had screamed, a couple of changes would have been made before dawn and nappy rash avoided.

Well, what can be done to prevent and treat nappy rash? There are a number of practical things you can do:

- Change wet and soiled nappies as soon as possible.
- Rinse the bottom well with water to remove excess urine and bacteria. Then dry well.
- Make sure that you have enough nappies. Don't be a Scrooge when it comes to changing.
- Switch to disposable nappies.
- Use a skin-protective product—your chemist will suggest a good brand. These protect the skin's own natural oils and create a barrier to keep the ammonia away from where it can cause damage.
- Night-time is when the baby's bottom is most at risk of rash. When preparing for bed, take extra care. Wash and dry carefully then apply a liberal coat of protective cream. Use a disposable, or a one-way nappy liner may be used and changed as soon as possible in the morning. Where a rash is a real problem, changes during the night may be necessary.
- Remember the basic rule. To have a nappy rash, first you need a wet nappy. When a rash is really bad, little bottoms need frequent changes or to be left exposed to air. Where there is no nappy in place it helps healing but is not very practical if you have a fully carpeted home.
- If you have tried all these suggestions but the rash persists or gets worse then it's time to seek help from your clinic sister or family doctor. It is probable that a medical treatment is needed and very likely that there is secondary infection with thrush (monilia).

Thrush

Thrush (monilia) is often a troublesome free-loader on the nappy rash which makes it hard to heal. Often, it is completely unnoticed, though sometimes it will have the appearance of raised round patches all over the nappy area. Sometimes it affects the creases. When in doubt, it's best to treat it anyway.

Treatment involves an antifungal cream such as Mycostatin (Nystatin) or Canesten (Clotrimazole), or a steroid–canesten mixture such as Hydrozole, which requires a doctor's prescription. If you're not sure which approach to take, then consult your clinic sister or doctor.

Conclusion

If you have a baby, you have to have nappies. Use the type that suits your pocket and lifestyle. Make things as easy as possible for yourself. There are going to be at least 7000 changes before you're finished. Nappy rash is extremely common and often strikes very well cared for babies. Change your baby regularly, keep her dry, clean her well, waterproof the skin and where it becomes a problem, avoid plastic pants. A rash on your baby's bottom is a sign of sensitive skin, not bad parenting.

Disposable nappies

- These come in various sizes, makes and designs.
- Shop around and look for deals: there is generally a difference on any given day between your chemist's discount offer, the supermarket special and the full retail price.
- Large packs are much more economical.

Nappy services

- Look under 'Nappy Service' in the Yellow Pages.
- Most companies require at least a one-month contract.
- The recommendation is for 60 (girls) and 70 (boys) nappies each week.
- Soiled nappies are scraped, no nappies need to be rinsed.

Feeding the natural way

H uman breast milk is a specially designed food that meets every need of the very young human infant. Its clever blend provides the exact nourishment required and even more remarkably offers a certain level of protection against infections. For these reasons it is the maker's recommended food.

Having agreed that 'breast is best', I know that with the best will in the world some mothers do not manage to breast-feed and they should not be made to feel like a failure at the first hurdle.

BREAST-FEEDING— THE ADVANTAGES

Natural is best

Presumably, after a few million years of evolution, cow's milk has been refined to suit little cows best, goat's milk to suit little goats, and therefore human's milk to suit little humans. Improved over millennia to meet the needs of the modern baby, it is in itself a miracle.

Body contact and bonding

Bonding requires closeness, warmth and eye-to-eye communication. Out of these comes the sense of wonder that connects us to our babies. You cannot get much closer than the feeling of holding your cherished infant as he feeds at the breast. Humans have been de-signed so that the most comfortable position to hold him in while he feeds is also the one where it is easiest to look into his eyes. There is no surer way to win you over. And just to make sure, breast-feeding releases a 'happy hormone' that makes you feel contented. Those who breast-feed successfully the first time almost always feel it is the only way to go with their next baby.

Scientifically-proven benefits

Before birth the breast was primed for the job. After birth the baby is introduced and though it might seem that initial sucking brings forth little in the way of food, it provides something very important in the form of the creamy-looking substance colostrum. This is rich in health-giving immunoglobulins that help protect against infections by coating the gut with antibodies. Volume of colostrum may seem low but there is plenty of nourishment. Baby was well topped up on food from the placenta and has plenty of stores to get him through the first few days.

By the fourth day milk is well established and the biological miracle continues. The first part of the feed is the foremilk which provides thirst-quenching fluid and an early hit of energy. Then comes the heavier substance of the hind milk, a fattier product with energy for the long haul. The foremilk sets us up for the sprint; the hind milk for the distance events. Both are essential.

Nature has by now provided the antibodies to get us off to a good start and the fuel for life and growth. She's done a good job!

Safe, clean and transportable

For decades the World Health Organisation has campaigned to increase breast over formula-feeding. This is an essential project in developing countries where a preference for formula-feeding is of great concern if water quality and sterile conditions are compromised. Contaminated feeds can be a death sentence in areas without adequate hospital care.

Breast-feeding is safe, clean and transportable, and crucially it gives a level of immunity that is valuable to all babies but especially those in developing countries.

BREAST-FEEDING— THE DISADVANTAGES

Keeping it in perspective

I accept that breast is best but I also accept that not all mothers are able to do it. Many give it their best shot but either do not provide enough milk or just cannot find a way to do it comfortably. In spite

of support from various organisations it does not always work out. Mum may do her very best to up the milk supply with a regime of pumping and although this can sort out the problem if it's about production levels, there may be a cost: to Mum, to Baby, to the family, in terms of emotional drain.

It's important to look at the big picture here. Our absolute goal is to raise a happy, well-bonded, cherished infant in a relaxed and loving family. Feeding is only one piece of the puzzle. After twenty years of keeping him safe, teaching him to share, helping him with his homework and worrying where he is at night you'll see that it was the first hurdle of many. If feeding has become a nightmare of tiredness and guilt, try to take a step back, inform yourself and make a decision that looks at all the options.

There is no doubt that there are advantages to breast-feeding. There is also, on the other hand, no doubt that bottle-fed babies can do very well in developed countries. Reluctant breast-feeding will always be a chore but may benefit the baby, while mothers persuaded to bottle-feed reluctantly will also be unhappy.

If you are uncertain as to what to do, opt for the breast for now. You can always stop if it doesn't work out and change to a bottle, but it's harder to do a swap the other way round if you think you might change your mind.

The decision on how you are going to feed your baby is yours and yours alone. The arguments around breast-feeding can take on a fundamentalist tone. You are not damned if you are lost to the faith. Around here we embrace all persuasions, particularly if they allow Mum to relax and enjoy her new baby.

THE PHYSIOLOGY OF FEEDING

There are three different stages in the process of breast-feeding. First of all, the breast needs to be prepared for the task that lies ahead and this is done by the action of the hormones during pregnancy. Next the glands in the breast need to start production of the milk. This happens after birth when the sucking of the breast sends messages to the mother's pituitary gland, which then releases the hormone prolactin which makes milk. Lastly the milk that is made and sits in the glands must be released down to the nipple. This release is called 'the let-down' and is brought about by the action of another pituitary hormone, oxytocin. This is again activated by sucking, but also by emotional cues. It sounds complicated, but it goes like this.

Throughout pregnancy the breast was being primed, ready for action. You knew this was happening as the size changed and there was discomfort. At birth the breasts are larger but making little real milk. When the baby first sucks he gets a substance called colostrum, which is low in nourishment but is jam-packed with anti-infection antibodies. The sucking stimulates the pituitary gland and prolactin is made which sets the breast to make milk. It takes a bit of time for proper production but in three to four days milk will usually be in good supply. The more sucking and the emptier the breasts at the end of the feed, the more prolactin is made. Prolactin is also inhibited by worry, tiredness or pain, and so milk production may fall when any of these feelings occur.

The let-down can feel like a pleasant tingling sensation (or occasionally like a stab) that comes after about ten to 30 seconds of sucking or when just thinking about a feed. When a mum is really sensitive to this emotional cue, the milk can be let down so fast that it can leak everywhere before you have got the baby near the breast. As oxytocin controls the let-down and is the same hormone which is produced to make the uterus contract at birth, it's not surprising that afterpains are often felt in the early days of feeding.

Please don't get too bogged down in the business of prolactin, pituitary, oxytocin and let-downs. What you need to know is that the best results come with ample sucking, good emptying and not too much emotional worry or tiredness.

If you think about it, breast-feeding is not unlike the financial management of a government department. You are given a certain volume of funds to spend. If you make sure you use every last cent and leave nothing to spare, then next time you will be rewarded with a bigger budget. If, however, you are an efficient, careful manager and save on your allowance, your reward is a cut of what's on offer next time. The same goes for breast-feeding. Constant demands and the use of most of the milk establishes the best long-term flow.

Breast-feeding—the technique

Start by getting yourself comfortable. Feeding is going to take up a lot of your time in the next half year or more so make it as easy and enjoyable as you can. The right posture is important, as is a suitable chair that's the right size for you and has firm back support.

In the early days the hospital staff will be encouraging frequent sucking. Remember that this is not a high-nutrition nibble, the baby will get a bit of colostrum and minimal milk, but that's all he needs as he is born with quite a reserve of food aboard. What is important is the sucking which gives a major message to signal the start of milk production.

To start feeding you first need to get the baby's mouth to the breast. Touch the baby's cheek or lips gently with the nipple and he will automatically turn towards it. This is called the 'rooting reflex' and is one of those amazing bits of pre-birth programming which ensures that little ones feed and survive. Now all they need is to be close to a source of food and off they go.

As the hungry baby approaches the breast, the mouth opens. If the mouth stays shut, nothing much is going to happen. With the mouth open and tongue down flat, move the baby onto the breast. Put the nipple and an amount of the surrounding breast tissue in the mouth. When the baby has had enough he will come off the breast.

Initially there may be a little tenderness but feeding should not hurt. If it is painful, the baby is probably incorrectly attached and you should start again. To move the baby away, insert a little finger gently into the baby's mouth, break the suction and you have release.

When feeding is properly established, your plan will be to feed for as long as it takes to empty the first breast, then burp and offer the other breast. Start each feed with the breast that was used last the previous time, if he got that far. This allows maximum stimulation and emptying to alternate. If you are as forgetful as the rest of us, put a safety pin round one bra strap and move it as a marker of where next to start.

With feeding you need a comfortable supporting nursing bra and ease-of-access clothes. You don't need to feed behind locked doors. Although it might take a bit of getting used to feeding in public, it's a normal and natural part of life. Those who take offence are really going the way of the dinosaur.

Increasing the milk supply

As you get the feeding pattern going there are a number of ways to give your milk supply a boost. The mainstay of the process is effective sucking and allowing Baby to finish at the breast. When milk supply is low, expressing milk for five minutes manually gives extra stimulation and some to store in the freezer for emergencies.

You should aim to feed your baby yourself at night, rather than letting him be given a bottle in the nursery. This does nothing for your tiredness but it keeps up stimulation and production, and prevents problems like low blood sugars and jaundice. Avoid top-up bottles as an instant fix because they won't increase your supply and may in fact reduce it further, but if you really think your baby is not getting enough milk seek advice about this from your baby health nurse.

If breast-feeding is obviously becoming an uphill struggle, there's nothing too smart about turning a pleasurable, natural process into an uncomfortable scientific obsession. When uncertain which course to take, you will get good guidance from your baby health sister, doctor or breast-feeding counsellor.

Worry, tension and tiredness all rob you of milk output. Try not to let the worry about the adequacy of the milk supply become the reason why that supply is inadequate! Give it your best shot, but if it doesn't all come together then it's not the end of the world. Just try and relax, put your feet up, especially in the afternoon when tiredness is greatest, and let Nature take its course.

When feeding really starts to get going, you will be using about a litre (1.8 pints) of additional fluid each day and perhaps 2000 extra kilojoules (500 extra calories). There will be lots of spare kilojoules to turn to milk and a need to drink more.

Is Baby getting enough?

With breast-feeding there is always one haunting unknown—how much is your baby actually getting? You know that your baby has latched on but you don't know how much is passing down the tube. At least with bottle-feeding you can count the empties at the end of the day. But remember babies will feed to their needs, sometimes this will be 450 ml, sometimes only 20 ml. Sometimes they want one breast and sometimes two.

There are, however, a few indirect ways of gauging intake. Let's consider them.

Weight gain

You should expect a weight loss in Baby for about the first five days and then usually weight gain. After the fifth day the average gain should be about 30 g (1 oz) a day. As weight fluctuates in an average baby, not too much can be read into one weighing. It's best to take a longer view over a one or two-week period. Some very normal babies will gain more than their average 30 g (1 oz), others less. Weight gain is no more than a guide and though helpful you must never be ruled rigidly by the scales. (See the weight-gain figures given on page 152.)

Contentment

The ideal baby has six feeds a day, sleeps for four hours between each one and is generally contented. The problem is that few of us seem to have ideal babies. In the early weeks the normal well-fed baby feeds between six and twelve times a day, sleeps between one and six hours between meals, and cries for between one and four hours in each 24. With these figures it's always hard to know how contented a baby needs to be before you declare him contented. There is also the problem of when he's irritable, not sleeping well and grizzly. Does this mean lack of food or is he just a grizzly little person? If you have an ideal baby then be reassured about feeding. If he is discontented then look at weight gain, the nappies and the overall appearance of the baby before blaming it all on hunger.

Nappies

What goes in the top must come out the bottom and if the nappies are pretty dry, fluid intake may be low. If there is a daily flood, then it has to be good. You should expect about six to eight good wet nappies each day and if you have these, milk production should be fine.

Test feeding

People don't go in for this much anymore but it's quite an interesting process to observe. One millilitre of breast milk weighs approximately 1 g—or to put it the old-fashioned way, 1 fl oz of milk weighs 1 oz. Armed with this information and an accurate set of scales it is easy to calculate Baby's daily intake. Weigh your baby before the feed and again directly afterwards before changing the nappy. With a bit of simple subtraction, you should now be able to record the fluid taken.

In the first few months the average intake should be approximately 150 ml for each kilogram of ideal body weight per day. (See the conversion chart on page 369.) I say 'ideal' because we feed the overweight baby less and the thin baby more. This sounds really accurate, but it is not. Each breast-feed is of a different volume and you would need to test feed quite a few to get a clear picture. What's more, quantities vary from day to day and also the anxiety generated by test feeding may itself diminish the flow so try not to get too academic about breast-feeding.

COMMON CONCERNS

Does your baby need extra vitamins and fluoride?

It appears that the vitamin wheel has turned full circle. In the past it was not thought necessary to give babies extra vitamins. Then it was deemed a good thing. Now we're back to advocating nothing extra in their diet again for babies born at full term. If Mum has a good balanced diet then Nature can do the rest. If the baby isn't getting any vitamin-containing solids by eight months, then some vitamins are advisable after that age.

Additional fluoride is not given to the totally breast-fed baby, whether the local water is fluoridated or not.

Drugs and noxious substances in milk

In my more cynical moments I wonder whether breast milk is as pure as we like to think. The cow munches through a monotonous diet of grass, which by rights is relatively unpolluted—that is, if the local nuclear reactor is in good working order. We humans, on the other hand, eat so much food that has been tarted up and fiddled with before it reaches us.

There are over 2000 legally permitted additives used in our food and on top of them there is an army of pesticides and other pollutants from our high-technology farming. Some of this must work its way into breast milk, though it is said to be benign.

When it comes to prescribed drugs, some will get into breast milk, but most stay out and have no effect on babies. While breast-feeding you should do as you did during pregnancy—only take medicines that are necessary and stay off drugs that you do not need, whether safe or not.

The following information is meant only as a rough guide to some commonly used drugs. However, the literature changes from month to month and you should always check with your doctor for an update.

Aspirin, paracetamol, ventolin-type asthma drugs, iron, penicillin, amoxil-type antibiotics and most vitamins are safe. So if you have a headache, wheeze, sore throat or anaemia, go ahead and treat it.

Sulphonamide antibiotics such as Bactrim or Septrin are a slight worry in the first weeks but safe later on.

Valium and other tranquillisers are generally quite safe in moderate doses but high levels are not recommended as they make a baby sleepy.

Antidepressant drugs are mostly safe, but your doctor must check the specific brand before prescription.

Most anticoagulants that stop blood clots, such as warfarin and heparin, are not a problem.

The anticonvulsants that we use for epilepsy are mostly safe and certainly safer than allowing an untreated mum to have a fit while nursing the baby. These medicines will have been given right through pregnancy and the levels a baby will get through the milk are minute in comparison with what would have been coming through in the womb.

Alcohol passes into the milk but seems harmless in small quantities. Chronic alcoholics and binge-drinkers are a hazard and should not breast-feed or have children at all.

Smoking reduces milk supply and some of the pollutant may enter the milk. In any case all health professionals agree that smoking and children do not mix in any form.

Marijuana and cannabis have so far not been identified as a risk as passed through breast milk, but again the use of drugs around children is clearly not advisable.

Caffeine from tea or coffee is found in the milk but the amount is so minuscule that there are no hazards if these beverages are drunk in moderation.

Contraception and breast-feeding

As many mothers have learned to their surprise, breast-feeding is not a reliable form of contraception. If your baby is under six months, your periods have not returned and you are exclusively breast-feeding, the risk of pregnancy is small but little ones can slip through unexpectedly.

The thing is that until Mum's body gets back into shape, most other forms of contraception are equally unsuitable. The sensible thing is to let the body settle down for some months before starting to take any contraceptive pill. This is a good time for husbands to take responsibility for contraception.

Engorgement

In the first few days Baby doesn't require much milk, but often when it comes it arrives in a flood. It will take some time to get this supply and demand mechanism in tune. In the meantime, breasts may get over-full and become tense, lumpy and painful. If this goes on they soon become too tender and distended to allow sucking and then the situation gets really painful. Don't despair, this is only a temporary problem. Some excess pressure can be lost by manual expression of milk and once the edge is off the tension, sucking can resume. A comfortable bra is a necessity. Ice packs are an old remedy that can provide a bit of pain relief. If a painful area of redness develops, this may suggest an infection (mastitis). Antibiotics may be needed, so consult your doctor.

Cracked nipples

In the early days of breast-feeding the nipples are vulnerable to small injuries or cracks in the skin.

The best course for cracked nipples is prevention. Ensure the baby is correctly attached, and don't pull the firmly fastened baby off the breast in mid-suck. Feed in a position which is comfortable for you and does not drag on the breast. Keep the breast area as dry as possible. Then there is the natural cure. Just rub a little hind milk (the milk produced at the end of a feed) on the area and let it dry. The milk fats soften the skin in their own gentle way.

Biters

This is obviously more of an eye-opener for the mum who feeds after the teeth are through than for those with little babies. Babies can't bite and suck at the same time, so they can't be too interested in feeding if they bite. Hold the head, insert your little finger and remove the baby from your breast. If he wants something to bite on, get a teething ring. He must realise that mums offer food and are not for nipping.

Afterpains

In the first days after birth the uterus will still be enlarged and pretty responsive to any hormones. Oxytocin is the hormone which sets the milk flowing and this is the same one that caused the contractions of the uterus during birth. So don't be surprised when crampy pains occur at feed times. This is only a temporary worry, so there's no need to worry! It is just your body helping the womb return to normal.

When and how to stop

Once feeding is going well it seems a pity to stop and not go on for most of the first year. The important thing is to do your own thing. If you and Baby are happy then get on with it. Feed for as long as you wish, the only limits are to introduce some extra iron and vitamin-containing food as well as the milk by around six months and give something with texture to accustom your child to chew and swallow by nine months. When it does come to stopping, however, gradual withdrawal is better than going cold turkey and stopping with a bang.

The gentle way is more comfortable, natural and to be advised. You start introducing solids at six months. At first the amounts will be so small that it will take over a month before you get enough each feed to knock the edge off your baby's appetite. Then, if you want to stop breast-feeding you should increase other fluids, leaving the breast as the comfort at the end of a fine meal, rather like a glass of brandy for the adult gourmet. If you want to be even more gentle, then introduce solids and when other fluids are needed you can wean your baby straight on to a cup. It's up to you.

The tough method involves determination, discomfort and is only necessary if feeding has to stop quickly for some medical or other reason. If you stop all sucking and emptying, within a week milk supply will cease. The first few days will be extremely uncomfortable. To see this through, both Mum and her breasts will all need good support. Also be aware that there is a risk of developing mastitis.

Feeding and breast shape

If you are worried about the shape of your breasts, it's too late! The stable door was left ajar nine months ago and the horse has long since bolted. It's not breast-feeding that stretches and deflates breasts, but nine months of pregnancy. Some women gain weight, some lose weight while breast-feeding. All who have been pregnant change in shape.

Weaning—an emotional time

When breast-feeding stops, this can be a time of very confused emotions for many mums. It can feel like the end of an era, a closeness that will never return. After all, your body has been the life-support system for your child since the cells began to divide all those months ago and it's natural to grieve as you go through this change. Parenthood is punctuated by many of these milestones. The sadness can be stressful for a while but it soon passes. This can also be a time of liberation. As you shake off the tiredness that may come with nourishing a growing baby you can more easily leave him in the care of others for a little longer than may have been practical while breast-feeding, allowing you to return to some of the activities the old you enjoyed.

CONCLUSION

The choice of whether you breast-feed and when you wean is yours and yours alone. In the end it comes down to what feels right for you. Breast-feeding should be enjoyable and undertaken in a relaxed way. You should continue it for as long as you and your baby wish. And if there are difficulties, please try to remember that support is available and feeding is only one element of the care of a child in a loving family.

Resources
Antenatal classes for breast-feeding are available in most hospitals and are given by lactation consultants. These experts are also on hand for first-timers and mothers who've previously had problems. They can visit when you're in hospital for the birth and will be happy to see you after discharge as well.

- **National Breastfeeding Helpline** 0300 100 0212
- **National Childbirth Trust** www.nct.org.uk 0300 330 0771
- **Your midwife, health visitor or GP**

Infant feeding for breast-feeding and formula

Feeding to need is the recommendation today. Whether breast or bottle-fed, 'they get it when they want it'.

Approximate volumes of milk taken

Birth to one week: A small intake initially (e.g. 60 ml per kg body weight per day) increasing to full quantity by day five to seven.

One week to four months: Average intake 150 ml per kg body weight per day. (Usual range 120-180 ml per kg.)

Four months to one year: Reduces gradually from 150 ml per kg at four months to about 100 ml per kg body weight at one year.

Average number of feeds each day

Six feeds per day in first two months.
Four to five feeds per day thereafter.
Remember it is feeding to need, and the need may be four to eight per day.

Average weight gain

Birth to one week: In the first two to three days up to ten per cent of the birth weight is lost but regained again by one week in a full-term baby.

One week to four months: Gains 25 g per day (average).
Usual range 150-200 g per week.

Four months to eight: Gains 16 g per day (average).
Usual range 90-150 g per week.

Eight months to one year: Gains about 10 g per day.
Usual range 60-90 g per week.

Note: The rate of weight gain lessens as the months pass. Don't brood on daily weighings. It's much better to weigh your baby weekly or two times a week, always at the same time of day. That way you'll have a more accurate record.

Bottle-feeding

I f you have decided that you are going to bottle-feed your baby, there's no
need for guilt. Thousands of excellent parents bottle-feed. Commercial
infant formulas have similar amounts of macronutrients (lactose fats and
protein) as in human milk. And national food standards authorities have
strict quality control standards so you can be sure that formula is safe.

There's a lot of support available for breast-feeding. It's only right that
we should support bottle-feeding families too, and a good source of advice
will always be your early health sister if you need extra information. Here
we'll get to grips with the gear for the job, how to make the feed, hygiene
standards and health. And once you've got a handle on all that, there's no
reason why it can't be an enjoyable and fulfilling process for all concerned.
When it comes to comfort it's the warmth and care of the feeder that counts,
not the breast or the bottle. The bottle-fed baby in a developed country will
thrive, grow and develop.

Figures show that about two thirds of today's mums are breast-feeding
completely at three months after birth. That means a third are fed by bottle.
A baby needs milk whether it comes from the breast or the bottle.

Why the bottle?

Mothers have personal reasons for choosing to bottle-feed their
babies. Here are some of the more common ones:

- They've tried their best but cannot produce enough milk.
- They can't get the hang of the technique.
- It's painful/tiring/stressful.
- They don't enjoy it.
- The mother or baby has been ill, perhaps mastitis has been a
  problem.
- The focus on breast-feeding has become overwhelming.
- They need to get back to work and it is too difficult to express
  milk all the time.

It's a common story that Mum has been put on a schedule to express
milk, either to up the milk supply or make provisions while she's at

work. This may work out fine but for some it's a guilt train that they just want to get off so they can enjoy life again. I worry that mums can be fragile in the early days and if difficulty with breast-feeding risks being a trigger for depression, then formula-feeding is a very good alternative. If breast turns out not to be best for you, you are still a good mother.

Enjoying bottle-feeding

Human adults use eating as a social event. We communicate as we feed and some of our most enjoyable occasions centre around food. It's the same with Baby!

All members of the family are able to connect with Baby while they feed her. Hold her close and enjoy the warmth, eye-to-eye contact, touch of her skin and the wonder of a little baby taking the food that will help her to grow and develop. Turn the phone off, sit somewhere comfortable where you can really have a good cuddle, and if a friend is visiting make sure this time is still about the baby. Take the time to enjoy this special moment.

THE MILKS

With the wide range of commercial infant formulas available today, you might well be excused for becoming confused and wondering which type of milk you should be pouring into that bottle.

Milk formulas

Most formulas come as dried powder in a tin, though some expensive brands come in the ready-to-drink form. All those on the market are safe, with lowered salt, balanced nutrients and added vitamins.

They are generally based on cow's milk which has been modified so that the protein is as similar as possible to that of breast milk. The fats are also blended with vegetable fats so it's easier to digest, and there is less salt than in straight cow's milk. So it's as close to human milk as humanly possible.

As you look at the rows of tins on the chemist's shelves, it's easy to become totally confused. I see all these milks as being pretty much the same. If your baby is going to thrive she will thrive well on any of them. One plea, however: please don't embark on a milk-swapping spree. One change at the start is fine, but continual chopping and changing leads to confusion and does nothing for the baby.

It is advisable to shop around before choosing a formula. Find one that's widely available, preferably at the supermarket and the local chemist, so that you can shop around for deals.

Doorstep cow's milk

Babies used to be fed the family's cow's milk from the beginning, but we know now that this carries a risk of dehydration, particularly to those babies with underlying problems. The safest milks until twelve months of age are either from the breast or from a recognised formula. You can use cow's milk for all custards and cooking without any worry, and most mums use it for making up cereals. After one year, then it's open season on cow's milk used without modification or restriction.

Special milks

Just as all that glitters is not gold, so all that is white and flows from a teat is not milk. You can obtain white non-dairy fluids that are made from a vegetable base, usually the soya bean. I may be old-fashioned, but I still think of milk as something that comes from a mammal, not a vegetable processing plant.

To be serious, occasionally an infant is not suited to cow's milk. This is to do with a reaction to the lactose (which is the same sort of sugar as that found in breast milk) or there's an allergy to cow's milk protein. It is even possible for the breast-fed baby to have a reaction to the cow's milk the mother is drinking. Infrequently the allergy is serious, but it is more usually mild. Symptoms are vague and diagnosis uncertain, but in general Baby is unsettled and hard to comfort and this seems to be related to feeding times. The difficulty is that a lot of unsettled babies are diagnosed with milk allergies, and not all of them can be allergy sufferers.

If you are worried that your baby is reacting to cow's milk formula, the first step is to talk to your health sister. She sees such things every day and will be able to provide sensible advice. Treatment is with either a soy milk or hypoallergenic formula.

FEEDING

This is where the one great technical drawback of bottle versus breast comes in. With breast-feeding all you have to do is undo a few buttons and, hey presto, it's all there, warmed, sterilised and ready to go. Not so with bottle-feeding. Before your baby is able to feed you need to assemble the basic equipment, mix it up, warm it and make sure you've got the volumes right. Here's what you'll need and how it's done.

The equipment

You'll need bottles, teats, a bottle brush, sterilising fluid or tablets and a container for soaking the empties. Though not essential, a sterilising unit can be bought for about $100. Microwave steamers are often cheaper than the plug-in unit.

The bottles can be made of glass, which is easier to clean but makes them heavier, or more usually of plastic, which is harder to clean but makes them lighter and able to bounce when dropped. Most mothers prefer to prepare the whole day's water at one go in bottles ready for warming. The only problem with this otherwise good idea is that you will need at least six bottles to cover the 24-hour period.

You should use a standard teat which releases the milk at about two drops per second when the bottle is held upside down. You can buy teats of silicone or rubber and of all shapes and sizes ranging from the trickle feeder to the Niagara model. Boxes of teats are generally labelled according to age and flow rate. There are also 'anti-colic' teats and bottles/teats with vents to let out air. You may have to experiment a bit at first to see which teat suits your baby best or ask advice from your baby health nurse, but don't chop and change as this confuses little feeders.

Cleaning and sterilising

Milk left sitting for hours in an unclean bottle is a health hazard. It is an excellent culture medium in which bacteria thrive and multiply. During your baby's first twelve months, cleanliness and sterility are of the utmost importance.

After feeding the bottle should be immediately thoroughly washed in warm, soapy water, teats washed both inside and outside, and everything rinsed and immersed in a container of sterilising fluid. There it should stay for at least an hour or until the next feed. When it is needed again, just shake off the excess fluid and use it without rinsing. The small amount of fluid that remains is safe and will be so diluted that your baby won't notice it. It tastes a bit like the chlorinated water in public swimming pools. You wouldn't choose to drink a glass of it with your dinner, but in small amounts it's perfectly harmless.

Though the soaking method has long been a simple and cheap way to sterilise, many now use electric or microwave steamers. It is also just as effective to boil them for ten minutes on the stove. Be careful with any method involving hot water, particularly if you are tired.

All milk formulas must be made up with cooled boiled water but not left sitting around for more than 30 minutes, and should then be stored in the fridge ready for use. It is best to use the main body of the fridge as the temperature of a shelf in a frequently opened door will vary. Don't keep unused bottles of water or made-up milk for more than 24 hours and never store half-used feeds. If a quarter of an hour has passed and there is no sign of a second sitting then dump the remaining feed at once.

Travel hygiene

If you are carrying made-up bottles around they need to be kept cool and safe until the feed or you can get to a fridge. There are special insulated bags for this.

Little breeding nasties thrive in milk during those long, lazy days in warm tropical temperatures. When travelling in summer it's safest to fill the bottles with cooled boiled water and not add the milk powder until feed-time. This helps prevent infection, and as most modern formulas mix so easily, it can be done in the bottle. Or there are long-life made-up cartons for the odd occasion when the expense is not a worry.

Sterility in food preparation

- Wash hands before preparing.
- Use cooled boiled water to make up formula for one feed.
- Soak bottles and teats for at least one hour in sterilising fluid, boil them for at least ten minutes or use a microwave steamer (make sure the bottle is microwave-safe).
- Spoons, measures, plates, etc. can be washed without special precautions.

Making up feeds

Cleanliness, accuracy and a minimum of effort are the three main ingredients of making up formula feeds. Although you have to sterilise bottles and teats and boil the water you use, scoops, spoons and measures are safe with just a simple wash under the hot tap. Before you start, read the instructions on the formula tin and do exactly what they say. **Don't compress the powder in the scoop**, fill it gently and shave it off level with a knife. **Don't be tempted to add a few extra kilojoules** or another scoop 'for the pot'. Making up over-strong feeds not only causes obesity but can also be dangerous due to salt and solute overload.

The volumes

The expected food intake is calculated by a simple formula. The volume required each day is 150 ml of milk per kilogram of the ideal bodyweight for the age of your baby.

Most babies will demand six feeds a day, some dropping the night-time feed around the sixth week, leaving them with just five a day. Unfortunately your baby won't have read this book, so don't be surprised when you find them demanding between 120 and 200 ml per kilogram of milk a day or between four and ten feeds. **The secret is not to get over-scientific about all this.** Leave your calculator in the drawer and use rule of thumb instead. **If your baby is happy, thriving and gaining weight, then you must be doing it right.** Babies are like adults, they each take different volumes at mealtimes. While you are trying to decipher your baby's feeding pattern, just put an extra 25 per cent of correctly made-up milk in each bottle and discard what's left. You'll soon learn exactly how much to make up each time.

Giving the feed

Feeding is on demand, like breast-feeding, when Baby is hungry.

The temperature we offer the milk at is largely a question of habit, rather like Australian cold beer as against the warm British variety. The habit is for warm milk, so if it's not too inconvenient, keep up the habit and use a jug of warm water to warm up the bottle. Warming the bottle in a microwave is generally discouraged but busy mums often find it convenient. If you do use one, research the settings carefully, and with any warmed milk, don't forget the ritual of shaking the bottle to mix evenly and then test a few drops of milk on your wrist for temperature before the teat goes anywhere near the baby.

Once you're arranged in a nice cosy cuddle, make sure Baby's properly attached on the teat—just like with breast-feeding—the bottle is tilted and the teat is full of milk, not air. If you need to start again, press under her chin gently with a finger and withdraw the teat a little to encourage sucking. The aim is a good strong suck without the intake of air that might cause wind.

Some dads find the burp the most satisfying part of the feed.

Most babies can wait until the end of a feed but some like to release the valve halfway through. Sit them up straight on your knee or over your shoulder (arm yourself first with a towel or cloth nappy) and give them a little pat if you like. If the burp doesn't come just make sure they're in an upright position for a while and don't worry about it. If a burp's there it will come.

Added vitamins, iron and fluoride

All formulas are fortified these days with the necessary vitamins to keep the average baby well for at least the first eight months. This includes vitamin C, so there's no need to start squeezing rosehips, blackcurrants or oranges into tiny mouths. In those areas where the water is fluoridated there is no need to add any extra fluoride. If you live in areas where there is no fluoridation don't worry for the first six months of life, then discuss the use of fluoride tablets or drops with your local dentist, who will advise you on usage.

Most babies should be getting at least a sniff of solid foods by six months and these will give an even wider variety of vitamins and iron. If bottle-feeding continues past this age as the only method of feeding, it's best to ask advice about what extra may be needed.

Although vitamin C–enriched drinks aren't necessary, a word of warning to those who use them anyway. It is best to dilute 100 per cent orange juice to avoid what in many babies may be an explosive bowel-emptying. Some blackcurrant products are appallingly sweet and can start the child off on bad dietary habits as well as being bad for teeth when they come through. We know that a little vitamin C is necessary for us all, but despite what some claim there is no evidence that large quantities improve health in any way.

CONCLUSION

Bottle-feeding can provide your baby with balanced nutrition, but it is important to remember a few main points. Here's a checklist:

- Choose the formula that suits your pocket. This may not be the one introduced by your hospital.
- Shop around when first choosing. See what brands tend to have specials at your supermarket or chemist. Price is not related to benefit.
- Then stick to one brand of formula, don't chop and change. It will not alter behaviour or health.
- Straight cow's milk can be used for cooking and making up cereals, but not for drinking in the first twelve months.
- Non-dairy milks are only of benefit to rare cases of true cow's milk allergy.
- Make feeds up cleanly and accurately.
- Sterilise all bottles and boil all water for the first year.
- Don't compress extra powder into the scoop. Over-strength formula can be dangerous.
- Don't pollute the bottles with custard or cereals. Drink is drink and solids should be taken as solids.
- No added vitamins or iron are needed for the average commercial infant formula-fed baby for at least the first eight months.
- Don't become obsessed by accurate intervals between feeds and exact volumes consumed. Feeding to need is what we practise and that's a laid-back approach. Feed them when they want it.
- If your baby is happy, thriving and gaining weight, you must be doing it right. For more information on weight gain see page 364.

It might be worth ending this chapter by observing a small wonder in the lives of children that sooner or later most parents marvel over. For the first twelve months of life you spend countless hours washing and sterilising anything that goes near baby's mouth and then suddenly one day they're eating worms in the dirt, and apparently none the worse for it. That day comes soon enough. In the meantime there are some bottles to be boiled …

Infant feeding for breast-feeding and formula

Feeding to need is the recommendation today. Whether breast or bottle-fed, 'they get it when they want it'.

Approximate volumes of milk taken

Birth to one week: A small intake initially (e.g. 60 ml per kg body weight per day) increasing to full quantity by day five to seven.

One week to four months: Average intake 150 ml per kg body weight per day. (Usual range 120–180 ml per kg.)

Four months to one year: Reduces gradually from 150 ml per kg at four months to about 100 ml per kg body weight at one year.

Average number of feeds each day

Six feeds per day in first two months.
Four to five feeds per day thereafter.
Remember it is feeding to need, and the need may be four to eight per day.

Average weight gain

Birth to one week: In the first two to three days up to ten per cent of the birth weight is lost but regained again by one week in a full-term baby.

One week to four months: Gains 25 g per day (average).
Usual range 150–200 g per week.

Four months to eight: Gains 16 g per day (average).
Usual range 90–150 g per week.

Eight months to one year: Gains about 10 g per day.
Usual range 60–90 g per week.

Note: The rate of weight gain lessens as the months pass. Don't brood on daily weighings. It's much better to weigh your baby weekly or two times a week, always at the same time of day. That way you'll have a more accurate record.

Feeding—from slushes to solids

*I*ntroducing babies to solids is not something to be scared of. It's a natural stage in the development of any little human and although this is where the mess really starts, it's usually a happy time for baby as he discovers the wonders of pumpkin and banana.

Weaning is a gradual process. It's not a question of the breast on Monday and a well-done steak on Tuesday, but rather a spoonful of cereal here and some squashed banana there until Baby starts to understand that not all food is liquid.

The best way to accustom your baby to this gastronomic upheaval in his life is by gentle trial and error. First see what happens when the chosen food is put in his mouth. If it is sucked up with the whoosh of a vacuum cleaner then you're probably on the right track. If it pops back out again like a yo-yo then try something else. If nothing seems to be working he may not be developmentally ready. Leave it a couple of weeks and then try again.

When to introduce solids

The recommended time to wean your baby lengthens and shortens like the hemline fashions. At one time doctors said that nine months was the best time, then that was reduced to three, and now it's six months. It seems to me that where such variations of view exist the actual starting time cannot be all that critical. Somewhere between four and nine months seems to be the time with a preference for about six months.

Wait until your baby is developmentally ready, has good head and neck control and shows an interest in solids. Like most things to do with your baby, a lot will be up to him in the end, though there are some good reasons for not starting solids too early and others for not leaving it too late. Breast-feeding advocates stipulate six months but if you're torn between the manual and a hungry baby, follow your instincts.

Early solids

It is well accepted that human milk is the best fuel for young babies. It's easily digested and provides all the nutrition a baby needs. Bearing in mind just how remarkable the rest of the design is, it's probably wisest to use the maker's approved fuel. In theory you could feed some solids to a newborn baby and after a month it would be reasonably successful, but there are some good reasons why you should not do this. First, solids will be incompletely digested in the early months. Then there is the worry that early introduction of solids can increase the risk of allergies in later life. Another concern is that feeding solids too early can produce weight problems. Certainly very early spoon-feeds coupled with milk are more likely to produce an overweight baby.

Late solids
Starting solids too late on the other hand also has a couple of disadvantages. First you run the risk of nutritional deficiency. Sometime after six months iron and some vitamins will start to run low. If you're bottle-feeding, second-stage formulas offer extra vitamins, but since Baby's gut is by now revving up for a bit of real food you might as well start to go the natural way. After nine months of nothing but milk some babies become milkaholics and are quick to tell you what you can do with anything else. It's best therefore to introduce some texture into the repertoire at around six months with some lumps and little chewy pieces at nine months. This can save a lot of problems later on.

The foods
At birth your baby is taking nothing but milk. By the age of one he is enjoying a cut-up selection of the family dinner. What happens during the intervening months is a gradual introduction and increase in textured food.

There is no one correct way to introduce solids. Having said this, most parents will start with an iron-fortified rice baby cereal. This dry powder is mixed with breast milk, formula or cool, boiled water. It's not that wheat-based cereals are inferior. It's just that very occasionally they precipitate what's known as coeliac disease, a chronic malabsorption–wasting condition. It must be emphasised that this rare complication would probably have occurred at a later age anyway when wheat was introduced, but that by starting later it is easier to diagnose and treat if it appears.

After rice cereal, most babies will move on to fine purees of fruit such as apple or pear, or vegetables such as pumpkin or carrot, and yoghurt, with lean meats and thicker purees coming in about one to two months later. When you start, use sieved or blended foods. The baby tins you buy in supermarkets have a big range of sieved foods or else you can make up your own in the blender. Most fruits and some vegetables melt to a textureless pulp after a long spin in the blender, but you'd better leave meat off the menu for a few months as it can tend to remain a bit stringy and it's harder for Baby to digest. At that stage, don't forget delicacies like liver. It may make the parents feel ill but most babies like it and it's pretty nourishing.

At six months, 'chewing' starts, or to be more precise, Baby starts to gum his food. Now food of rather greater texture can be tried. Baby tins can make way for junior tins, chicken can become scraggier, meat and vegetables no longer need to be a textureless pulp. By eight months a slice of bread can be chewed and a biscuit soggied and sucked.

At nine months you need hardly depress the blender button at all and finger food like biscuits, cheese, toast or fruit can be put on offer. Soon mincemeat, rice and pasta can be added to the menu and little cubes of food will be chewed. By his first birthday your little gourmet should be able to cope with cut-up food from the family table.

Please don't approach the introduction of solids as some scientific ritual. Just relax and find the sequence that suits you best.

The technique

Try to introduce one new food at a time. In this way you can easily see what's popular and what's not, or if there is an allergic or intolerant reaction. Aim to rotate food so as to give a variety of different tastes and textures. Give the food straight, don't add sugar, salt or seasoning just to make it palatable to you. Baby food is for babies and would never be a big taste sensation at the Ritz. If you pollute it to coincide with your palate you may run up against a mouth shut as tight as a bank safe.

At the start don't expect to see vast quantities of food disappearing, as the swallowing mechanism at this stage is pretty immature and it will take some time for your baby to get the hang of it. It's best to begin by offering him one spoonful during feeds and see what happens. If he enjoys it, offer him a couple more and then more the next day. There is no magic to starting solids. It is mainly about taste, texture and colour—the experience of food—so don't blend them into a tasteless beige-coloured mush. Be prepared to experiment and be flexible. All you require is a spoon, a bib, some slushy food and loads of patience. If your baby won't take the food this week, don't worry. Try again next week.

The bowels

It is said that 'what goes up must come down'. With baby feeding, it is 'what goes in must come out'. It's only logical that the gut, having been used to an all-milk diet for so long, will show some changes when faced with solids. The result of course will be much more solid bowel motions and dirtier nappies. Different foods produce different results. Some fruits and juices scoot through as if by jet propulsion, while some vegetables can appear to pass right through the baby without any hint of digestion. Sometimes they re-emerge so untouched that there is not even a change in the tone of their colour. Not to worry, that's not malabsorption, it's perfectly usual, especially with carrots and corn. Now's a good time to start using disposable nappy liners if you are using cloth nappies. These make waste disposal a bit easier and much less intimate.

Tins or home brand?

Pre-prepared food in tins or jars is certainly convenient and provides all Baby's nutritional needs. Much of it is a blend of various substances and can be of a rather monotonous texture and taste. It can also become rather expensive. Home cooking, on the other hand, leaves you in no doubt as to the contents. It also gives you greater control over the consistency of the food and allows you greater scope for experimentation. Your baby is going to get all the nutrition he needs whether he is fed on tins or home brand. I am all for home cooking but opt for convenience.

Convenience cooking

Good nutrition for babies means a proper balance of protein, fats, carbo- hydrates, vitamins and minerals. The truth of the matter is that once that food hits the stomach it doesn't matter at all whether the protein was steak or lamb, the vitamin C orange or rosehip. When time is short don't provide the sort of widely varied menu you expect to find at the Hilton, opt for convenience.

Armed with a blender, a few sterile ice-cube trays and some freezer space it becomes very easy to store meals. Set aside a little food from the normal family meal, blend it and store it in the ice trays. In no time you'll have enough little frozen squares to provide an à la carte selection. Now mealtimes can be as easy as watching an ice cube melt.

Good nutrition habits start early

Good nutrition is a family affair. If you want to have healthy children then parents need to create a healthy lifestyle and example for their children. There are four main aims for adults and children when it comes to improving nutrition:

1. Increase the complex carbohydrate level.
2. Cut down on highly sweet and refined foods.
3. Cut down on salt intake.
4. Reduce the intake of fats in children over two and in adults.

To modify the complex carbohydrate level we need more unrefined energy foods like bread, rice, pasta, potatoes, vegetables and fruit. These are fine in themselves and shouldn't be greatly polluted with fat, salt or sugar. If the bread has some extra grain or fibre in it, better still, but its benefits are soon lost if it is heavily greased with butter or margarine and loaded with jam, honey or salty spreads. Potatoes and vegetables are excellent nutrition. They have lots of fibre and few kilojoules so long as they're not fried or buried under a tonne of butter.

After the age of two years it's important to reduce fats by buying low-fat products, less frying, less fatty meats, fewer fatty spreads and generally watching fat intake. Saturated fat in particular should be reduced and if you must have fat, use mono- or poly-unsaturated fats. As for salt, it should be taken off the dinner table altogether and used less in cooking.

Now, this is all very smart for adults, but how does it affect babies?

Taste starts from day one and it's best to introduce your baby to a wide variety of foods as early as possible, without allowing him to get hooked on a sweet or a salty diet. By the age of one your child will be eating the same meals as you, so if your diet is a healthy one so will his be. There's no need to go completely overboard about it on the other hand. Your baby isn't going to collapse if he doesn't get stone-crushed wheatgerm bread and sticks of celery a foot long. Less refined carbohydrates, less salt and you're in business.

Weaning the milkaholic

Most babies take to solids like a duck to Peking. There are a few unfortunately who will refuse point-blank, as they are now hardened milkaholics. For them spoon-feeds become a miserable failure and they leave you in no doubt whatsoever as to what you can do with your spoon.

It's best to approach this situation gently. Start by reducing Baby's milk intake by a third, offering extra non-milk fluids as a substitute and try to give him a little solid food early in each feed. If this doesn't work, next reduce the milk by half and see what happens. It usually brings a cure within one week.

If you suspect that your baby has a problem with either chewing or swallowing, then have this checked out. But if there appears to be no problem, then you'll have to be firm and keep up the regime.

Other fluids

- Babies less than six months old who are on human milk or commercial infant formula don't need other fluids, except for the option of cooled boiled water for hot days and illness.
- Older babies should also be offered cooled boiled water on hot days. Whatever they take is the right amount. They don't need fruit juices, cordials or other liquids. If you do give juice, dilute it heavily and use sparingly.

The hooked-on-baby-food baby

Rather in the same way as some teenagers are hooked on junk food, some babies get hooked on no-texture baby foods. Nothing will they allow past their lips unless it has been mashed to minutiae or passed several times through a sieve. You can prevent this unfortunate habit by ensuring that a bit of texture and variety are offered by seven months and a few lumps by nine months of age. Here you will find that home food preparation will give you the most flexibility.

If your baby is used to taking only food of some bland, highly filtered variety, don't disappoint him. Continue with this, but gradually readjust the contents. You can start by adding a speck of home cooking, and increase the amount until after a few weeks, unknown to him, it's all coming from your blender. You can hurry this along by reducing the milk volume which will tone up the appetite.

Beware and prepare for the toddler backlash

Once weaned most babies enjoy their solids, which they attack like lions at the kill. They will accept an extensive range of meats, fish, fruit, cereals and vegetables—and even smile as the last trace of spinach slips out of sight! Oh, that this would continue, but regrettably for some it all falls apart around the first birthday.

It is as though someone has turned off the mains switch and the eating mechanism refuses to function. It's nothing to get unduly worried about. This is all due to an interesting stage of life called toddlerhood. The toddler may only reach up to your kneecap, but as anyone who has met a leprechaun will tell you, this doesn't stop him telling you exactly what he will and will not do. The toddler has a lot more determination and stubbornness than sense, which makes food fights a monumental waste of time.

Another factor is temperament. I believe God made two types of feeders: those who take food very seriously and those who think of it as some sort of joke. The serious won't lift their eyes until they have practically scraped the pattern off the plate, whereas the joker will play with his food, doing just about anything he can with it except eat it.

The first rule is never to fight about food, as it will get you absolutely nowhere. Forget for now dreams of introducing your child to the entire contents of your Jamie Oliver cookbook and narrow it down to a few palatable essentials. If you are still getting nowhere, you may even have to forget about formal meals altogether and resort to eating on the hoof. Grazing is good for millions of sheep and it must be good for toddlers too. Now it's cheese and crackers, chicken, a cold sausage, fruit and lots of nutritious sandwiches all washed down with a good vintage white (from the milkman).

Conclusion
- Don't start too early or too late. Four to six months seems ideal.
- Introducing solids means trial and error with gradual introduction.
- If the food you offer reappears, check your baby is developmentally ready or try something else. If it disappears you're probably on the right track.
- Rice cereals are best before six months. Start wheat cereals later.
- Baby rice, vegetables and fruit are the favourite starters.
- Little kilojoule intake from solids is achieved in the first month after introduction so don't take it too seriously.

- Baby tastes and adult tastes are different. Don't season Baby's food to your palate.
- Honey can carry infection. Avoid it until the first birthday.
- Egg yolks are out until six months and egg whites until one year, due to allergy.
- A healthy diet is a family affair. Aim for more complex carbohydrates, less fat, less over-refined sweet food and less salt. Healthy parents teach by example to their healthy children.

Foods to watch

Foods that may cause loose bowel motions

- Most 100 per cent fruit juices, especially apple and orange

Foods that may reappear undigested

- Carrots
- Corn
- Sometimes peas

Foods that may alter the colour of the bowel motion

- Iron tonics and medicines (black)
- The artificial sweetener sorbitol (pink diarrhoea)

Foods that may change the colour of the urine

- Beetroot (red)
- Some food dyes
- Vitamin B supplements (yellow)

Foods best avoided

- Egg yolk—first six months (allergy)
- Egg white—first year (allergy)
- Wheat-based cereals—first six months (possible coeliac disease)
- Bottled cow's milk to drink—first nine to twelve months
- Honey—first year (botulism)

Crying—what does it mean?

M ost new parents find their little ones cry considerably more than they ever expected. Often they feel overwhelmed and exhausted as this crying will usually come on for no apparent reason and, what's worse, will be devilishly difficult to stop.

We are told that the average young baby cries two to three hours each day, but the reality is that there are few average babies. There are some angels who are almost too good to be true and some who cry so much that their parents are reduced to quivering blobs of jelly.

Parents are further confused by all the folklore that clouds childcare. We are told that the properly fed baby sleeps peacefully for four hours, wakes, smiles, cries gently, is fed, burps and goes off to sleep once more. Some children certainly behave like this but it will be unusual and you will be privileged if your child does.

Other unfounded myths tell of the dangers of letting a baby cry. Belly buttons blow out, children have convulsions and hernias drop down. Then there is the fable which gives a stern warning not to spoil your baby. It implies that the little baby who is comforted when he cries becomes spoilt silly and will be demanding for years. This is not a true tale and in fact there is some evidence that the babies who receive the most comfort become the most secure and least demanding.

So, I hear you ask, why do little humans need to cry? Unfortunately, no-one really knows. My feeling is that it's about exercise and circulation while they're waiting for proper movement to begin, a bit like all that ankle and wrist flexing you do on a long-haul flight.

Let's look at what the different types of cries mean, the effect of temperament and finally what crying does to us poor parents.

TYPES OF CRIES

The newborn nursery in a hospital is filled with a chorus of cries indistinguishable to the untrained ear, but most mothers can identify the chirp of their own chick after about three days of age. At first all sorts of crying sound identical, but as the weeks pass, different patterns emerge indicating different needs. There will be a cry of pain, another of hunger, while a lesser cry may simply signify boredom or grumbling. Often you just won't know what it means.

Please don't get too scientific about this as it's often very difficult to distinguish crying accurately.

The cry of pain

When it comes to the cry of pain there is generally a gasp and then a loud bloodcurdling screech, which is followed by a short pause while Baby winds up to start all over again. The knees draw up, the face goes red and the child is inconsolable.

Though we know that this is a cry of pain the cause of it is often obscure. Many will have colic (see Chapter 17). Others will wake from a deep sleep with a jump and then scream, and some just wail for the hell of it. By all means check for nappy pins sticking into little bottoms, wet nappies and assorted illnesses, but by and large painful crying usually occurs for some reason known only to God and the baby.

The cry of hunger

The hungry baby communicates with a more regular cry which lacks the pitch, knee drawing and intensity of the pained cry. It occurs some time after the last square meal and, though it can be stopped briefly by comfort, it is really only a large dose of kilojoules that is going to provide proper relief.

Grumblers

Bored, lonely, tired, cold or uncomfortable babies are likely to grumble. Others, who have none of these problems, will grumble anyway because, rather like some adults we all know, it's just in their nature. This sort of crying is of a lower pitch, coming and going before winding up to a real cry. Alternatively they may just grumble themselves off to sleep. Generally speaking, with a bit of comfort and instant entertainment, matters can be relieved. Grumbling seems to become an art form after about the first four months. Before then most babies seem either to cry properly or not at all.

TEMPERAMENT AND TEARS

As everyone knows, all babies are not born the same. Each baby from his first cry will show an individual temperament. Some are quite content to lie gazing at the ceiling for hours, while others want to be up and about observing the world at its business. Some will sleep for long periods, while others will wake every two hours whether well fed or not. Some are fussy, some are jumpy and others just don't want to be disturbed. Some are comforted by the slightest touch, while others will remain inconsolable despite feeding, bouncing, driving round the block, the tuneless drone of the vacuum cleaner, Willie Nelson records or other such sounds. Of these, it's the hard-to-comfort, tense and active babies who cause the most anguish.

Tense babies

Some babies are tense and jumpy from birth. They will jump as the nursery door closes, hate any changes, prefer not to be handled too much and take great exception to being stripped and put in a bath. They respond best to quiet, firm holding, gentle movement, dim lights, swaddling, sucking, gentle massage, soothing talk and music. Noise, tension, bouncing and any frantic movement is best avoided because it will stir them up.

Active babies

These bright-eyed little humans want action. They have neither the time nor the inclination just to lie on their back being a baby. No lying flat in a pram for these babies, thank you very much, they want to be upright and on the move. They like to be strapped to your back or sitting in a stroller where they can see everything going on around them.

Though entertained by activity and movement, these little people are easily bored when the merry-go-round stops. They are happiest when the house is full of action and noise with lots of dogs, children and adults romping around.

Active babies tend to be more irritable in their first year and

demand a lot of individual attention. They improve dramatically once they are upright on their own feet and independent.

The most important time that active babies need to be soothed and calmed is when they are tired and it's near bedtime. At this time activity will wind them up and make sleep difficult, so soothing care is necessary if you are going to cool down their fast-moving brain enough to permit sleep. This is the time for quiet holding or just putting them down to settle in the same way as you would with a tense baby.

WHAT ABOUT THE PARENTS?

Easy babies produce relaxed, confident, competent parents. Inconsolable, irritable children inflict immeasurable psychological pain on their unsuspecting parents. Sometimes it is hard to understand why your baby responds with nothing more than continuous crying and apparent unhappiness when you are heaping love, care and attention on him. Where are you going wrong? Why can't you cope when all those other mothers out there seem to be doing so well? Crying is a real confidence crusher.

The answer of course is that you are doing nothing wrong at all. You are every bit as good a parent as the next one. It's just that you are unlucky enough to have been dealt a difficult baby.

Soothing the unsoothable is one of life's most soul-destroying experiences and is guaranteed to reduce the competent to a feeling of utter impotence. Excessive crying, especially when coupled with a lack of sleep, can easily lead to parents with numb, befuddled brains. This in turn leads to tension and irritability which is in turn communicated to the baby who then behaves even worse, and so the vicious circle spins round even faster like a Catherine wheel.

There are, I'm afraid, no miracle cures for such babies, but hopefully some of the ideas in the next chapter will ease the burden a little.

How to comfort
a crying baby

W*hen it comes to comforting crying babies I'm afraid there are no hard and fast rules. The whole thing falls into the category of 'seat of your pants' science.*

In this chapter I'll be discussing a wide selection of comfort ideas. Some are effective for the majority of children and some for a select few. Comfort is a peculiarly personal affair and certain techniques which may be good for one type of child may not work on another.

For most first-time parents, the right type of comfort is discovered by trial and error. By consulting the lists in the following table, hopefully you will have more ideas for trial and less room for error.

Top tries for different cries

Before you get totally bogged down in what follows, let's steer you towards the best strategies for the main types of crying. As you scan the lists you may wonder what happened to milk allergy, gastric antacids and tapes of pretend heartbeats. I have to confess that I have moved heavily towards all the old-fashioned, well-tried remedies. I am sure that they leave what's new and trendy for dead. Soothing by gentle movement, postures, swaddling and sound is as old as civilisation itself. These forms of soothing have stood the test of time and are still streets ahead of anything new.

The list that follows is beautifully black and white, but don't let this fool you for a minute. Nothing in your life or mine is as cut and dried as this. Use these suggestions as a guide from which to choose your next move. Use a package of three or four ideas at the one time. There's no guarantee of success first off but some guidance beforehand has to save a bit of emotional energy in the long run.

Posture

For every crying, unhappy baby there is a particular position of maximum comfort. The trouble is it takes a lot of experimenting before you find it.

Most babies just like to be close to their parents, probably held up against the chest, where they can snuggle in, hear a heartbeat and

Tips to try

Colic

- Posture—over knee, arm or bed
- Apply gentle pressure to abdomen
- Movement—firm, one step per second
- Patting and rhythm
- Sucking
- Swaddling
- Medicines

The active baby

- Slings, frontpacks and strollers
- Baby bouncers
- Allowing baby to sit up and look around
- Baby walkers may even be worth a try in extreme cases (she'll be more content when she starts walking alone)

The tense baby

- Swaddling
- Firm holding
- Firm stroking of the back
- Gentle rhythmic movement
- Leaving in peace

The grumbler

- Patting
- Dummies
- Music
- Changing nappy
- Leaving her alone

When all else fails

- Get out of the house with Baby.
- Visit friends, playgroups, baby health clinic.
- Ask for help.
- Ask friends or family to mind Baby for a while.
- When you can take no more, put Baby in the safety of her cot and move away.

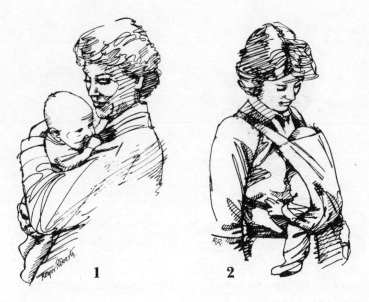

1 2

possibly peep over the shoulder (picture 1). A simple sling made from an old sheet or a commercially made frontpack will give comfort to both the holder and 'holdee', and frees up Mum's hands to continue with her work (picture 2).

The tense baby will accept most positions so long as she is held firmly and not fussed over. The active ones prefer to be upright, on the move and able to see what's going on. With them, slings, strollers and baby bouncers are the answer.

The colicky baby is usually happiest when held in a position that puts some gentle pressure on her tummy. This can be achieved either by lying her tummy down over an arm (pictures 3 and 4), knee or pillow (picture 5) or folding her gently in the middle which enables a little squeeze to be given to her troubled tummy. By 'folding' I mean letting her sit in the crook of your left arm with her knees drawn up and her body flexed forward (picture 6). Another favourite fold is with your baby's back against your chest, facing out in front with her legs held up against her abdomen or moved gently in a bicycling movement (picture 7).

Try a number of positions until you find the one that suits you and Baby best. Some, such as carrying her over an arm, give portability

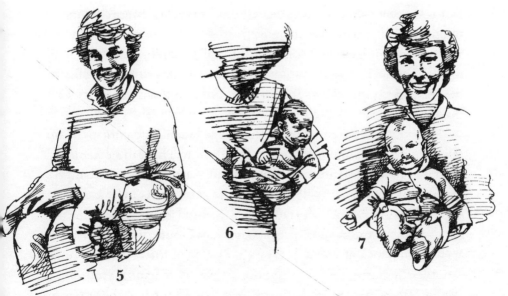

These illustrations were compiled with the help
of the staff of Torrens House, Adelaide.

while soothing over a knee or pillow ties you down.

The correct posture will help most criers but there may come a point when whatever you do does no good. When that happens, it's probably best to put your baby down in the safety of her cot. Being glued to an inconsolable child can create more tension and frustration than is good for you or your baby. There is a time when it's best to separate, in the name of safety, before something snaps.

Movement

Movement has always been recognised as the great baby soother. Mothers have always rocked cribs, sat on rocking chairs with their babies or walked them around in slings. Gentle rhythms give comfort, but wild gyrations do nothing but stir up and unsettle young ones.

Most babies like to rock gently in the arms of a parent as they walk slowly round the room with her. One small step per second will give the right rhythm.

Quiet babies enjoy long periods of horizontal meditation in a pram. If your baby is harder to settle, a very effective technique is to position the pram over the edge of the carpet or any small bump and push them back and forth rhythmically. Active babies are often too alert for this. Being compulsively curious creatures, they like to be propped up on pillows so that they can see what's going on. The stroller is a device which is ideal for the active baby. She can then face the oncoming world at eye level (well, at knee level, perhaps). The only problem is when the stroller stops. You will find that long chats in the shopping mall are out if you want to keep a busy baby happy.

Movement in a car often soothes the active or colicky baby, but she won't cope well with traffic jams and red lights. On the other hand, many an exasperated parent has had welcome relief from a trip around the block at 3 am.

Soothing sounds

Since the Dark Ages lullabies have been used to soothe babies. The words are irrelevant, but the rhythm and tones are low-pitched with long, drawn-out syllables.

If you can sing then let your baby have the full works. If you can't, then forget the words and just hum along the best you can—the effect will be the same. If, however, you are tone-deaf you can always buy the latest tape of womb sounds. These may not feature in the Top 40 but the gushes, whooshes and gut rumblings are said to soothe some babies as surely as a choir of heavenly angels.

Babies are not quite as discerning as their parents when it comes to soothing sounds. Some babies will relax to the roar of the vacuum cleaner, while others positively purr to the strains of the washing machine, and even the white noise of an untuned radio station is another popular soother.

The important thing here is experimentation. You never know what's going to be best until you try it.

Swaddling

Back in biblical times swaddling was very popular, and it's still good value today. Remember that the newborn has been effectively swaddled for nine months inside Mum's tummy and it's not surprising that she likes returning to the pretend womb of a tightly wrapped blanket.

In the first weeks most babies prefer to be wrapped firmly. They are ill at ease when stripped off and left lying free in space. Swaddling is particularly good for tense babies who gain great comfort from being bundled up. Wrap them up, leave them alone and they are at their happiest. Many babies will be happy to be swaddled until they are six months old.

Active babies in particular object to being restricted. After the first weeks they will begin to resist. You may swaddle them as much as you like but they will jack up and kick their way to freedom.

Always use 100 per cent cotton wraps to keep them comfortable and follow your instincts if they begin to resist strongly.

Sucking and dummies

A great many criers are helped by sucking. It's not the kilojoules that they're after but the soothing sensation of a breast, bottle, hand or dummy. Colicky babies don't want food, but they do like to suck. If they're not hungry it may be that a dummy is the answer. Walk them at an appropriate speed or pat them with perfect rhythm, and try a bit of sucking at the same time.

When it comes to grumbling babies, a dummy will be most useful. They can lie in their cots, sucking and grumbling a bit at the same time. For them this little bit of oral entertainment keeps their minds off the woes of the world.

Don't be frightened to introduce a dummy for fear that you will not be able to break the habit later. If it helps keep the peace now, then that's most important.

Massage

Babies can be soothed by a gentle touch. You may have heard about baby massage at antenatal classes and shown what to do in hospital after the birth. There are books available and you can ask your baby health nurse but once you get the hang of it it's not difficult. The benefits are that it is soothing, quiet and bonding for both of you, it will help circulation and it's a lovely, natural way to get Baby off to sleep.

To keep things moving smoothly, get a few things ready before you begin. The room temperature should be comfortable for a naked baby, around 22 degrees. Massage works best when it is unrushed. A warm, dimly lit room with your favourite CD playing softly in the background is the ideal setting. Make sure things are going to be quiet—turn off the telephone. Have your gear ready before you start: a nice oil, perhaps almond (although be careful of nut allergies), choose a comfortable position for you and for Baby, and have a nice towel or her bedclothes ready to wrap her up in afterwards. You should first experiment with your baby in times of peace and wakefulness. Once you have found the best technique for her, then you can give it a try when she is tense and crying.

The job now is to focus on Baby. Talk gently and make slow, light strokes, sliding your hands gently over her skin. Cover her body from shoulder to abdomen and legs and over her hips and bottom. Make circular movements with your fingers. Aim for a lovely flow and pay attention to what she enjoys and finds restful.

Massage is potentially valuable for all babies. Some may be too irritable but give it a go; if it does work it'll be a real treat for both of you.

Warmth

Just as the rest of us soothe our cramps with hot water bottles, babies who might have crampy abdomens can also be soothed with heat.

Hot water bottles are too dangerous for babies. Microwave a wheat bag instead so it's warm rather than hot to the touch. They smell comforting too, a bit like someone is making porridge! Lay Baby down, holding the bag against her abdomen. As the warmth makes contact, start to massage and gently pat her to produce a super soothe.

Upset babies won't thank you for being stripped off and put in a baby bath all alone unless it's something she loves, but an adult bath may be a different matter. Get the temperature just right, comfortably warm, and then slip in with your baby. This allows togetherness, body contact and for some is as therapeutic as a plunge in healing hot springs!

Wind and gas

Wind has been blamed for many an unhappy baby. I fear that it is greatly over-diagnosed but experiment for yourself and if you find that releasing the last gurgle of gas brings relief then by all means go ahead. I'm certainly convinced though that the gentle rock–pat–burp routine gives closeness, rhythm and movement, and that must be good for any upset baby.

Changing the formula

If my car starts to smoke and backfire I know that there is something wrong with the motor. This needs a mechanic, not a change from one brand of petrol to another. Likewise if your baby is crying and colicky on one formula, changing her fuel to another brand isn't going to do much more than perhaps change the colour of the exhaust products.

There's no need to go on a formula-shuffling spree. If your baby is breast-feeding and thriving, don't stop. It may occasionally help if you cut out dairy products from your own diet for a while, but even that's uncertain.

It is true that occasionally babies do have a real allergy to cow's milk and become extremely sick, blotchy, pale and wheezy. Lesser allergies are also said to cause a multitude of minor symptoms from a runny nose to colic.

Although many do not share my view, I have rarely been impressed with claims that crying has been cured by a switch from cow's milk to a different kind, but if in doubt, talk to your early childhood nurse about giving it a go.

Extra kilojoules and solids

Starving babies cry, but most crying babies are not starving. If your baby is unsettled, is thriving poorly and homes in on food like a famished vulture, then it is time to investigate her intake. If, on the other hand, she is robust, healthy and cries regardless of her nourishment, then the answer does not lie in food.

Although not everyone agrees with offering complementary feeds, I have seen some totally breast-fed babies do much better when offered a bottle as well. There are babies who just seem to need a little top up. This is an area you should approach with a little caution and discuss with your early childhood nurse who will be able to help you decide whether your baby needs a little extra nutrition.

Wet and dirty nappies

New mums are always told to check for wet nappies and sharp pins when their youngsters cry. I don't believe that most babies are that sensitive to damp. After all, they are submerged for their first nine months and then dribble, spill and wet for most of the next two years, without too much upset.

As for being impaled on a pin, it must be pretty rare if proper nappy pins are used and if the parent who uses them pokes them through with care.

I admit that the grumbling baby may fuss less when dry, but I am afraid that the screamer is usually as vocal whether there is a flood or drought down there in the bottom paddock. If you are in doubt then change the nappy; a change of scene and a little one-on-one time may do the trick in any case.

Medicines

Many parents with a consistent crier will eventually experiment with a few medicines. These range from homoeopathic drops to camomile tea, or from gripe water to sedation. While there's nothing wrong with using any safe medical or alternative preparations, my own experience shows that they rarely seem to work.

Once upon a time, gin was the stand-by of the professional baby minder, but this use of alcohol is best left as an interesting relic of the past as we know now that it's dangerous for the developing brain. Gripe water has been popular for generations of mums with criers. It has its devoted followers, but there is not a lot of convincing evidence that it works.

Other medicines are said to break up gas bubbles in the gut and guide them gently towards an opening. This sounds most commendable, but I don't really believe that gas is the cause of continuous crying either.

Some doctors will prescribe night sedatives when crying is constant and inconsolable and the parents are close to breaking point. I don't see them as a great evil and when the chips are down, if they are going to help keep the family intact, then they probably should be used, under medical supervision.

However, before you decide to use medicines I think you should try the simple, soothing ideas mentioned above. Then have a chat with your doctor or paediatrician if these methods are not helping.

Although it's not easy to remember when the tears are flooding and your befuddled brain has zero confidence, colic and crying are very short-term problems. Time is an amazing healer, and it should be of some consolation to know that your baby will soon move on from this distressing stage.

Time to oneself

It's not hard to imagine what happens to a parent's self-confidence when Baby has been crying long and hard and all efforts to comfort her have collapsed. Optimism is replaced by a focus on failure. Now this is the time to down tools and get out.

Load up the pram or stroller and head for the wide open spaces. Crying is often soothed by movement and if not, it is always less upsetting out of doors.

Isolation is the curse of many families. Now's the time you need Grandma, Aunty or support from any kind, caring friend. You need time to get out, to unwind from tension, to clear the brain and to regain an identity other than that of a mother under pressure.

Isolation can be deepened where fathers are working very hard or travelling and most of the childcare falls to Mum. And many mothers find it easier to stay in the rut than muster the energy needed to get up and go. Some become sensitive that others are coping where they feel they are not.

Time to oneself is a must for all mothers, not just for those in strife. Time to recharge the batteries helps both you and the baby, and everyone around you. If you can get some time to go out, grab it with both hands and don't let anyone make you feel guilty. Mix with other adults, do some exercise or just involve yourself in something quite different from the daily grind of baby-related chores.

When all else fails

When all comfort fails, there is no help, you can't get out and you can't take any more, then you and your baby must separate. Take the inconsolable baby, put her in the security of her cot, close the door and move outside or to the most distant part of the house. This is time out for Mum and is much better to take than being driven over the brink.

Accepting advice

One of the first tasks of parenthood, even from pregnancy, is to develop your advice filter. One thing is absolutely certain in this world: there is no shortage of free advice from well-wishers telling you how to manage your children. When the going gets tough, advice should only be accepted from friends and family who offer to roll up their sleeves and help. The others can keep their theories to themselves.

It is important too to choose your helping professionals with care. Whether it be clinic sister, psychologist or doctor, you need a listener, a communicator and someone who understands how you feel. They must be able to boost your confidence and send you off with a list of practical ideas that work for real people.

Conclusion

All babies cry with different duration, style, intensity and response to comfort. Those parents with easy babies have no idea just what their friends are going through.

Continuous, inconsolable crying transforms the confident, optimistic parent into a demoralised defeatist. Parents matter too. When the crying is getting to you, seek help and don't feel guilty about taking time out to cool off by yourself. Helpful friends and family are to be blessed.

There are no sure-fire cures for crying. You must experiment and pick a package of ideas that will give some relief, while time does its healing work. Don't give up. Crying always improves as the months go by. I've been there, with my own children and thousands of others. I know how hard it is. You are not alone. It will get better.

Colic

C olic is an imprecise term used to describe a pattern of unsettled behaviour and crying common in the first months of life. It usually occurs in the late afternoon or early evening and comes on shortly after feeding. The baby is distressed, seems in pain and is extremely hard to console.

The definition of colic is vague and it means different things to different people.

Most view it with very loose limits. For them it describes any fussing or unsettled behaviour that occurs after feeds, especially in the late afternoon and evening. Others try to adhere tightly to a definition such as crying in the first four months of life in a healthy, well-nourished baby, who cries at full force for a total of at least four hours in one day, this occurring at least four days each week.

Although it has been around for centuries, no-one knows for certain what causes colic. It makes children cry and almost impossible to comfort. It can turn happy, confident parents into defeated and demoralised ones. Though an anxious mother may make it worse, it is the colic which causes the anxiety in the first place, definitely not the reverse.

Many academic doctors find the whole concept of colic beyond them. The descriptions are too vague, there is no pathological explanation, and it can't be measured by blood test, biopsy or any medical machine. Whether or not you can measure it, colic is a very real condition and one which causes considerable stress for both Baby and parents.

The picture

Your baby has been a model of good behaviour in hospital and you go home full of the joys of life. Parenthood seems a breeze and your thoughts turn to having another child next year. Then after a few days the crying starts. You have just fed Baby that afternoon or evening and your first impulse is to give her more. But after the first few sucks the screaming returns, louder than ever. You burp, bounce, pat, change the nappy, give yet more food and start to feel thoroughly incompetent. Nothing appears to help.

Her face is red, her knees are drawn up and the cry is now like one who is in great pain. This goes on for between one and six hours day after day. With this you gradually disintegrate, and while this is going on your baby is thriving, gaining weight and generally looking a picture of rude good health. Confusing, isn't it?

Colic occurs somewhere between a few minutes to a full hour after feeding and is usually made worse, not stopped, by food. The most usual time for it to happen is between 5 and 10 pm, but it can occur at any time of the day or night. It usually starts when the baby is about ten days old, though it has been known to commence right from birth. It usually eases up by two months of age and stops altogether by three months, though again in some cases it can continue until six months.

It is estimated that five per cent of all babies born will have severe colic and probably around 25 per cent have a mild degree at some stage in their early lives. These figures of course depend on the definition you use.

THE CAUSE

The most plausible theories focus on some immaturity of the gut or nervous system, or imbalance in the body's hormones. The gut at birth is a poorly exercised bit of tubing that has never before received anything that resembles food. It is possible that it hasn't quite got its act together by birth and resents having food run through it. Maybe, on the other hand, the nervous system that controls everything is not quite up to it. There is also the possibility that the baby is suffering from a withdrawal of Mum's hormones, which she shared before birth. Some of these hormones have a muscle-relaxant property which allowed Mum to stretch enough to permit the baby to be born. Possibly removing these relaxing hormones causes spasms.

All this is unproven speculation, and there are a number of popular theories.

Wind
Being a keen sailor I know a lot about wind. I can tell an ill wind when I see one, be it in boats or babies. Each day all around the civilised world,

billions of babies are bounced and burped in the ritualistic pursuit of expelling the last knot of wind from either end.

These wind watchers will tell you confidently that this is the cause of colic as they lift their baby up from the horizontal position of the cot, and lo and behold exhibit a small gas explosion. There is, however, one major flaw in this argument. Gravity affects colicky and normal babies alike. Any baby lifted from the horizontal to the vertical will tend to burp.

Many health workers I greatly respect are still convinced that careful feeding and winding will help some colicky babies. For me I am still not sure and believe that no amount of wind-free feeding, patting or burping is going to relieve colic.

Anxious parents

My own interest in writing about babies began after the birth of my first son, who is now in his thirties. My goodness we were pleased with ourselves. What a perfect baby! What clever parents! And then, about three days into parenthood, came the colic. My wife and son were still in hospital—they didn't shoo you out quite so quickly in those days—and the nurses asked me when I arrived for visiting hours if there was something wrong in our relationship, as the baby was crying out of control.

That was often the way, parents were blamed for being anxious and infecting the baby with it. We could well believe it. We didn't have our own parents around and it was all new to us. It went on for six months and with the second baby it was even worse. I learned from our experience that colic is real and parents truly suffer with it. Without the experience I would never have written my parenting books. I wanted parents to know that the difficulties they face with problems like colic are not a product of their own failings. They say it's slightly more common in first babies. Perhaps that's because if you experience it the first time round you may never get to number two!

We really know only this: colic is awful, and they will grow out of it.

It may be that the anxiety caused by colic feeds back into the vicious circle and this is hardly surprising. It may be the same with postnatal depression. If you are struggling with parenthood, and colic isn't helping, then you need to take care of yourself as well as baby. Please see the tips in Chapters Five and Six about looking after your own wellbeing and be assured that colic is not a symptom of your own personality.

Incorrect feeding

Hunger pains and colic are definitely not the same. A hungry baby will cry before food and stop when fed. Lack of milk may certainly cause hunger, but it won't cause colic. Another myth is that it is the quality of the breast milk which causes colic. This is utter nonsense. The quality of breast milk is always grade A. You either have top-quality milk or none at all. It is also true that colic is about as common in bottle-fed babies as it is in the breast-fed.

There are those who are sure that colic is due to feeding too fast and still others who believe it is caused by feeding too slowly. Some quite unnatural feeding positions have been devised to act on these theories, and while these may help a few, I have to say that I am unconvinced.

Substances in mother's milk

It is true that certain substances eaten by the mother can pass into her milk. Some babies find that second-hand garlic, spices and broccoli are not to their liking while others find their mothers pleasantly soothing after a well-lubricated party, though this is not a method I would ever recommend.

Dairy products cause the most interest and dispute. Some mothers have found that relief comes when they stop all dairy products in their own diet. Though I am not really a believer in this, it's so simple to do, so if you're in doubt, why not cut them out for a week and see for yourself?

Cow's milk allergy

There is a very strong anti-cow's milk lobby who claims that cow's milk may be fine for little cows but that it is no good for little humans. Colic, they believe, can be improved by removing cow's milk from all bottle-feeds.

Most studies, however, have not been able to support these claims, though there are occasional babies who certainly seem to get relief. Once again I am not convinced that there is a connection between cow's milk and colic, but as it will certainly do no harm, why not try removal of cow's milk as a short trial when all else has failed?

Oesophageal reflux

It was recently discovered that many colicky babies have a leaky valve at the top of their stomach. 'Eureka!' cried the scientists. 'At last we know the cause of colic.' The theory was simple. Acid leaks up from the stomach to the sensitive oesophagus to cause pain and crying.

Unfortunately this has now gone the way of most such theories—out the door. Certainly some colicky babies have this leaky valve, but so also do many normal, happy babies. And those who have specifically studied the oesophagus of colicky babies have found that there is not much sign of any inflammation or irritation in these children. This must make the theory of regurgitation causing pain unlikely. Another group of scientists who placed an acid-sensitive recorder in the oesophagus of babies who had colic and reflux found that the acid leak bore no consistent relationship to the time of crying. One would have thought that if colic were due to the irritation of acid, the leak and the crying would always come together.

There must be some colicky babies who have pain from reflux and it must be worth keeping in mind, but from my experience, it is not common.

Temperament

Temperament cannot be said to cause colic, but certainly there is a type of baby who is more prone to this affliction. The active, awake, busy, tense baby is more likely to have colic than the more placid ones. It is possible, I suppose, that babies with a tense temperament also have a tense brain and tense guts. Possibly they also have taken their genes from tense parents!

In later life it is often found that those who display active, inflexible and tense tendencies have frequently suffered from colic as a baby. Colic does not come from one clear cause. Unknown physiological factors, the child's individual temperament, factors in the environment and the parents' tolerance to crying all play a part.

TREATMENT

Many professionals and parents can see one, and only one, possible treatment for colic. It is easy to make great claims for your chosen treatment of colic, particularly if you persist long enough, as all babies always get better in the end.

God matures and cures, but we experts are quick to claim all the glory. There is no lack of remedies for colic and crying, the trouble is that few work really well. If you are prepared to be flexible, to experiment and to work for a percentage improvement, not a 'bolt of lightning' type miracle, then I guarantee that things are about to take a change for the better.

When you seek treatment, I believe you can't go past a professional who is practical, understanding and knows what it means to support. I believe that spirits lift and the situation improves significantly once you realise that you are not alone and that there will be light at the end of this relatively short tunnel.

For treating your baby, Chapter 16 is cram-packed with ideas. It's best to start with finding the most soothing posture, then introducing certain gentle movements. Patting, rhythms, soothing sounds, sucking and medicines may also help.

Use not one but a package of ideas together. Experiment and keep adding new ones until you get some relief. If all else fails, you may be driving round the block at 3 am to try and soothe Baby, but let's hope you don't get that far.

CONCLUSION
....

We don't know the cause of colic but we know it is real. When you can't help or soothe your baby, you become exhausted and confused and may question your ability to be a good parent. Get help, use whatever you can from the previous chapter on soothing that you think might help, take shifts so you get a break and know from a survivor that it will pass.

Sleep problems— how to solve them

H ow much does a new baby sleep? Probably a darn sight less than most parents ever expected. Though sleep is a big part of our lives, we are still uncertain how it revives tired brains and bodies. What is certain is that without sleep we would soon fall apart.

Sleep deprivation is not just unpleasant, it is a form of torture. Secret police use it to soften up those they bring in for a chat. Come to think of it, after a week of disturbed sleep the average parent is about ready to confess to anything.

Most babies in the first three months are going to wake once or more each night. You may become resigned to this fact and when it happens view it as normal. If by some great fortune you score a super-sleeper, then that's a bonus and a pleasant surprise.

By six months about three-quarters of all babies sleep through to sunrise but this still leaves one-quarter who continue to wake, many of whom keep up the antics right through toddlerhood.

This chapter looks at the science of sleep and how you can work with it to help your baby sleep more continuously. If we understand a condition we can often help it. Of course, you can't cure the incurable, but if you have sensible expectations, introduce a good sleep routine and use my Controlled Crying technique, all should gain improvement and most will find a cure.

THE SCIENCE OF SLEEP

Most of us take sleep for granted, and may feel as though we go out like a light at bedtime and don't register a thing until the alarm goes off. But in reality it is impossible to make any adult or baby sleep deeply and continuously all night—this is just not how sleep works. Sleep is not one unbroken, dead-to-the-world state, but a glide through a standard sequence of levels of consciousness. Deep sleep—light sleep—a period of dreams—a brief awakening and roll over—then down into the depths once more and so the cycle goes on all night. Deep sleep allows the body to build, grow, repair and remain healthy. In light sleep our brains are active and buzzing. It's as though the files from the day's work are being sorted so that everything we've learned is in its place and ready to use when we need it again.

How adults sleep

If you attach electrodes in a brain-wave test (electroencephalogram—EEG) to a sleeping human, the tracing tells us much about the states of sleep. This shows if they are deeply asleep, dreaming (REM sleep) or floating on a lighter plane. It measures the length of the cycle and tells us how much time is spent in each state along the way.

From this we discover that adults sleep a 90-minute cycle from start to finish. This means that every 90 minutes we may wake briefly, open our eyes, stretch, grunt, roll over, register that it is still dark and then go back to sleep again. When we wake we keep it to ourselves and don't wake our partner to share the moment. We don't even notice it ourselves most of the time.

We learn as adults that good sleep needs a consistent routine. If we want to get a good night's sleep we plan to go to bed at roughly

the same time every night and beforehand we wind down. We try to leave the day's stresses behind, forget about unfinished work, avoiding feverish activity, undue exertion and terrifying television when we're just about to hit the hay. We might snuggle under the covers, read a couple of pages of a book by lamplight and fall quietly to sleep.

What happens next? Well for the most part, we'll slip between cycles, unaware of the joins between them. If someone were to wake us during deep, non-REM sleep, we'd be stunned, and it would take a while to wake up properly. If we wake in a dream sleep we're already fairly alert. Left alone, we'll manage six or seven 90-minute cycles a night, barely aware that we moved between the cycles at all.

How babies sleep

Babies don't sleep continuously all night either, as you may well and truly know by now. They too sleep in cycles. New babies ride a cycle with a shorter frame, one which measures only 60 minutes. Being shorter it increases the potential number of wakes possible each night, leaving the daunting possibility of a wake every hour on the hour if you are really unfortunate. If that wasn't enough, they spend a larger proportion of the cycle in lighter sleep, about half of it rather than a third, so that means trouble for someone, generally the frazzled parent on night shift.

As parents, we can recognise some of these light periods of sleep. Sometimes the baby will stretch, grunt, yawn, open a sleepy eye and drop off again. Sometimes they start to cry in a half-hearted way, uncertain if they want attention or whether it is better just to grumble themselves back to sleep. It is also at these times that they move around the cot, kick off the blankets and may well wake and shout for attention. It is nigh on impossible to make little children stay deeply unconscious all night, they will always wake. What we as parents can do is to teach them to wake quietly, get themselves back to sleep without help and not to disturb their parents.

The brain-wave tests also show that little children fall asleep much faster than adults. While we glide through every level down to deep sleep, they drop like a brick in a bucket. Then when they're asleep, you can take them to restaurants, parties and at home generally be as noisy as you like.

All this talk of the science of sleep has probably left you yawning but if we understand what's going on we can help the process become a little smoother:

- Sleep occurs in a series of cycles.
- We all have the potential to wake in the night, little children more so.
- Adults drift to sleep; babies plummet.
- Babies sleep deeply and are relatively immune to noise.
- Adults when they wake have learned to put themselves back to sleep. Little children must be taught this social skill.

HOW MUCH SLEEP IS ENOUGH?

No-one can stipulate exactly how many hours your baby should sleep. Each child is an individual with his own sleep needs and patterns, and will go his own way whatever I say. We do, however, have some idea of the range of sleep habits you can expect at different ages.

The newborn

At birth, the sleep periods are spread out evenly throughout the 24 hours, with no preference for night or day. In the first weeks of life, most babies will sleep between fourteen and twenty hours each day with an average of about sixteen and a half hours, though I never met an average baby yet. They take this as a series of snoozes, each lasting between one and six hours, with an average length of three to four hours.

It is interesting that before birth the setting of the sleep clock is actually loaded against night sleep. They act as though they're permanently jet-lagged, snoozing it off in the day and then getting ready to party while Mum is trying to sleep.

It's best not to expect too much rhyme or reason from a newborn's sleep patterns. Most parents quickly come to view this time as one of survival when it comes to sleep and not much more.

At two to three months

For the next few months the 'average' baby sleeps fifteen hours (or about fourteen to eighteen) in 24. But there is a refreshing change on the wind. You will see a gradual preference toward sleeping at night rather than by day.

At three months

By now the average baby still sleeps fifteen hours each day, with two-thirds of this at night. About half will be sleeping right through (that's perhaps 11 pm to 4.30 am) to the delight of their lucky parents, with the other half still keen to call for room service at least once before dawn. This is an important phase because now we can begin to separate day from night by giving full attention, playing and laughing in the daytime and being much more low-key about 2 am contact, which is probably what comes naturally in any case. At 2 am you might change, feed and comfort but not play or communicate deeply.

At this stage sleep is moving towards the 90-minute cycle of the adult. This is a start, as there's less chance of waking up so often, but they still sleep lightly a full 50 per cent of the time.

At six months

By six months Baby is on about fourteen hours and the sleep pattern has become much more predictable. Now about three-quarters will be sleeping right through the night. If you're finding sleep is still erratic and the baby is healthy and of normal development you can steer lightly or even go in a bit harder if you want to now, to start moulding the poor sleeper towards a more sociable habit.

At nine months to one year

The usual pattern is of thirteen to fourteen hours each day with two daytime naps, the longest after lunch and a shorter mid-morning one which will soon drop off. Most sleep is at night by now.

At two years

About one-fifth will still be waking most nights and many more will be very reluctant to go to bed. There's now only one nap, this usually being in the afternoon. At this stage some of the busier little bees will be all for losing this and will go to their cots with a fair amount of protest. If they show no fatigue, it might be best to forgo this sleep and maybe read to them instead. Some sleep well in the afternoon but at the cost of making them hard to settle at night. So a choice has to be made. The daytime nap usually disappears before the age of three, though a few would gladly snooze up to and even while at school.

Older children

After this, sleep patterns are all very individual. For example, most ten-year-olds sleep for about ten hours, whereas late teenagers often come down to just seven or eight. Whether that is due to bad habits or is simply all the sleep they need is unclear.

Even adults have completely different needs. Some declare that they cannot function with less than ten hours, while the Churchills and Thatchers of this world, in common with many other driven individuals, seem to thrive on as little as four hours a night.

To sum up . . .

- Each baby is very individual when it comes to sleep patterns.
- In the first three months expect most babies to wake once or more each night.
- From three to six months expect about half to wake, but you can begin to create expectations about day and night-time attention.
- After six months the sleepless reduce to about one-quarter, but you now have the ability to change the situation.

SETTING GOOD HABITS FROM THE START

Some babies are built to sleep soundly no matter what you do. Others are lousy sleepers and will wake up at the drop of a pin, making the night shift a long and difficult one. A great many of these, however, have the potential to sleep really well but somehow have lost their way and got off on the wrong footing. Here are some ways to encourage a better sleep pattern.

A consistent routine

Just like adults, children thrive best on a consistent sleep routine. The time of going to bed and getting up should, as far as possible, be the same and late nights should be avoided whenever you can. Children of all ages like routine and quickly come to accept it, and although such a sleep routine may not make an enormous difference in the first months, it should bring its rewards later on.

Cues and rituals

As adults we tend to lead much of our lives with our brains in neutral and our bodies locked into automatic pilot. We go about the day's routine firmly guided by previous programming and cues from our environment. For example, we know it's time to get up because it's daylight, we eat lunch when we do because the clock says midday, we prepare for bed with a ritual of teeth-brushing, undressing and reading a book to help us unwind. All in all we function like factory robots, taking our cues from our environment and being creatures of habit.

These cues and rituals which get us so comfortably through the day are also important for our children. Try to develop a standard sequence of cues and rituals to prepare Baby for sleep. Don't make them too complex or it will take all night to get ready for bed. But once you've worked them out, stick to them each night and always maintain this good pattern. First there can be a bath followed by a nice warm rub-down and then get Baby dressed in his sleep attire. Take him into his bedroom, dim the lights and give him his goodnight bottle or breast. From here on consistent cues should be given such as gentle patting, talking quietly or even singing (if your voice is up to it). Then before he has fallen asleep you should just walk out saying 'Goodnight'. Go through this ritual every night and your baby should very soon catch on to what is expected of him.

The put-down

If you are graced with the kind of baby who drops like an autumn leaf from a twig every night, then whatever it is you're doing must be right so keep on doing it. If, on the other hand, his night-time antics are more akin to a bedroom farce, then it's time to look at how you're dealing with Baby at bedtime.

As we have already seen, babies, like adults, come close to consciousness at regular intervals through the night, but whereas we adults can open our eyes, see that it is still dark and crash back into sleep again, some babies may find this difficult without you coming in to comfort them. This difficulty is often caused by never being allowed to fall asleep without your comfort.

If your baby is put to sleep every night by being rocked, bounced and cuddled tight, caring and charitable though this may be, it could well lead to big trouble when it comes to the 3 am eye-opener. At this ungodly hour your baby may well refuse to go back to sleep unless you turn on the full show again, and understandably you will be less than enthusiastic about it. Though most parents may want to cuddle their little babies to sleep, there is more chance of establishing a good habit if you let them fall asleep in the comfort of their own cot without too much parental intervention. If they manage to fall asleep without your close contact at bedtime, they are more likely to drop off again without it later on. Just pop Baby in the cot, pat him gently, talk soothingly and be in the room but don't lift, rock or cuddle him. Your presence alone will suffice, and if he drops off to sleep this way then the chances are he will do the same when he wakes in the wee small hours of the morning.

SLEEP—THE CHOICES

Now we understand how humans of all sizes sleep we can think about how we want to manage the situation. Though babies have different cycles to adults, they need the same sorts of routines to prepare them for sleep and to ensure smooth transition from one cycle to another. The piece of practical information to take away from the science is that when we adults slip between cycles we turn over and go back to sleep. When babies make that shift they may well register that they are hungry, uncomfortable or bored.

A non-sleeping baby can enfeeble the most robust of parents, yet there is not too much you can do about it in the first three months. From three months until six months is a time to concentrate on good routines and prompts. Where sleep is a problem after six months of age you have the power to change things, and now you must decide whether or not to be tough and how tough you want to be. This will depend on three factors:

The baby

Babies are individuals. If your baby flows easily from cycle to cycle on most nights and seems to self-soothe it's probably best to leave well enough alone. Other babies seem to jar between cycles and can cause real problems for their parents. Those who complain noisily in transition are the most ripe for intervention.

The parents

Whether or not broken sleep is a problem for you will depend on your attitudes to parenting and how you function on reduced sleep. Some are happy to go with the flow until it sorts itself out. Some have lower tolerance for disruption and/or have work commitments.

Outside influences

Society always has an opinion, expressed by the media, family and friends, about what the current view is on sleep management. Even the toughest of free spirits can have trouble disregarding these.

The choices

i. The 'let it be' approach (or do nothing)

If you're happy, Baby's happy and anyone who lives with the baby is managing all right, then there is no harm in just going with the flow. Feed for comfort if you want to, day or night, for the first months or even years. Rock them or cuddle them to sleep. If they like a dummy give them a dummy. Accept that it is a short chapter in life and do what you feel is right. As long as the health and emotional strength of the family is not compromised, there will never be anything wrong with this.

ii. The gentle nudge in the right direction

At birth

If you want to try and set good habits, you must think about the three stages of Baby's sleeping patterns. At birth to three months, you can't change very much. Sleep is erratic and you will need to grab your own rest where you can. Your baby health sister may have some settling ideas and may help to give you some perspective on this phase. It can all seem a bit hopeless but a little structure may help you feel a bit more in control. A stay in a mother and baby unit, if you have the opportunity, may even be a good idea. Most mothers who went in feeling disordered and out of control leave feeling much better about life with Baby.

Three to six months

Now we can start to steer our way out of the chaos a little more. Here we aim to show that night and day are different, that daylight is for play, fun and communication and night-time is for sleep and very little else.

For day sleeps, learn the tired signs—eye rubbing, grizzling, etc.—and put Baby down before he deteriorates further. Your instinct will be to comfort Baby to sleep but it is helpful to leave him in the cot to settle himself to sleep. He may grumble a bit but he'll learn to self-soothe this way. Leave the room light on so he knows this is his daytime nap.

In the evening there is a winding-down time for the main sleep, a routine that's followed pretty much every night. Then into pyjamas and into his cot. Ideally we'd avoid dummies but if he's happy and you're happy then go ahead and give him it. Have a low light on in the room. Be gentle and loving but leave him to it, even if he grumbles a little bit. If he's unhappy (or you are!) sit close by but leave him be. If he's crying leave for a very short time, give him a warm pat, but try to avoid taking him out of the cot.

If he wakes in the night, give him a few moments before you go in so he knows it's night-time and attention isn't quite so on tap (and to give him a chance to put himself back to sleep), change him if necessary (which it may well be at three to six months), give him a feed and a quiet cuddle. We are establishing that this is not the time for play or excitement or a lot of feeds, and that's all we need worry about for now.

Six months

At this age you can choose how tough you want to be but if we are continuing the 'steering' approach we follow along the same lines. A healthy older baby doesn't need night feeds so you can choose now whether to give night feeds or not. If there is still a 2 am wake-up call, go to the baby after a few moments, feed if you really want to but try to avoid comfort feeding. There is always the option of sterile water if you're worried he's thirsty. By now this wake-up call is to do with habit and wanting a bit of attention from you. He'd like food but it's probably not necessary.

SLEEP—THE CURE

There are those who believe that it is every parent's duty to be up all night every night, ready to rush in the moment their child makes the slightest squeak. This is one of those wonderful childcare theories that looks fine in books, but when you are faced with the constant crier it's not so wonderful. Multiple nocturnal disturbances may suit

some who feel you must suffer to be a good person, but for most of us it's a one-way ticket to collapse.

There is another group who believe that all babies should be handled firmly from their earliest days. If they wish to cry at night then that's their problem and they should be left to get on with it. The theory is that if left, they will soon get the message. The problem is that babies often become very upset if left like that and so do parents. The answer, I believe, has to be somewhere in the middle, with a bit of firmness but always knowing Mum and Dad are never too far away. Babies may feel a bit of separation anxiety at night. The aim is to show that we're close but help everyone to get better sleep.

The Controlled Crying technique

I developed this technique in Sydney in 1975 as a postgrad at the Prince of Wales Children's Hospital. It grew out of a blend of the tough and 'go with the flow' schools of thought, and took about six years of trial and error to finetune. I published an article on Controlled Crying in *The Journal of Maternal and Child Health in the UK* in 1980. Throughout the late 1970s and early '80s I lectured in Australia and the UK, and the technique is now pretty widespread and used by many mothercraft organisations. After *Toddler Taming* was published in 1984 it was used all over the world. Many parents use it without having a name for it or knowing where it came from. It's possible that many did well before I ever thought of it because it seems like a natural balance between extremes. It's pretty straightforward and this is how it works.

The aim is to let them cry for a short period of time, but not long enough for them to get very upset. You come in and give them some basic comfort, but the moment the crying abates and turns to sobs, you leave at once. They will protest immediately but this time you extend the time by several minutes before going back in to comfort them. Then you go in, comfort them and again put them down the moment they stop crying and leave at once. This will build up by small amounts each time until eventually the little one realises that the parents will always come if he needs them, but that it's really not worth all the hassle. Then he sleeps without calling for you.

If sleep disturbance has become a major problem after six months of age and you have decided you want to fix it, follow this technique firmly and do not give up until you see considerable relief. As every child and every parent are different, you have to adjust the method to suit your stamina and style. If in doubt start gently but never back off, and hard as it may be in the early days, don't give up.

SOME PRACTICAL POINTS

Expectations—work with what you're given

All children are not born with an equal capacity to sleep. A few will sleep perfectly, right from birth, many will wake a bit and others will be total disaster areas. The most difficult sleep problem I ever cured was a boy, who at eight months had never slept for more than one single hour at a time and never for more than four hours total in a day. When I say 'cure', he eventually slept for six hours each night and none by day. This may be unimpressive to the average mum but for this particular one she felt it was a miracle. I followed his progress

Controlled Crying—step by step

1. When the baby first starts to cry resist running in to give instant comfort.

2. Wait five minutes if you are feeling tough, three minutes on average, one if you are a bit fragile, and go straight in the first time if you're really delicate or worried about the baby.

3. Go in to Baby and make your presence felt. It is preferable to pat and soothe him where he lies but lift, cuddle and comfort him if you must.

4. When the crying has ebbed to a series of soft sobs and sniffles, that's the sign to cut the comfort and clear out. Once you hear that sniff Baby is saying to himself, 'Aha, now I've got them!' But this is where he has it all wrong. If you leave him he will say to himself, 'Hey! What's going on here? My audience has walked out.' Nevertheless you must be firm and go, even though the crying will start again with gusto.

5. This time allow the crying to go on for a slightly longer period before returning to comfort him. If, for example, it was three minutes last time, then this time try and leave him for five.

6. Each time you go back remember just to comfort Baby until the cry stops and the sniff starts, then put him down and scram! Don't feed or cuddle him off to sleep. That's not part of the deal.

7. Eventually the message will get through that Mum or Dad will always come when he cries, but is it really worth all the effort?

8. Keep this routine going tonight, tomorrow and for as long as it takes to work. Don't give an inch whatever you do. The cry periods should rise to a maximum of about ten minutes and plateau then.

9. With babies over six months of age you should get about an 80 per cent cure within one to three weeks, while many of the remaining twenty per cent should show a significant improvement. Most cures are actually secured well within the first week. I find those who have been terrible sleepers from birth are usually more difficult—they take a little longer and have a lower complete cure rate. Those who have slept well and have wandered off-course along the way are generally much easier to cure.

10. If you are feeling particularly fragile or the crying is going on too long then see your doctor or paediatrician, who may recommend a short period of sedation. If you choose to try this, combine it with the method. After half an hour of being awake and using the Controlled Crying method, the child can be sedated. This will guarantee a good night's sleep but gives the child a major message while the sedation is working. Sedation takes half an hour to act and you keep the technique going until they finally drop. (See section on sedation on page 222).

into his teens. He grew up to be a lovely kid who just had an unusual approach to sleep. They are all different, but this method does bring improvement.

Night feeds and the milkaholic

When babies are very young they feed to gain nutrition, but by the age of six months the night-time nibble is moving more towards comfort than kilojoules. If he's healthy, by six months it is only a soothing suck they are after and so now's the time you can discard it, safe in the knowledge that you won't be the cause of night starvation!

Feeding a baby until he drops off to sleep is a bit like rocking him off to sleep. It might all be very cosy and comforting, but you run the danger of making a rod for your own back. In time you may set up a dependence that creates a no-suck-no-sleep situation.

If your baby has a reasonable sleep pattern and the night feeds suit you, please feed. It's only when you are becoming exhausted that the firm approach is needed. Then you move to water or nothing and cut out the night-time milk feeds.

Breast comfort and the night-time curfew

Babies love a night-time breast-feed, and as they get older this is generally just about comfort. I believe it's best to feed and comfort your baby in the first six months. After that you can keep the night shift going if you are happy with it, but if it has become an exhausting experience then it's time to call for a curfew.

You do this by giving the child his last breast-feed on going to bed and refusing to offer it again until morning. If the baby wakes up in the meantime then by all means give him comfort, but don't feed him. The most effective way of ensuring this works is getting Dad to sign on for the night shift. After all he doesn't have the equipment to feed so the only thing he can give is comfort.

Dummies and sleep

Many babies love to suck a dummy to soothe them to sleep. Unfortunately there is one great drawback to this. The dummy eventually dislodges and all hell breaks loose. Trying to play 'hunt the dummy' in the dark at one in the morning is not much fun and you may wish you'd never introduced them, which is certainly one option, as is banning them when they start causing trouble. Having gone down the dummy route though, parents can either provide extras and/or get up and help the dummy back into the mouth. Sometimes it is much easier to go in and insert a dummy than to fight over sleep. If this approach suits your style and brings night-time peace, then do it.

The light sleeper

On going to bed most babies will drop quickly into the deepest sleep. One minute they're all smiles and gurgles, the next nothing short of a ten-megaton blast will make them blink. These young babies are oblivious to such things as whether the lights are on or off, and can sleep happily through the noisiest party. There is, however, a small group of children who seem to have their senses tuned to a supersensitive level and who will wake at the slightest disturbance. This can become an utter pain for parents who then have to tiptoe around the house avoiding squeaky floorboards, keep the TV turned down and leave the toilet unflushed.

If the situation becomes quite unbearable, there are ways of desensitising Baby. First, introduce a little noise into his life and then build it up gradually until he becomes immune. You can do this with the help of a radio. On the first night leave the set on a zero volume. Next night turn it up a little, and then night by night thereafter turn the volume up little by little until it's pretty loud. Actually, gentle music from an all-night radio station is probably the best choice, but sometimes the very sensitive children may even wake with the gaps in the records. If this is the case, tune the radio to an FM station and then shift the knob a fraction so that you get the static instead of the station. Start this as a gentle hiss on night one and increase it to the sound of the Niagara Falls; it will have the same effect.

Other children sharing a bedroom with Baby

If your baby is over six months old with disturbed sleep patterns and your poor, tired brain cannot cope any longer, then you need a cure. The Controlled Crying technique should sort things out for you, but if the baby is sharing a bedroom with a brother or sister who is a sensitive sleeper then you have a problem. Once the Controlled Crying starts you end up with two non-sleepers instead of one!

Don't despair. The treatment is easy, though somewhat unjust. Put the better of the two sleepers into another room and if another bedroom isn't available, then use the living room, kitchen or a passageway for a bit. Since this is only a temporary measure nobody need feel he is demoted. Now that the coast is clear, set up the Controlled Crying technique and when peace returns you can restore normality.

Remember that current SIDS advice is to keep the baby close by in the first six to twelve months, so bear that in mind when rearranging the beds.

Whose bedroom?

For the first months babies will sleep close to their parents. Having Baby next to the parents' bed is convenient for the night-time feed, but parents may not sleep very soundly, tending to keep one ear open to monitor all the little snuffles of their newborn. Eventually it may help Mum and Dad's sleep for him to move out and by the time you are applying Controlled Crying, this may well be the best option. They can always come back if you miss them after the few nights or a week it takes to get them back on track.

Deaf dads

I've never actually seen it published in a scientific journal, but there is good evidence to support the theory that many husbands go stone-deaf once the lights are out. 'Did you hear the baby crying at 3 am?'—'No, never heard a thing!' I bet if he were expecting a phone call to confirm he had won the lottery he would bolt out of bed on the first ring. Of course what we are talking about here is not a permanent problem, but a well-known male affliction called selective deafness. Luckily this is not incurable. A sharp kick in the shins at 3 am seems to help tune in the male hearing once again, most effectively.

When to start curing sleep problems

Things will usually get worse before they start to get better. Once you commence the Controlled Crying technique you can expect at least two difficult nights before the benefits start to show. With the very young it can sometimes take a couple of weeks before you get relief. Unfortunately many parents do not have sufficient spare emotional energy to cope with this initial disruption. They are exhausted and go from day to day hanging by the thinnest of emotional threads. It seems easier to trudge on than to lose what little stability there is.

Don't start a sleep program unless you feel you are together enough to see it through. Start when you are in your strongest frame of mind, there is some chance of support and you have time to catch up on some lost sleep. If you enter this program without commitment it won't work. If you are going to embark on the technique, try starting it on a Friday night. Most people don't have to go to work on Saturday so there's some chance of support and time to catch up on lost sleep. Don't start when the baby is sick, or when you are about to go on holiday, or there is some family disruption.

Is it sickness?

It is almost impossible to be firm if you suspect that your child may be sick. Certainly if the baby has dull eyes, fever, is off his food and is unwell both day and night then this is genuine enough and you are going to have to expect to be up all night every night until it passes.

Chronic illness as the cause of sleep problems is, however, greatly overrated, I believe, and extremely rare. In my work with toddlers, many children sent to me have had sleep problems blamed on conditions ranging from glue ear to constipation and everything in between. I don't believe a child will wake up two or three times each night for months or years on end due to these sorts of problems. To my mind these children either have a non-sleep temperament or, more likely, they have just got into a bad habit. If you have any doubts about your baby's health, get your doctor to check him out, but once given a clean bill of health, get on with your own treatment.

One word of warning about acute illness, however. Many long-term sleep problems start following an acute illness. Your child is no fool. He enjoyed the attention and fuss he got when he was sick and will try to keep this going once he is better if you will oblige. So once the sickness has settled, be firm. It will save you a lot of trauma in the future.

Sedation

I don't believe children should ever be sedated unless there is a very good reason for doing this. There are a number of occasions when it is called for.

When a family is disintegrating due to chronic sleep starvation, then sedation can provide a valuable safety valve. When the going gets really tough and you feel you are being pushed over the edge, then short-term sedation may save the situation. If you have a disabled child who is irritable most of the day and cries much of the night, then talk to your doctor about sedation. This may only be a bandaid but sometimes a bandaid applied at the right time can be a lifesaver.

When the Controlled Crying technique is failing due to a re-sistant infant or fragile parents, then giving sedation along with the program can provide the catalyst that 'saves the night'. Sedation given alone, however, without the technique will have no long-term ben-efits, as once you stop it the problem returns. Sedation given after half an hour of Controlled Crying on the other hand has ensured that the message has been given loud and clear before the sleep sets in.

Until recent times, parents could buy children's sedatives without a prescription. Now, however, most can only be obtained with a doctor's script. These prescription drugs are quite safe as long as they are administered in the proper doses and for the correct reasons.

It is important to realise that all children respond to sedatives in different ways. Some drop into the deepest sleep with little more than a sniff of the uncorked bottle. Others are more resistant and the trick with them is not to give the sedation at bedtime but to wait until they first wake up during the night. It is always more effective at this time and usually guarantees sleep in those important hours from midnight till dawn.

Sedatives don't suit some little children at all. They can turn an awake child into a little drunk who will tumble around walking into furniture, or if not at the walking stage, become noisy and restless. Be particularly careful with this group and if you are planning an overseas trip, whatever you do, don't try your first sedative on a long airflight. Travelling for hours at 33,000 feet with a little drunk is no fun for anyone. Try out the medicine at ground level first and test the effect!

In conclusion, yes, I do agree with the occasional use of sedatives, but only when prescribed sensibly, and sensibly means for short periods, in times of crisis or as the catalyst to make a faltering sleep program work. There is a sedative and dose to suit every child, but it often takes careful adjustment by your doctor to get it right.

Changing the clocks

'A thousand curses on the man who invented daylight saving!' I hear you cry. I'm sure it had to be a man, as no mum would have been so keen to reshuffle their children's sleeping patterns.

Just when you have got yourself organised with a 5 am start to the day then that certain Sunday rolls around—bang! You have a 4 am start instead. Give it a week to realign. It's all done by gradually readjusting the whole routine, bedtime, feeds and cues. It doesn't take too long to get back on an even keel.

Sleep programs—do they damage children?

When I first started to work with sleep problems, many asked such questions as: How do you know that setting limits at night won't cause long-term psychological scars? The answer is frankly that I don't know. I cannot say with 100 per cent certainty that giving

Baby an injection to prevent the measles, removing a perforated appendix or going to the dentist isn't going to cause psychological upset either. What I do know, however, is that the proven benefits of these actions far outweigh any theoretical concerns, and so it is with sleep programs.

Of course if we lived in an ideal world where every mum was Wonder Woman and every dad Superman, then we could give comfort all night every night. But in the real world, sleepless children make for tired, irritable parents who give very poor care to their children by day. The sleep-deprived mum can be spotted at a distance of a hundred paces. She has bags under her eyes and the defeated stoop of someone who has run (and lost) a marathon. Such is her exhaustion and despair that anyone who could cure the problem would probably be left money in her will.

Sleep problems certainly put enormous stresses on some marriages. Many parents have told me that getting some sleep is literally a marriage saver. Children must never be allowed to become the instrument of their own destruction or yours! Treat sleep problems seriously.

CONCLUSION

This is a big chapter because sleep (or lack of it) is a big part of new parents' lives. It affects how we function and enjoy our babies. Understanding the science enables us to begin to make the changes we need to set good habits and eventually, fix bad ones.

It is your baby, your family and your life. Make the decisions about sleep management that are right for you. You have the power to make things so much better. Not next week or next month, but today.

Common baby illnesses

*A*ll babies fall ill from time to time and often parents worry because they're not sure how serious the illnesses are. In this chapter we're taking a quick look at the most common problems. If you are still uncertain or worried about any condition your baby may appear to have, you should not hesitate to seek a medical opinion. It is always better to be safe than sorry.

The common cold

Common this may be, but when your perfect little newborn baby catches her first cold, what a drama! The main problem with colds and babies is that little ones of this age don't like living with a blocked nose. It makes them uncomfortable and upsets feeding as they attempt the impossible and try to suck milk and breathe through their mouths at the same time. Colds can cause poor food intake, fever, irritability, disturbed sleep and even vomiting, but often there is nothing more wrong than a snuffly nose.

The common cold is caused by a number of viruses, none of which unfortunately produces any sort of long-term immunity to all the other types. It's not like measles or mumps which you catch once and that's it for life. With colds you can be infected this week, catch another variety next month and then be smitten again by the original some time later.

Little babies generally lead relatively isolated lives and are therefore not quite as prone to outside infection as are toddlers and schoolchildren. Nevertheless it is still possible for Baby to catch a cold. As the cold virus is not helped by antibiotics, your doctor won't prescribe these. He is not being negligent, just practising good sensible medicine. Occasionally a secondary bacterial chest or ear infection can come along following a cold and of course these need treatment, but that is a different matter.

Despite what your granny may have told you, you cannot catch a cold from being cold, and getting wet or chilled will not move a cold to your chest. Also, despite several decades of claims that vitamin C prevents and cures colds, there is still no conclusive evidence to support this.

Treatment

The best treatment for a cold is no treatment at all. Of course if there is a fever or some irritability, a little paracetamol may help, and if the nose is blocked and making feeding really difficult, a decongestant could be prescribed, but reluctantly.

Don't poke cotton tips up your baby's nose either as this will do nothing for a cold and may harm the nose.

Vomiting and diarrhoea

All little babies will have some vomits and diarrhoea. If they vomit once or twice or have occasional loose bowel motions, this is generally nothing to worry about. You start to worry when it is persistent and the child obviously looks sick.

Gastro-enteritis is uncommon in young babies and exceptionally rare in those who are totally breast-fed. The very little baby who vomits more often than not has a benign problem of regurgitation due to her immature stomach. Slightly loose bowels are usually caused by such things as fruit juices and certain solids, and often for no very apparent reason.

When infection is the cause of vomiting or diarrhoea, it's more likely to be the result of a cold, flu or a sore ear rather than due to a primary gut infection. Where there is a genuine gut infection (gastro-enteritis), its danger has little to do with the number of times the baby vomits or the number of dirty nappies, but rather by its effect on the baby's body fluids and salts. If these get low the urine output reduces, the skin gets dry and the baby looks withdrawn, dull-eyed and unresponsive. This is dangerous and your baby should be seen by a doctor immediately.

Treatment

With gastro-enteritis the aim is to prevent dehydration and its dangers. Please forget the kilojoules and concentrate on getting the fluids in. Never mind any weight loss, this is irrelevant at this time.

If the problem is very mild, just ease back and be selective with the solids and give the milk as small, more frequent feeds. If there is a significant problem, however, then stop all solids immediately to give the baby's gut a rest.

If the baby is being breast-fed, carry on with this but with greater frequency and added clear fluids—cooled boiled water if the problem is mild. On the other hand, if your baby is being bottle-fed, then stop the milk for half a day or so and replace it entirely with clear fluids. These will be much easier for Baby to digest and a whole lot easier to clean up if returned.

If gastro is more severe, the recommended fluid is a commercially prepared electrolyte-sugar rehydration solution bought from your chemist (e.g. gastrolyte). **Whatever you use it must be given only in small amounts and offered frequently.**

Don't be impatient to reintroduce solids as this can unnecessarily delay the cure. Go easy when you restart the first few bottles of milk. It might even be an idea to dilute these to half-strength for the first day.

Antibiotics have no place in the treatment of gastro-enteritis and often can make it worse. Medicines to stop vomiting are not recommended for small children as they can have undesirable side effects and do little good.

Vomiting and diarrhoea by themselves do not harm a child. It is the dehydration they may cause that is very dangerous. If your baby becomes dull-eyed, unresponsive, passes little urine and clearly looks sick, get medical help immediately. Babies can deteriorate quickly and must be seen by a doctor early on.

Fevers and high temperatures

Fever is the body's signal to tell us that there is an infection in the house. Maybe as the body heats up it helps kill off the unwanted visitors and certainly in moderation raised temperatures are harmless. Strangely the level of fever is usually out of proportion to the severity of the illness. For example, the fever associated with severe meningitis is often lower than that of measles, and an acute perforating appendix may produce a lower fever than, say, a kidney infection.

Most childcare books suggest that you keep a thermometer at

hand and check your child's temperature the minute you have any concern. Personally I have never taken my children's temperatures and I tend not to place much emphasis on what a child's temperature is.

The main concern with high fevers in the young is the risk of fever fits (febrile convulsions). The immature brains of little children can be sensitive to raised temperatures and it is possible for a fit to occur. This may affect up to five per cent of all children, but is extremely rare under six months of age and unlikely before nine months. In older babies and toddlers there is a case for keeping fevers under some control.

Treatment
- Leave the child dressed only in a nappy and singlet or covered by a sheet depending on the room temperature. Don't put on extra clothing or blankets.
- Don't give the child icy-cold baths or point a fan at her.
- If there is a chance of fever fits, a gentle sponge down with tepid water or a lukewarm bathwater will help to cool her.
- Keep fluid intake up (small amounts frequently).
- Use baby paracetamol to lower temperatures.

Rashes and spots
Babies, as we've already seen, get lots of different sorts of rashes and very often even the cleverest doctor is at a loss to diagnose the exact cause of some of them.

There is a school of thought which says that all spots that are accompanied by a fever must be measles. Rubbish! For a start measles is almost unheard of in the first year. Rubella (German measles) could possibly occur but it is likely to be so mild that it is doubtful if it would even be diagnosed. Chickenpox is usually a very mild illness in a baby. All you're likely to see are one or two little spots like flea bites and nothing else.

The message here really is: don't get unduly wound up over every little spot and rash that appears. Most of them are due to

Baby's delicate skin getting accustomed to the real world, minor viral illnesses and allergies of uncertain origin.

If in doubt, by all means see your doctor, but I suspect that most of the time he is likely to turn a blind eye towards the skin and say he sees nothing to worry about.

There is one rash that signals a serious disease and that's the rash of meningococcus. It is not usual in the first year but it can happen. It can come on rapidly and without warning, and if not treated immediately the results can be devastating. In spite of its ferocity, this bacteria is one of the easiest types to treat, responding to even the simplest antibiotics.

If infected, the bacteria causes sudden septicaemia (blood stream infection) or meningitis (an infection of the tissues that covers the brain). Most children I have treated had both the septicaemia and the meningitis.

Early on, the rash of meningococcus is identified by fine, dark red spots, 1–2 mm wide, which don't disappear when you press them. The rash is accompanied by a fever and in the more advanced stage of the infection the skin looks bruised. Septicaemia is suspected if the child has a bruised-looking rash that increases every minute and is extremely sick. Dial the emergency services immediately if you suspect meningococcus. Treatment will be immediate injection of antibiotics and if it comes quickly enough will be very effective. **The key is early diagnosis and speed of response.**

Ears and throats

Tonsillitis is not a baby illness, but rather more a problem for the preschooler. When a baby has a cold, the back of the throat may become a bit red, but this is part of the cold, not tonsillitis. Frankly, it's hard enough even spotting the tiny tonsils in a baby, let alone calling them infected.

Ear infections, on the other hand, are much more common. They develop in the inner part of the ear called the middle ear, which lies hidden behind the eardrum. When this gets infected it is called otitis media and can often follow a head cold.

The infection can cause great pain but unfortunately the baby cannot tell you where it hurts. She will tend to become irritable, sleep poorly, feed badly and will be miserable and restless all the time. If your doctor looks into the ear he will see the eardrum red and bulging and this will alert him to the fact that there is an infection trapped inside.

Treatment for otitis media is usually through antibiotics given by mouth coupled with paracetamol for the pain and fever. Sometimes the first you ever know about this condition is when you find a speck of blood on Baby's pillow which shows that the eardrum has burst. This is undesirable, though not a major problem as most heal again completely without any residual problems.

A few helpful pointers

- If your baby is bright-eyed and bushy-tailed, alert and responsive, then generally speaking there is unlikely to be any serious problem.
- If your baby starts to look withdrawn, distant and sickly then call for help immediately.
- Watch out for the frightened-looking baby who is pale and has a cold sweat. She is certainly sick and needs urgent help.
- Watch for rapid or laboured breathing that continues for some time.
- Watch out for any severe pain that comes on unexpectedly and cannot be eased.
- Watch out for any strange postures, odd eye movements or periods when your baby stops breathing.

To sum up in one sentence: well children look well and sick children look sick, but if you're ever in any doubt, seek help. Little children are too valuable to put at risk.

When to seek help

It is difficult for a new parent to look at his or her sick baby and know when to sit tight and when to shout for help. Since little babies are in no position to tell us anything about how they feel, you must always play it safe and seek help when in doubt.

Getting the best out of your doctor

I believe that it is every person's right to be made to feel at ease, be given a listening ear and be spoken to in clear, everyday language. Getting the best out of your doctor is not difficult. Here are a few suggestions:

- Know what you want to ask before you even get to the doctor's surgery.
- If you get flustered, write a list and don't leave until you get your answers.
- If you don't understand what has been said, ask again and again if necessary.
- Request to be told in everyday English, not medical mumbo-jumbo.
- Don't bury the doctor in an overwhelming fog of vague complaints. Bring the important problems to the top.
- Similarly, don't introduce new complications and problems all the time. This prevents your doctor from gaining a clear picture of how to help.
- Although I believe that it is every person's right to seek a second opinion and that no doctor has a right to obstruct this, beware of multiple opinions (shopping around). If you're not careful no one person will feel a direct responsibility for your baby's care and when a crisis hits you will be left totally unsupported.
- Don't put too much pressure on your doctor when there is really nothing more to be done. When pushed past a certain point, he may feel obliged to do something useless and irrelevant, just to clear you out of his office. Be careful!
- A good doctor is prepared to tell you that he doesn't know what is going on with your child. This is called honesty and must be respected.

- A good doctor will not always do what his patients request. If he believes you have a viral cold and refuses to give you the antibiotic you demand, this is called good medicine and should be applauded.
- Often there are several drugs that will cure the same ailment. Don't be afraid to ask for the one with the best taste and the least number of doses needed each day.
- If doctors recommend investigations it is every parent's right to ask as many questions as they need to establish whether they are necessary.

Doctors have feelings. They get frustrated and upset when unable to help those they care for. We all have good and bad days, and doctors are just like anyone else. At times there is just not enough emotional energy to provide as much support as one would like. You don't need a scientist, you need a human doctor, but remember humans are only human.

Temperament and behaviour—the great debate

D espite the writings of idealists, all humans are not born equal. At birth each of us possesses a unique predestined package of heredity which will influence physical growth, academic achievement, behaviour and temperament. It is no longer believed that each little baby is born an amorphous blob ready to be moulded into any shape his parents wish. Those of us with a number of children have discovered to our cost that once we started to mould, we found that the concrete had already set and all we could do was to round off a few rough edges. All children are born unique individuals and we must then give our best to ensure they realise their full potential. As parents we can gild the lily, but we cannot change a lily into a rose. Not so long ago many people believed that achievement, intelligence, misconduct and one's place in society were exclusive products of heredity. But, as with many theories, these ideas changed with time, eventually to be replaced with the exact opposite view.

By the mid-1950s most childcare experts were teaching that child behaviour and temperament differences were produced directly by the parents—Mum in particular! If you had a child with a simple behaviour problem, you were made to feel guilty, inadequate and incompetent. These experts believed that parenting and the child's environment were all-important and every little environment imbalance was thought to leave its scar and had to be put right. Commonsense, instinctive parenting was no longer good enough.

Fortunately, in the midst of all this there remained some professionals who continued to view life with their eyes partly open. They saw the different qualities and temperaments present in each newborn baby. They looked at their own children and noted that, though equal care was given, each was endowed with very different behaviour and temperament. The gurus of the time were quick to explain these differences in terms of one child bonding closer and getting better care than the other. When parents objected, as they knew that their children were loved equally, some were then told that obviously one child was nurtured on the good breast and one on the bad! Others who found the dogma of the day hard to swallow were the staff of the special care nurseries. They saw each baby as having a very different temperament long before his mother had even touched him.

STUDIES IN TEMPERAMENT

In a classic study from 1950 to 1977★ a group of over 140 newborn American babies was thoroughly assessed to see if patterns of individual temperament could be measured. Those 140 babies, adults by the end of the study, were followed and observed, and from this study we have objective evidence to show how temperament differs right from birth. As the group was observed, it seemed that there were nine dimensions of temperament. Some of these were clear cut but others overlapped greatly. Some were to be of great influence when it came to whether a child was to be easy or difficult to manage, while others were interesting but pretty irrelevant. These dimensions outlined below are not black and white, and may come in many combinations and shades of grey. Sometimes I feel that such is the overlap between some that maybe only six clear groups exist. At any rate, don't get bogged down with the detail and grey edges—just look at the overall concept, which is fascinating.

Activity

All babies enter life programmed to function at a certain level of activity. Some are destined to sit quiet and content, to smile placidly and do little else. Others hit the world like a tiny tornado and, as babies, need to be bounced, carried, wheeled up and down in the stroller and whizzed round the block in the car. They hate lying flat, they wriggle during nappy changes and seem able to move about the floor long before they can actually crawl.

These are usually the early walkers, climbers and specialist cupboard re-arrangers. As toddlers they are active, sleep restlessly and have forever fiddly fingers. Later they fidget during homework, find it hard to sit still through mealtimes and on wet days they pace around the house like caged animals.

Activity is usually a life-long characteristic, only partly influenced

---

★Chess, *Temperament and Development*, Brunner Mazel, New York, 1977.

by the activity of those around you. There is a large hereditary component where active parents tend to produce active children. This is most clearly demonstrated when an active, driving father produces an active, driving son.

Rhythmicity

The rhythmicity of a child refers to the regularity and predictability of how he functions. Some babies are really predictable. They sleep at a fixed time, get up at a fixed time, eat a certain amount of food at a regular hour, even their bowels have set opening hours. Other babies function in a totally haphazard way, their exhausted parents never knowing what is going to happen when.

A child who is programmed to an easy rhythm tends to continue along that path. The irregular ones may change a little, but they will never run like clockwork.

Approach/withdrawal

This describes a child's initial response to meeting new people or situations. Some will approach the unknown with adventurous ease, while others withdraw, hide and cry.

The approach-type baby accepts new foods and enjoys his first bath. As a toddler, he will greet strangers openly and when he starts school, it is well accepted. When he is away from home, he will sleep well, even in a strange bed.

Withdrawing children initially resist new situations and avoid trying out any new food. They often cry when they see strangers and it takes time for them to fit in with other children. When school starts there are separation problems and lots of difficulties before they settle in. Such children are not adventurous in approaching new activities.

To some extent all these characteristics continue throughout life, making children either easy, or not so easy, to cope with.

Adaptability

This is the quality of adapting to the demands put on us by new situations, our parents and life in general. The adaptable baby accepts

and complies without fuss. The unadaptable baby is unaccepting, digs in his heels and makes life far from peaceful. There are some obvious overlaps between this and the approach/withdrawal type of behaviours mentioned above.

The adaptable smiles his way through nappy changes, baths and dressing. As a toddler he learns quickly what is acceptable and what is not, and tends to be compliant.

The unadaptable may resist nappy changes, baths and dressing. Haircuts may be a hassle and new foods resisted. He often disobeys and does not seem to learn easily from experience. He will be more difficult no matter how he is handled and parents may find that discipline is about as effective as whistling to a duck.

The parents of the adaptable generally breeze through life oblivious to the great difficulties experienced by those of the unadaptable.

Intensity

This refers to the intensity of the reaction to a given situation. Some greet life's joys, griefs and frustrations with the laid-back acceptance of a Buddhist monk. Others always react at full throttle with the intensity of an Italian taxi driver.

The quiet reactors are not too fussed by a wet nappy and put out a low-key grumble when hungry. When, as a toddler, their favourite toy is snatched by another child, they look startled but never think to retaliate. When hobbies or homework are not going well, they whisper 'Oh, bother' and plod on.

The intense react in a way that makes a drama out of everything. When food is not wanted, they spit it out, arch their backs and the dogs of hell are unleashed. Childhood is always sparky with no-one left in any doubt about whether they are pleased or displeased.

High-intensity children tend to feature more strongly in politics and other behaviour problem groups. They are generally more fun to look after, but like old gelignite they are pretty unstable, highly explosive and need to be handled with extreme care.

Threshold of responsiveness

This refers to the amount of stimulus needed to engage or distract a child. Some will ignore all but the most major events. Others will be distracted by the slightest trivia.

The low-threshold child may for instance stop eating when the dog barks and cannot achieve academically in a noisy classroom. When it comes to hardship and discomfort, it only takes a little upset and he is soon shouting.

The high-threshold child gets on with the serious business of living and reacts only to the most major stimuli. As a baby he will tolerate wet nappies and will eat just about any food put in front of him. Later he fusses much less about change, noise and what is going on around him. Most probably, when he learns to read, he will become hypnotised by print and oblivious to all sorts of commotion going on around.

Mood

Here we have the friendly, happy child versus the one who is grumpy and dissatisfied.

Some babies are sunny and full of smiles from dawn to dusk. They are a joy to be with and nothing seems to be a bother. Others, however, wake up grizzly and may continue to grizzle. Nothing ever seems right and the air seems tense with negative vibrations.

Distractability/soothability

This is the ability to pacify a baby and divert him to a different course. Some babies are soothed and diverted quite simply, while others need volumes of enthusiastic input to achieve anything near the same result.

The soothable baby stops crying when lifted and takes little effort to comfort even when hungry. As a toddler, he is easily diverted away from unwanted behaviour and quick to steer in the approved direction.

The hard-to-divert, unsoothable baby cries a lot no matter how much comfort he is given. As a toddler he is hard to console. When a favoured toy is removed, all hell breaks loose and no possible substitute will ever bring peace.

Attention span and persistence

These refer to the ability to stick to a task and see things through to the bitter end. It is hard to score these in an infant as concentration and stickability are not too prominent at this age. By six months the attentive, persistent baby will probably watch the mobile above his cot intently. At a year he will play happily in a playpen and listen to stories with pleasure. The toddler will enjoy sitting still and doing puzzles, which he will perform with great care. He listens intently when shown how to do something. As a schoolchild, homework is done carefully and reading is usually a pleasure.

The inattentive and non-persistent baby sucks the dummy for a few seconds and spits it out. He will be bored with the playpen and will lose interest in toys quite quickly. When learning new tasks he is quick to give up if things do not go to plan. He will use toys only briefly and will give up a puzzle when it proves a bit difficult. At school he fidgets and fails to get things finished, while with homework he is up and down like a yo-yo.

Obviously attention and persistence must have a strong bearing on the quality of a child's academic work in the school years.

Clusters of features

When these nine dimensions were analysed, there appeared some clusters which were usually associated with problems and others that seemed to assure peace.

Five adverse features kept coming up in the most difficult children—irregularity of rhythm, poor adaptability to change, high intensity of reaction, initial withdrawal and a negative mood. The opposite five features seemed to make up the easy child.

This analysis of behaviour was then taken one step further to find out how common the various groups were. About ten per cent of babies fall into the difficult category with about 40 per cent falling into the easy group. Looking again at the figures, it seemed that another fifteen per cent have many of the difficult characteristics but with very close supervision and high-quality care, parents could keep them on the straight and narrow reasonably reliably. As this group took some time and effort to get going they were referred to as the 'slow to warm up' group. That then left 35 per cent who were called the 'intermediate', who had the middle-ground, non-extreme patterns of behaviour. These are the children we call average.

WHAT DOES THIS ALL MEAN?

If these figures are correct, it follows that about 40 per cent of all parents will have an easy baby, who will tend to graduate into an easy toddler and schoolchild. Little ones like this endow their parents with a great feeling of competence and even superiority. From this position it is all too easy to criticise those less fortunate or to even believe that super-parenting alone has brought about such a perfect child.

Ten per cent of parents will not be in such a happy position and a further fifteen per cent will suffer less but still have considerable worry. When your babies are far from easy it doesn't take long for your confidence to be shattered. Friends who have been fortunate enough to have one or two easy children presume you are just an inexperienced and incompetent parent.

You will get no criticism from me—parenting is quite hard enough without the interference of meddling outsiders. If you are being criticised by parents who believe they have moulded their God-given perfect child, all you can do is ignore them, secretly hoping that next time they conceive a really obnoxious little terrorist.

I don't mention these figures to strike despair into the hearts of good parents, but I want to show that life is by no means the same for all of us. What works for the mother next door with her particular child may be quite out of place in your household. Just as children have individual temperaments, parenting and childcare styles also need a certain amount of individuality.

Finally I have to admit that nothing is quite as black and white as this. Some very difficult babies move on to become angels and sometimes the opposite will happen. **Temperament is important and interesting, but fixed typecasting at birth is unwise and counterproductive.**

CONCLUSION

Temperament certainly has a constitutional basis but can be greatly modified by a child's environment and is further helped by the maturation that takes place with age. We can't send back our little ones for some genetic engineer to adjust their temperament with his silver screwdriver, but with good handling by confident parents we can get the absolute best out of what we have been given.

Discipline—how much does a baby need?

W *hereas toddlers and adults can most certainly behave very badly, when it comes to babies there is no such thing as a true behaviour problem. Your little one may be irritable, sleep poorly, cling to you like a leech or repeatedly turn your cupboards inside out, but she will not have acted with premeditation. Her behaviour will not be bad, but rather the usual antics of a baby who doesn't think too deeply about what she does.*

These acts cannot possibly be seen to be in the same class as the Oscar-winning performances of toddlers who perfectly stage-manage tantrums, selectively refuse food and perform all sorts of other attention-seeking antics.

We have looked at the behavioural concerns of crying, colic, sleep and general irritability. In this chapter, however, I want to focus on two areas of confusion which generally arise in the minds of new parents. How much discipline does a baby need and what makes all easy-going babies suddenly become clingy?

DISCIPLINE

Discipline has its origins in the Latin 'to learn'. Go one step further and, from a biblical viewpoint, a disciple was someone who learned through love and example. Now if that's what discipline is really all about, then I think we could all do with a lot more of it. If, as parents, we're happy and in control of our lives, then love and our own good example should be all that a baby requires in the way of discipline and the word need not conjure up anything negative.

There is another positive definition of the word, as in leading a disciplined lifestyle. This means a life of structure, healthy habits and sensible routines which can't be bad for anyone, Baby included.

So do babies need discipline? Yes, if we use the word according to the definitions above. They need love, example, routine and good healthy habits right from the start.

Can you spoil a baby?

In the 1940s parents were taught to be firm with their offspring. They fed them with a strict regime and if they woke at night they were left to cry. It was thought that babies who were lifted too often became spoilt and difficult. The teaching then swung to the opposite extreme. We were told that babies didn't need any discipline at all and that you could never spoil a baby. If they cried, you comforted them. If they were hungry, you fed them. If they were bored, then you entertained them. It's probably somewhere in between now, with a preference for kindness and comfort. Many believe that babies who get the most comfort in fact become more confident, independent and will cry less. So, that's the position at present, but these things change with the wind!

Personally, I believe that there is no such thing as too much love and that it's true that you can't spoil a baby. They're little for so short a time. Let's enjoy the wonder of it.

Do all babies need equal discipline?

No, of course not! Each baby has her own individual make-up and some need minimal guidance to keep them on the straight and narrow, whereas others need the reins held more tightly. You should judge for yourself what is best, always remembering that what is needed for the child next door may be totally different to what is appropriate for your own child.

Can a ten-month-old be disciplined not to touch?

I get depressed when I hear boasting parents tell me how they are teaching their ten-monthers not to touch things. Every time the child's natural curiosity gets the better of her and she comes near one of her parents' precious ornaments, she gets a tap and a firm 'No'. Their view seems to be that they lived in the house first and Baby will just have to smarten up her act and keep to the rules and behave on their terms. So it goes on: 'Don't'—'Stop it'—'Don't'.

Throughout this ritual, the child smiles benignly or cries noisily, utterly incapable of understanding what's going on. It would have been so much easier just to lift temptation out of reach! Of course, if you persist long enough, you can teach any young animal to perform tricks. All you need is enough conditioning. But does this sort of conflict benefit anybody?

Sensible parents keep valuables and breakables shut in a cupboard or up on a high shelf out of harm's way. If Baby then turns to dropping teaspoons down the toilet, then tie, jam or otherwise immobilise the cutlery drawer. Batten down all cupboards with special baby catches or sticky tape, or put elastic bands around the door handles. These allow the adult instant entry but totally defeat even the young Houdini! Safety plugs should be put in all power sockets not in use and dangerous items should be kept under lock and key. All drugs, medicines, caustic cleaning fluids and suchlike should be securely locked away from ever-prying little hands.

This just leaves the big things that you cannot easily lift out of the way, like the television. You could even put a playpen around this. With a small repertoire to protect it's relatively easy to divert their attention and train them to stay away. It's not a bad idea to leave a couple of your cupboards for them to play in. They can't do much harm to the saucepans or the vegetables but it gives them hours of fun juggling onions or rattling saucepans.

The message here is simple. You can eventually teach your baby not to touch things, but by taking the bait off the hook you are unlikely to catch so many inquisitive little fish!

Strict or permissive?

I believe that we adults are much happier in life if we know exactly where we stand at any given time. We may complain about rules and regulations, but from them we get a kind of mental security. Children too thrive on this sort of consistent limit setting and like to know just how far they can go. The question is just how strict or lax should those limits be?

To be honest I don't think it really matters at this age. We should be guided by what feels comfortable to our own particular style of parenting. I doubt whether you could see any great difference between a child who has been brought up strictly and one who has had a rather more relaxed upbringing by the time they both reach the age of twenty. The real difference will come out when they themselves become parents because they tend to echo the behaviour of their parents.

I think the secret really is just to be positive, enthusiastic and above all consistent. Yes it's important to give them guidance but let's not forget to support their learning and marvel at the wonder of a little person investigating life.

> ### Discipline—the recommendations
>
> • Start to introduce routines and good habits from the early month.
> • Punishment is not for babies.
> • Don't expect a ten-month-old to behave like a mature adult.
> • Feed the hungry, comfort the crier—you can never go too far wrong with a cuddle.
> • Start to mould the behaviour from the end of the first year. Praise and reward the good behaviour, deliver a low-key response to the undesired—attention is the best reward for any young child.
> • If sleep problems are shattering your sanity and grizzling has you tearing your hair out, forget all this philosophy and be as firm as is needed to keep the peace and repair the emotional health of the parent.
> • Children thrive equally well on both strict and permissive discipline. What they can't take is parental conflict, inconsistency and long-term tension.
> • In short, the best way to bring up children is to lead through love and example. If what you are doing feels right and works for you, do it!

SEPARATION ANXIETY—WHY DO BABIES BECOME CLINGY?

This may come as a bit of a blow to some of you, but it is a fact of life that babies are not totally attached to their parents in their early months of life. Early on, bonding is a one-way street, although they need good care of course. However, this state of affairs changes rapidly at about seven months. From here it's a two-way street. Parents will be very aware of this change as after this age they become strongly attached to one person, usually Mum, with other close caregivers gradually being allowed into the select inner circle.

Separation anxiety and its attendant clinginess start to intensify at this age, reaching a peak soon after the child's first birthday. At this stage some mums are so clung-to that it begins to seem as though life is being led with a little child permanently attached to her skirt hem. Even a short visit to the toilet can become a conducted tour!

At the age of two the child likes to play close to her mother. She may pop outside briefly, but she'll be back every couple of minutes just to check that Mum's still there.

By preschool entry most children are ready to be separated from their mums, though a few are still far from ready for this big step. By school age, however, this urge to cling has diluted to such an extent that they can go off to school quite happily, but come 3 pm and they are still mighty pleased to see you.

Well that's all very fine, but what bearing does it have on the practical management of our children? For a start it means that up to the age of seven months the child can be left quite happily with a babysitter and handled by strangers without any protest. After this age they gradually become more and more clingy and they suffer from separation anxiety. Don't let anyone tell you that this is a pathological state. It's a perfectly normal part of childhood. It just means that they love you so much they don't want to let you out of their sight.

As a doctor I am made very aware of this sensitive stage of development. When I examine a tiny baby I whisk her up onto the couch, where she lies gurgling without a worry in the world. Try the same at ten months and the chances are I will be quickly told to get lost. That's why we tend to examine older babies and toddlers with them sitting securely on their mother's knee.

When hospitalisation is necessary, I believe that the very young baby suffers little from the traumas of separation, but the same cannot be said for Mum. She is devastated. When separation is a major problem, we aim to keep little children out of hospital as much as possible. Out-patient investigations and day-stay surgery are a help, and when babies have to be admitted, there is 24-hour visiting and parents are encouraged to live in.

When it comes to babysitters, obviously you have fewer problems if you are lucky enough to have grandparents or other emotionally close people to call on. With other sitters some babies will object noisily when left, this protest making you feel a heel for deserting them. What's worse they often start up again when you return, to punish you and let you believe they cried non-stop all the time. Don't feel concerned or guilty. As long as they were happy and settled between times, that's OK.

The life of a parent is subjected to such extremes of behaviour and emotion. At one year many mums are so clung-to that they would give anything for a life lived without an infant permanently clamped to their leg. By primary school age they have become so independent, you look back longingly at that long-lost time of closeness and total trust. Childhood passes so quickly we must always try to savour the current stage. Once gone it won't come back.

CONCLUSION—ATTENTION IS THE KEY

Babies need an immense amount of attention and luckily it is part of the bonding process for us to want to give it to them. Babies need to be noticed and they need lots of time with the people who love them paying them quality attention. You can't give them too much.

As they grow attention is the key to discipline, rewarding good behaviour with lots of positive attention and minimising it for all else where possible. This is central to surviving the toddler years, but that's in another book!

22

Normal development— bringing out the best in your child

A ll of us would like to have clever children who achieve well in life. Some parents pursue this goal to extreme lengths with their young placed firmly in the academic rat race almost the moment the umbilical cord is cut. Others appear to do equally well by adopting a much more laid-back style. Though I favour the gentler approach there is certainly room for both philosophies. In this chapter we will look at the normal patterns of development, see their value to predict intelligence and then see how we can bring out the best in our children.

WHAT MAKES CHILDREN CLEVER?

How much of our children's intelligence comes from the genes and how much is the product of enthusiastic encouragement? It is a combination of both. Our children are born with a certain potential to succeed which is then modified by the environment in which they live. Einsteins are not made by the academic cramming of parents. They are born brilliant and then brought to full potential by the love and efforts of their parents.

We can bring about great changes to our children's development but we can't work miracles. For example, a girl who is destined to be walking on her first birthday might walk at eleven months if given intensive physiotherapy and encouragement, but no amount of early intervention and bouncing up and down is going to get her on her feet at nine months. Likewise a boy who is destined to be of average ability at school, when helped by enthusiastic parents and teachers may rise towards the upper stream, but will never be the top brain in the school. Equally common, unfortunately, is the possibility of a poor environment causing children to fall below their potential.

Then there are other attributes. The child with a poor eye for the ball can be coached to play social tennis, but will never go centre-court at Wimbledon. Exercises can help the clumsy, awkward child, but he will never reach a rugby final. The impulsive accident-prone schoolboy can become more reliable but would always be a menace in the bomb-disposal squad.

Development is a product of our genes and the living environment. We can never achieve the impossible but with love, enthusiasm and a stimulating upbringing we can make a difference.

What is normal?

The terms 'average' and 'normal' can be very confusing. I know lots of normal children, but very few who are average. The average child sits unaided at six and a half months, walks at twelve and a half months, and will be dry through the night at 33 months. At the same time the normal child sits between four and a half months and nine months, walks between nine months and eighteen months, and will stay dry at night somewhere between eighteen months and eight years!

We don't need average children, all we need is for our children to be normal. The range of so-called normality is very wide, and even outside these generally accepted limits children can still be normal. Being behind in one or two specific skills is usually quite OK, it's only when a child is behind in a very important skill or many areas that we should start to worry.

AREAS OF DEVELOPMENT

Development is best considered under a number of headings. First there is gross motor, which refers to the big movements of head control, sitting and walking, then fine motor, which is all about hand movements. Next there's self-help, which includes feeding and toileting, and after that you've got speech, hearing, seeing, play and general behaviour. (See Appendices—Milestones in development.)

Gross motor (big movements)

Gross motor skills tell us that the movement part of the brain is working well, but little about the child's intelligence. So even if little Willie is up and walking at eight and a half months, he won't necessarily gain university entrance and a Rhodes Scholarship. There are many animals who move superbly, but don't think too deeply. The greyhound, for example, walks early and runs like a speeding bullet. But let's face it, any animal whose only aim in life is the pursuit of a stuffed hare can't be too bright!

To add to the confusion, phrases like 'Remember, you have to crawl before you can walk' are also quite misleading. Many babies never crawl in their lives. (They're probably too busy thinking about climbing at the time.)

Motor development works like this: you must learn to control your head before you can learn to sit. You must sit before you can stand. You must stand before you can walk round the furniture. You need to walk round the furniture holding on before you can walk alone. You must be able to walk alone before you can climb stairs. You then have to be able to climb up before you can climb down. That's what gross motor development is all about, starting with the control of the head and spreading like a bushfire throughout the rest of the body.

At birth a baby has absolutely no neck control. If you pull him up to sit, his head will flop back without support. If he is lying prone and you put a hand under his tummy to lift him up, the head will flop forward. By six weeks, however, the head will be level with the body when you try this and by three months will come up with the body when he is pulled up to sit. At six months there is full head control and almost complete trunk control. In fact a baby can almost sit in a somewhat unsteady and ungraceful fashion, though with one puff of wind he'll fall over!

Having achieved sitting somewhere between six and eight months the rest of the first year is spent getting into an upright position. A little weight can be taken on the legs at six months, but they quickly recoil like springs. Not until the eighth or ninth month can weight be borne reliably and soon he'll be able to pull himself into a standing position.

Just before the first birthday most children will be walking round the furniture, fingering trinkets, pulling off the tablecloths and starting to get into everything. Then one day they will come to the corner of a table, see something across the room that impresses them, forget to hold on and, hey presto, they'll be walking unaided.

Once that stage is reached walking soon becomes more sophisticated and in no time at all they are able to stoop, kick and run. Some may go straight into the mountaineer mode and begin climbing everything in sight. With little fear and considerably less sense, this can make for a very tense time for parents. They scarcely dare turn their backs for a minute without finding their Edmund Hillary on the benchtop.

By the age of two they can climb the stairs and not long after that they discover how to get down them again. At three they can pedal a tricycle, at four they can graduate to a bicycle with trainer wheels and some ride solo at five. The skills of a Roger Federer, Tiger Woods or Lance Armstrong may take a little longer to develop.

Though not impressed by advanced gross motor skills, I do worry about delayed and different patterns. If your baby is floppy, stiff or holds any part of his body in a strange posture, or is abnormally slow to sit or walk, please have an expert check him out—it's best to be sure.

Fine motor (hand movements)

At birth a baby's hands are blocked by the grasp reflex which locks them involuntarily onto anything placed in the palm. This reflex disappears by three months and the hands become free to hold and wave at will. By six months young ones can pick up toys in a somewhat primitive way, using all the fingertips to close against the palm. Items are passed from hand to hand at this age and then into the mouth.

Just before the first birthday comes the big breakthrough—the pincer grip. Here the index finger and thumb start to act together as a team and are used for all fine work. Now a marble can be picked up out of a cup and blocks can be put in a container. At eighteen months, three blocks can be stacked on top of each other, and at two years a pen—perhaps not as mighty as the sword at this stage but rather held more like a dagger—starts to scribble. By age three they can probably hold the pen properly and copy a 'V' and a circle.

Scissors can also be used at this age, though generally not so much for cutting paper as snipping bits off the dog and trimming their hair. At age four buttons can be done up and by five most children can write their own name and tie their own shoelaces.

It is generally thought that fine motor skills are better indicators of intelligence than gross motor ones. However, just having the skill is in itself not enough, you have to be able to do something clever with it. An eighteen-month-old may have the best pincer grip in the country, but if it is used only to bang blocks together or chuck them down the hall, then it's no great help. If, on the other hand, he's already started using the blocks delicately to construct a mini Taj Mahal then that's pretty impressive. Advanced fine motor-skills which produce advanced actions are what we really want.

Speech and understanding

Young babies may have no readily understandable speech but they sure do a lot of communicating! One cry says 'I'm hungry', another 'I'm tired', and there's no doubt when it comes to pain. Whole chapters can be written with their eyes and the body language they use.

Babies will experiment with a whole range of various noises in the first months. However, it's not generally until about nine months that the first recognisable speech-like sounds are heard. We call this pre-speech babble and it consists of a tuneful rendering of 'bababababa' and 'dadadada'. Rather like an orchestra tuning up, this lets us know that the big performance is about to begin.

The first meaningful word slips out at around the first birthday and it has always seemed one of the great injustices of being a mother, who generally devotes more time to Baby than anyone else does at that stage, that this first word is usually 'Dada', or worse still 'Doggie' or 'ball'! It's just that 'Mmmm's are harder to say than 'Dddd's.

These early words are supposed to be appropriate and meaningful, but it is my experience that Mum often gets called 'Doggie' and Dad called 'Baba', so there is a degree of confusion still as to the exact meaning of words. Doubtless your baby knows exactly what he means!

Between the ages of one year and eighteen months there is a great variation in the number of words each child uses. Some children can only use one or two words, others may be veritable walking dictionaries. Interestingly the word 'no' is more often picked up before the word 'yes', which may be a reflection of how we speak to our children. After eighteen months most enter a great speech explosion with their vocabulary mushrooming daily.

By the second birthday two-word phrases are being used, the more common being 'Me want' and 'Don't want', and these are closely followed by three-word utterances. By three years old the speech is relatively refined and by four most can debate like a parliamentarian as they justify why they aren't going to do what they know they should be doing.

Of course it can be argued that parrots can also be taught to speak clearly and this is no great feat. What separates us from the birds, however, is the use of new appropriate meaningful speech and comprehension. Intelligent humans do not repeat and echo like parrots. We are also way ahead of our expressive abilities when it comes to understanding what is said. Although there may be no speech at nine months, babies understand the command 'No!' (whether they decide to act on this understanding is another matter!).

Soon after their first birthday babies' comprehension is such that they will close a door or fetch a ball on demand, and by eighteen months they can point to various parts of the body if requested and are interested in pointing to all the cars, dogs and balls when looking at a book. From here comprehension rapidly speeds up, and in no time at all they understand the differentiation between bigger and smaller, now and later, under and over, and before you know it they're into generalisation and lateral thinking, which is the real evidence of intelligence.

Good appropriate speech coupled with good comprehension is by far the most valuable predictor of intelligence. Lack of speech on its own very often means nothing at all, but if associated with delayed comprehension can be a serious sign of slow development. There is also the possibility that a late talker could be deaf, and if you have the slightest doubt you must get hearing tested.

Hearing and seeing

I am still surprised in our advanced societies how many children with hearing problems slip through the net. This situation is being improved by screening at birth but we still need to be vigilant. It is so easy to show that a young baby can hear but still we don't seem to be very good at spotting the obvious signs of deafness.

Babies begin to hear during the last months of pregnancy and are born with full hearing. The fact that tapes of uterus noises and mothers' heartbeats can calm some newborn babies suggests that they have heard those tunes before. It has also been reported that expectant mothers living directly under the flight path of Tokyo's main airport say that their newborns were more restless in the maternity hospital but soon to settle when reunited with the 'soothing' sound of the 747s.

There is no doubt that at birth babies respond to loud noises. If a nurse drops a tray on the nursery floor twenty newborns will startle in unison. They can also hear quiet sounds. If a baby is crying in his cot he will change the rhythm of the cry if you talk softly and soothingly to him. Even the smallest baby moves his eyes and mouth to show that he is taking in every word his loving parents drool over the cot.

At six months, babies will start to turn their heads to locate sounds, and it is now you will find that if you walk quietly and unannounced into your baby's room he will turn with surprise and joy when you whisper.

Unlike many other animals who are born blind, human babies can see right from the moment of birth. As you hold the baby and move your head slowly across his plane of vision, the little eyes will light up and his face will be animated as he follows Mum's gaze. At six months the normal baby is visually insatiable. His interest spreads from close to far as he watches the dog moving round the room and then switches his attention to a far-flying aeroplane.

When it comes to either hearing or vision, please shout for help if you ever have the slightest concern. If it turns out there is a problem, early intervention can work wonders.

Self-help skills

Self-help usually refers to dressing, feeding and toilet-training. Of course babies do none of these things, but let's take a sneak preview anyway.

Dressing

You won't find your baby giving you much help with dressing until the end of the first year when his little arms will start coming up in anticipation to help you. Try to build on this by dressing your child in the same order of clothing every day.

At two years old most children can strip off all their clothes, like a streaker at a soccer match. However, they can put absolutely nothing on themselves. At age three many children go to preschool and it is a convenient coincidence that at this age they can take care of their dressing almost unaided. Tight T-shirts, buttons, shoelaces and getting clothes the right way round all come a bit later.

Feeding

Feeding is a pretty passive affair up until the eighth or ninth month when an attempt will be made to hold a bottle or some finger food. Most one to one and a half-year-olds still like to be spoon-fed, though a few militants will shut up shop if not allowed to hold their own spoon. Independence is an admirable ideal, but where it outstrips technical ability it gets you nowhere. Your child may be able to load the spoon up well but cannot quite stop the cargo shifting on the way to his mouth. The result? Splat goes the food all down his front! Don't fuss, however. Go out and buy one of those plastic bibs with a gutter at the bottom that catches any dropped food, leaving it ready to recycle. This allows him to be as independent as he wishes, feeding away while you patiently transfer all the dropped food back to the plate, slipping a few spoonfuls into the mouth as you pass.

By two and a half years they can get a drink and pour most of it into a cup. By four and a half they can tackle a knife and fork, or even poke about with chopsticks.

Toilet-training

This is not for babies. Despite what the grandparents may have told you about their toilet-trained babies, there is a world of difference between toilet-training and toilet-timing. Training is a deliberate, voluntary action, while timing is a mindless reflex which requires nothing more than a full stomach, a potty and an IQ over ten. They sit, the full stomach gives the bowel a reflex 'tweak' and the feel of the potty triggers some action. Success is not guaranteed, but if you sit them on the potty after every meal the law of averages says that you must have a sporting chance of success every so often.

Toilet-training is more useful and more permanent. It's pointless, however, to start thinking about this until the child is capable of knowing when he is either wet or soiled, a situation not encountered before eighteen months. It is successful somewhere between this age and two and a half.

The average child will stay dry at night at 33 months, though the 'normal' range is between eighteen months and eight years! Though it may be of little comfort, let me tell you that one in ten of all children is still wetting his bed at the age of five. All you can do is to make sure the washing machine is in good order and hope that your baby is in the nine out of ten.

Play

Young babies don't need toys to play with. Everything they need comes already attached: feet and arms to wave and fingers to chew. At six months your baby will grab his first toys. Usually, however, it's for the rapid transit to his mouth. Not until about the first year mark will toys become more important. Toy blocks will start to be banged together and posted into a container. Teddy will start to be flung out of the cot, and when you pick it up and put it back, out he will go again. A comedian once claimed that babies throw teddy bears out of their cots because they don't want them in there in the first place. It's a nice thought, but not true. They just like to play. At this age the game of peekaboo is as entertaining as a night at the opera. Rearranging the kitchen is another favourite, saucepans and vegetables seemingly giving the utmost pleasure and leaving Grandma's sparkling new toys for dead.

It is at two years that the real play breakthrough is seen. This is generally when imaginative, pretend play starts. Before this a toy car is seen as a fairly dull object with wheels, but now it screeches its way round the house with deafening vrooms and numerous crashes on the way. With the aid of imagination a cardboard box can become a boat and the innards of a toilet roll some super-shuttle that keeps blasting noisily into space.

Play in the two-year-old is not very sociable. He likes to be with other children, but playing beside them rather than with them. Working together, sharing and taking turns doesn't come until the preschool years. Team games with rules will not hold any interest until the age of five and even then the game is more important than the code of rules.

EARLY MILESTONES AND THE PREDICTION OF LATER INTELLIGENCE

There is a great selection of developmental milestones, but when it comes to predicting intelligence they are not all of equal importance.

While parents marvel over the age at which the first teeth appear, the time of walking or when the child stays dry at night, these are not pointers to intelligence. Kicking a ball, repeating nursery rhymes and holding a pen are also fairly unreliable and depend a lot on how much the child has been taught.

The one area of high predictive value is speech and language. No child with advanced quality speech is going to be a slow learner, but first make sure that the speech you are hearing is of high quality. Quality means more than just the volume of verbiage. What you should be looking for is new, appropriate, well-constructed communication that is relevant to the matter on hand. A child may say 'Good day' with perfect intonation, recite a nursery rhyme faultlessly like the kindergarten parrot, count to 1000 and know all the words to the national anthem, but this may have little relevance to intelligence.

Intelligence can be seen in children who answer questions clearly, cleverly and appropriately, who can use generalisation and lateral thinking. It's not difficult to recite 'Three Blind Mice' by rote. It takes cleverness to work out how many tails the farmer's wife cut off! Knowing the numbers one to 1000 is all very impressive, but using them to do simple sums is the real skill.

Advanced speech is my favourite milestone, but remember there are some children who are slow to speak yet are still very clever. Einstein was one of these children. He seemed to turn out OK, despite his quiet start.

When speech is delayed, focus on your child's comprehension. This is not as easy to test but if he seems to have a good comprehension of words and to understand how to manipulate his environment, then he's fine.

The other milestone I like to use is watching children at play. I like to see children playing with rich, inventive imagination, responding crisply to what is going on around them and showing a great interest in life. In assessing the abilities of a young child it is often these features that tell us most. It's not just what they do, but the way they do it. It's quality that counts. The top horse trainer at the yearling sales decides who will be a future winner not by measurements or horse IQ tests. He looks at the quality of how they move and behave, and makes his prediction.

Development—doing the best for our children

If you are the sort of parent who is planning early music lessons, junior gym, swimming lengths by one year old, reading by three years and playing the classics on the violin by four then you will find my ideas a trifle old-fashioned. I believe in the old well-tried methods. I don't know if the fad for super-stimulation helps in the long run nor do I know if it makes children better balanced and happier. Some children are pushed so hard that they seem to miss out on childhood. Many of these must be destined to become just as boring as the parents who push them. Often I worry that all this is designed more for the benefit of the parents' own egos than to help their child to a better life.

Helping them to fulfil their potential

Here are a few old-fashioned principles that can make parenting more effective:

- Warm, loving parents create warm, loving children.
- Touch, hold, carry your baby. Be close, be there.
- Talk, chat and talk some more. Even the tiniest tot needs words and these all help speech development and understanding.
- Horseplay, having physical fun, being roughed up by Dad are worth more than a season ticket to junior gym.
- Education is not just the three Rs, it's also social competence, communication, loving life and those old values like good manners.
- Play is not only enjoyable, it's a great way to learn.
- Parents are a child's main teachers. Set good examples and then teach them as your apprentice.

Premature babies

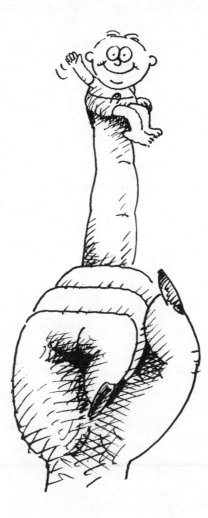

A bout twelve per cent of all babies born in the UK arrive at less than 37 weeks gestation. We think of the normal term as 40 weeks, and before 37 weeks a baby is called premature or more correctly preterm. Where prematurity is great the baby will be immature in all her body functions and will need months of very special care. In this chapter we will be looking at the problems these babies may have and how parents can hold together while modern technology and expert care attempt to sort out the difficulties.

THE PRETERM OR PREMATURE BABY

When I first started in paediatrics, babies weighing under 2500 g (5½ lb) caused us great worry and those under 1500 g (3½ lb) would rarely make it. In the last twenty years, however, all this has changed with the great advances that have been made in the area of newborn intensive care. Nowadays a baby born eight weeks early has about the same chance of survival and future success as any other baby. Babies born between 30 and 32 weeks certainly give some cause for concern, though not too great, while those born at 28 weeks still have a reasonably good chance, but it's a long and hazardous haul ahead.

If prematurity is between 26 and 28 weeks, life becomes extremely hazardous. When they're this small, specialists do not approach resuscitation in an automatic, unthinking way. The amount of medical interference is carefully considered against the likely long-term outcome. In the long term some will survive and fare extremely well, while others will have ongoing complications which continue to be a big worry.

Caring for these very small babies has become so specialised that it really has to be done in the biggest and best-equipped medical centres. Getting the baby to one of these centres often involves a very special transport service and a highly trained team will fly or drive to another hospital to administer intensive care to the baby and bring her back to base.

Where there is adequate warning of prematurity it is best to plan ahead and move Mum straight to the main maternity centre. The safest form of transport for a very small baby will always be inside Mum's tummy!

Living through the initial stormy weeks after such a baby is born puts a great strain on any family. There is a lot of worry, concern for the future and restrictions of the normal close contact one expects with a newborn baby. Nowadays, however, newborn nurseries not only care for babies, they also care for their families as well. Technology has certainly raced ahead, but happily humanity has managed to keep pace alongside.

CHALLENGES FOR THE VERY SMALL

Because premature babies have entered this world ahead of their appointed time, they have immature, unprepared lungs, brains and bodies. The earlier they are born, the greater the problems, but strangely no two babies of the same premature gestation period will have the same severity of symptoms. Some seem to handle prematurity with difficulty, while others manage quite well. Let's consider the practical implications.

Breathing
A baby born ten weeks early will have lungs caught in a totally un-prepared state. They will try to move sufficient oxygen across the immature membranes but this process will initially be pretty inefficient. If the baby is mildly affected, her breathing will be fast, laboured and will require some extra oxygen. Those who are badly affected will need mechanical ventilation to keep enough oxygen in the blood and for some very small babies this assisted ventilation can go on for months.

The control of respiration is another problem. It's not only the lungs that are immature, so is the brain which sends the messages telling the baby to breathe. Very small babies have a tendency to forget to breathe, a condition known as apnoea. During the first weeks these tiny babies are wired up to a monitor that sounds an alarm if the breathing stops. In special care nurseries the staff spend much of their day running around the nursery giving babies a little prod to get them going again—that's generally all it takes.

Temperature control

Premature bodies were never designed to survive outside the womb and they find the big world a chilling experience. Initially the prem is nursed in a crib which has its own in-built central heating system linked directly to the baby's temperature monitor. If the baby has to be taken out of the crib, her body temperature is maintained by the use of special heat lights.

Sucking and feeding

When babies are very preterm, they don't know how to suck strongly and even if they did, very often their gut wouldn't be ready to digest food. In these cases, they are fed through a tube directly into the stomach, or if they are tiny, directly by drip into a vein. Don't panic when you see tubes and drips on a premature baby. They are normal and to be expected, and they will disappear as soon as the baby is mature enough to take real food.

Jaundice

The liver of every newborn baby is pretty inefficient and immature. The premature baby, of course, will have even greater problems with it. During the first month, the liver is kept busy processing and cleaning out the body's overload of bile products. Since initially it doesn't always work up to full power, most normal babies tend to have a tint of jaundice and the premature baby is even more vulnerable to this.

The bile products are mostly cleared by the liver, but some can also be broken down by the action of sunlight on the skin. It is quite common for some small prems to have a special bright light shining on their crib. This photo-therapy, as it is called, eases the load on the liver and reduces the risks of excessive levels of bile in the blood.

The jaundiced prem lies stretched out under the lamp like a sunbather on a nudist beach, but for her it's a bit of reverse sunning—she's trying to lose her tan, not develop it!

Vitamins and iron

Full-term newborn babies arrive in the world with their little bodies filled with reserves of vitamins and iron. These supplies keep them free from anaemia and vitamin deficiency in the first six months until they can start a properly balanced mixed diet. These important stores are transferred across the placenta in the last couple of months of pregnancy, so the premature baby slips her mooring and sails into life without the stores having been loaded aboard. This early embarkation can cause problems so iron and vitamin supplements have to be given for at least the first four months of life.

THE SPECIAL CARE NURSERY

The first sight of a special care nursery can be a mind-boggling experience. There laid out before you are so many tiny humans amid a mass of electronic gadgetry which would seem more at home in the cockpit of a jumbo jet. But these are friendly skies and the staff navigating them are experienced and gentle.

There have to be quite rigorous rules, however, and first among them is sterility—not the super-sterility of the operating theatre, but enough to keep out major infections and germs. Visitors to the nursery will be asked to wear a gown over their clothes, remove their watches, roll up their sleeves and wash their hands and forearms. If you are suffering from a cold, flu or any other infection, it may be best not to enter and just watch through the glass for a couple of days. If in doubt, the sister in charge will guide you. Wearing a mask might be an equally effective approach.

On your first visit you will be welcomed by one of the staff who will show you round the nursery and explain how they are helping your baby. There may be drips, tubes, alarms, monitors—a whole array of paraphernalia whose purpose will all be explained to you. Don't be daunted, it's only there to keep your baby well, safe and properly monitored. You are there to get to know, love and become attached to your little one, so focus on her and ignore the machinery.

The human touch

These nurseries are not just centres of high technology, they also specialise in great humanity. The staff will know that you are worried and ill at ease in such strange surroundings and will help you overcome your fears. As time goes by they will encourage you to do more and more of the caring, and they are on hand 24 hours a day to answer any questions you will have.

PARENTS' FEELINGS

At first most parents of premature babies are bound to feel a bit shell-shocked and numb. You never thought that the pregnancy would end like this and you can hardly believe that this is happening to you. As you lie in the postnatal ward you may feel very lonely, knowing that you cannot have your baby with you. When the time comes to go home it will feel strange leaving without your baby and those treks to the hospital to visit will seem to consume most of your life.

In the early days when a baby's life may hang in the balance, it is common to have doubts about just how close to allow yourself to get to a child with such an uncertain future. You cannot deny your feelings, however, and you just have to let Nature take its course. You will also get all those nagging questions like: What did I do wrong? Is it all my fault? Why can't I produce a normal baby like everyone else? It's also very easy to feel guilty and blame yourself quite incorrectly for not eating a better diet, not giving up work earlier or a multitude of other inappropriate causes. And of course there is the most common question of all: Why me?

You may start to feel angry and while you are having a go at yourself, it's not uncommon to kick a few passing heads at the same time. This is very normal human behaviour and acts as a defence mechanism to cope with your confusion.

Another typical problem at times like this is the way in which different people cope. Mum may become completely obsessed with the baby, while Dad distances himself by burying himself in work. Mum may want to talk about it while Dad copes better by trying not to think about it. It's not always easy to remember at times of high tension like these, but different people cope with a crisis in different ways and all you can do is try to understand the other's reaction. Also, try not to forget the other children in the family if you have any. They will feel the tensions and be worried and frightened themselves. I know you probably won't have a great deal of spare emotional energy left, but try and leave a tiny bit for them.

Asking questions and getting answers

The surest way to create confusion in your mind is to ask an opinion of every passer-by from head doctor to the junior cleaner. Make up your mind exactly who you are going to listen to and trust them and confine your questions to them. When you shop around you get conflicting answers which will only confuse you more.

Don't feel a burden if you want to ask a lot of questions. Everyone expects it, even when the same one comes up several times over. When the mind is stressed it sometimes takes more than one answer to sink in. It's not a bad idea to write down questions as you think of them so that you are well prepared when you next visit your doctor or whoever you are consulting.

Don't be afraid to ask direct questions. The answers may hurt but the sooner you know exactly where you stand the quicker you can make provision for them. Questions like: How good are the odds? Will she be OK in the future? How long will she have to be in hospital? What caused the problem in the first place? All these need to be answered at some stage but people may be wary of volunteering the answers unless they know that you want to hear them.

Going home

Most prems make it home at about the time they were meant to be born, though those who have had a really rough ride or severe breathing problems may take a little longer. By the time they are well enough to go home, all the problems of temperature control and feeding will have been ironed out and you can treat your baby like any other.

If you have had a lot of worry and the baby has had a long session in special care, it's bound to leave its mark. It's hard to stop worrying and over-protecting your little one, but nevertheless try to loosen up a bit and start focusing some more of your attention on other members of the family and getting your own life back on the rails.

Remember that the doctors wouldn't have let you take your baby home if they didn't think she was perfectly fit to be there, and that you were very capable of taking care of her.

THE OUTLOOK

The whole science of looking after very small infants is itself in its infancy. Each year new techniques are developed and more and more babies survive at earlier and earlier ages. It's still the really small ones of less than 28 weeks that cause the most worry, with other tinies causing significant but much less concern. The year following birth will be one of frequent reviews as your doctors keep a close watch on health and development to check for any complications such as squints, poor vision, hearing difficulties, cerebral palsy, possible delayed development or residual lung and breathing problems.

When assessing development, allowance has to be made for the baby's prematurity for the first two and a half years. A baby who was two months preterm is not expected therefore to have her six months skills until eight months, her one year skills at fourteen months or her two year skills until 26 months. After two and a half they have to forget the past and get on with it like the rest of us. You can't plead prematurity when you're booked for speeding or fail your final year at school. By that time it's all past history and by rights you should be sparking away on all cylinders like anyone else.

24

Twins—twice the trouble, twice the pleasure

W hen parents are told they are going to be welcoming twins into their family, they are delivered a mixed bundle of emotions which may well include joy, disbelief and anxiety. Certainly there may be twice the pleasure, but with that comes twice the work and twice the tiredness.

If there is a key to surviving and enjoying your larger than expected family, it's that you should accept all useful offers of help and not be afraid to ask for extra. Your life is going to be full-on for a while and those that share in the joys will not mind sharing the work.

Let's use this chapter to look at what multiple births entail and the sorts of things that worry most parents who are blessed with them.

TWINS

Twins occur in about one in 40 births, but if there is a strong family history or Mum has been taking fertility-stimulating drugs then the incidence is much more common. The ratio of identical to non-identical twins is about one to eight. The non-identical twins come from two separate eggs being released instead of just one. These are fertilised by different sperms and the twins will be just as different as any other two siblings. The only things they will have in common are their parents and their birthday. They can both be boys, or girls, or one of each. Identical twins occur when one egg and one sperm join and then split into two halves, each with an identical genetic make-up and usually fuelled by one cord from one placenta. This works well as long as both twins are nourished equally, but there can be problems, which is one reason why we monitor twin pregnancies so closely. Early delivery may be necessary which is not what anyone would choose but the outcome is generally good.

For most twins, though, they have a placenta each and the only issue is usually cramped quarters towards the end, and so they may need to come out a little earlier than single births. In general, twins have the same prospects as individual pregnancies, but they are monitored a little more closely to avoid problems.

The pregnancy

The first suggestion of twins may be that you are bigger than expected for your dates. Then you might have an early scan. These days it is usual to have an ultrasound at about ten to thirteen weeks. If not suspected earlier, a twin pregnancy will be detected at this time. In any case, once twins are confirmed, there will be many more scans ahead, as your obstetrician will be watching this pregnancy more closely than others. You'll have all the same sorts of blood and urine tests but your visits to the doctor will be more frequent.

Twin pregnancy has all the discomforts and difficulties of a normal pregnancy but usually to a greater degree. The enormity of the situation can become a real trial towards the end, especially for smaller women. Tiredness is often more of a problem and in these later stages the obstetrician will keep a sharp eye on your blood pressure and if it rises, order rest to reduce the risk of early delivery.

Figures show that about half of all twins will be delivered before 37 weeks, which is about the average for twin births, and they will tend to weigh around 2.5 kg (5½ lb).

Delivery can be natural but there is an increased chance of assistance or caesarean section with twins. All that matters here is the health of the mother and the babies.

Hospital

During her time in hospital Mum learns how to feed and manage her two babies. Apart from the obvious challenges she may find that hospitals aren't always designed for twins—the chairs aren't wide enough and the beds are too small to hold one mum and two babies. Initially breast-feeding seems like an acrobatic event but many will take to it very quickly and easily.

It is usual for the mother of twins to stay in hospital for some extra days just to make sure that feeding, weight gain and day-to-day management have got off to a reasonable start.

Home

When the twins first come home they are greeted as an epic attraction, a real double bill which draws a big audience of admiring friends and neighbours. If you have other children make sure they aren't ignored in the rush. The balance of power is going to be shaky enough as it is with the arrival of the twins without well-meaning outsiders disturbing it any further.

As with any other baby, an easy-care existence is what's needed for the first three months. Cooking should be kept simple, housework to a minimum and rest should be snatched at whatever unusual time chance allows. Put your phone on voicemail when you are snoozing. Encourage those who offer their services to come bearing gifts of precooked food and then roll up their sleeves and pitch in. Don't be too proud to accept help when it is offered, you are going to need all the help you can get and if you turn people down they will soon stop asking.

Feeding

The months of pregnancy give you time to get emotionally prepared for the task of feeding twins. Approach the job equipped with the information and resources you need and start off with a positive approach. Breast-feeding twins can be done very successfully and most give it at least a try.

It may seem daunting at first but there is a lot of support available, starting in hospital, where they will show you how to get comfortable and encourage greater milk production. If you encounter any problems the National Breastfeeding Helpline or Multiple Births Foundation will be at the end of the phone when you need them. And of course your health visitor or GP can also provide advice and practical assistance.

Bottle-feeding is slightly more complicated as it takes twice the volume and requires twice as many arms as it would for a single baby. But once you get the hang of managing all the washing and sterilising and the feeding technique you will progress nicely, with your babies getting all the nourishment they need. Whether breast or bottle, feeding is a special time to hold babies close and marvel at the double miracle in your life.

Feeding solids will require a couple of suitable seats, one bowl and spoon, a dextrous arm and possibly a splash mat.

Clothes

Although you may have twice as many bottoms to cover, most mothers find that one and a half times the usual cloth nappy quota is sufficient, but disposable nappies are usually a much easier option. My advice would be not to worry about being 'green'—this is basic survival! Use unisex outfits if your twins are of different sexes. Blue-pink coding may be very smart but you can be sure that you'll get one messy twin and one as pure as the driven snow and end up with piles of unnecessary clothes in reserve.

Make sure that the clothing you buy is simple—the gift givers can provide the fancy show-off outfits. And don't pay any attention to what the amateur psychologists tell you about dressing your twins identically. It doesn't matter what you do, they're both unique little people and as soon as they're old enough they'll very quickly decide the way they want to dress, whatever you may say.

Sleeping

In theory twins offer the prospect of twice as many night visits if their sleep cycles are not in synch with each other. It may help to know that most young babies sleep so soundly that a crier close by is unlikely to cause any disturbance. This means that it's probably unnecessary to rush in every time you hear a squeak. The noisy one usually won't disturb the sleeping partner. Some mothers I have seen though decide to get everyone up at once for night-time feeds so they don't have to get up again. In these days of cost efficiency this seems like the way to go!

If after six months one of the twins is proving to be a light sleeper and a sleep program is being used, then they will have to sleep separately for a week or two until there is success.

Having lived very intimately for the nine months since conception, twins can generally tolerate being pretty close thereafter. They will sleep quite happily top to tail in a single bassinet when you are out visiting, and even at home they can sleep top to tail in one cot if you want. They'll soon tell you if they are happier apart.

Mobility

Whereas the mothers of single babies tend to carry their babies around like a bomb-disposal officer nursing a ticking parcel, those with twins find themselves a little shorthanded for such gentleness. Nevertheless their twins seem to manage and the situation can be greatly helped by using a clever combination of slings, backpacks, frontpacks, prams or strollers.

The first necessity will be a pair of baby capsules for car travel. It is a bit expensive to buy two of these, but they can usually be hired relatively cheaply. The only problem is that they are rather too heavy to carry for any great distance. Strollers are useful for all babies, a double one being the order of the day for twins, or you can put one in a single stroller and carry the other in a backpack.

If you are buying a double stroller the 'side by side' model may be better than the tandem version, even if harder to get in shop doorways. Both babies can lie down and there are no arguments about which twin travels first class and which is in the back.

Actually mobilising yourself to go out is rather like organising an expedition to climb Mount Everest. At times you feel as though you need a team of sherpas to carry the stores between camps, but it's well worth it once you are out and the admirers will make up for the time spent in planning and preparation.

Will I love them equally?

When any parent expects a second child they wonder whether they can possibly love him as much as their firstborn and miraculously they always do. Although twins share the same birthday most of them are far from identical. It is a mistake to compare the two, though difficult to avoid as you watch them growing up side by side. Milestones will never be identical, they will develop like any two different children in a family, each with their individual strengths and weaknesses.

It's not just the development that differs, so does the temperament and behaviour. This makes it very hard to give absolute equality of love and attention to both parties. Human nature being what it is, the most noisy and demanding half of the duet is bound to get more attention than the quiet one. Although human nature may dictate a certain inequality of attention, this doesn't mean that there is a similar bias in the allocation of love.

Parents who only have one child at a time have little idea what a difference two makes. When they become toddlers they seem to work as a team, perpetually devising ever more ingenious ways of getting up to mischief. If one toddler can stay a step ahead of his parents, imagine what a long way in front two can be!

When it comes to identical twins, some can be so similar that even the parents find it hard to tell them apart. However, as you get to know them better you learn to recognise differences and don't have to rely on skin spots or putting nail polish on one of their hands to avoid confusion.

If you feel that coping with two babies is a bit of a handful there's nothing like support from someone who has been through it and understands. The Multiple Births Foundation and the Twins & Multiple Births Association (TAMBA) are only too ready to help you with good ideas and practical support if you feel you may be sinking under the double weight load.

CONCLUSION

Twins may be double the joy, but also double the trouble. Life can be much easier if you are sensible about your expectations of yourself:

- Don't be too proud. Don't knock back genuine offers of help.
- Organise an easy-care routine with easy meals and little housework.
- Try to rest whenever the opportunity presents itself.

- Dress your twin babies in simple clothes and avoid colour-coding them.
- Force yourself to get out even though the preparation may seem to take forever. It's always worth the effort in the end.
- Don't worry about trying to be absolutely fair in each situation to each twin. The attention may not be equal, but the love will be and that's what counts.
- If you feel weighed down, ask for help. The Multiple Births Foundation and TAMBA are always ready to assist.

- **Multiple Births Foundation** www.multiplebirths.org.uk
- **Twins & Multiple Births Association (TAMBA)** www.tamba.org.uk
- **National Breastfeeding Helpline** 0300 100 0212

The special baby —birth defects and disabilities

I would be a very happy doctor indeed if it were possible to write my baby book without mention of birth defects, disabilities and SIDS. Sadly we live in a tough world, one in which children's health problems are unfortunately all too common.

An ultrasound is usually done at ten to thirteen weeks and then at about eighteen weeks into the pregnancy. Many but not all congenital birth defects will be picked up then. If the foetus is found to have birth defects (e.g. heart defects or spine, gut and other problems), this early knowledge allows a management plan to be implemented as soon as the baby is born.

In this chapter we will take a brief look at some of the more common concerns that may occur in our babies. Then let's think of the parents and what this does to them, and lastly see how those of us around can help.

Congenital heart disease

The formation of the human heart is one of the great miracles of Nature. In the early weeks it starts as a thin sausage-shaped tube and by birth has become a complex system of channels, chambers and valves. The greatest miracle is the total change of circulation that occurs within seconds of birth. While the baby is in the uterus there is no need for lungs because all the oxygen needed comes from Mum via the placenta. Half a minute later, now out in the wide world, the placenta has become dislodged and the lungs have full responsibility for providing all the oxygen that is needed to preserve life. At birth the lungs expand, the cord is cut and within seconds channels close, new ones open and an entirely different plumbing system springs into action.

Amid the complexity of all this it's hardly surprising that sometimes things go wrong—valves don't work, holes stay open and abnormal channels remain. These are the defects that make up congenital heart disease, which affects almost one in every 150 babies born. Some conditions mean that the baby is not ready for unassisted life outside the womb and she will become very ill in the early days either with blueness (cyanosis) or with heart failure which shows as rapid breathing and a greatly enlarged liver. A number of these defects are extremely serious and difficult to treat, while other major problems will respond well to surgery. With all the modern techniques, success in heart surgery is now remarkably good.

Some heart defects give no signs or symptoms at birth. Parents find this hard to understand when a problem first comes to attention some time later. A number are so mild that they are diagnosed as a chance finding in an otherwise healthy child, and some of these are small holes in the heart that close themselves with age. The majority of heart problems that are amenable to treatment will cause no barrier to a long, normal and healthy life.

The message therefore is:

- Congenital heart defects are quite common.
- This usually presents as blueness, breathlessness and tiring at feeds.
- Not all heart problems can be diagnosed at birth. Sometimes there are no signs early on.
- Many problems need only diagnosis, yearly review and little further treatment.
- Surgery, when necessary, is much safer and more successful than parents may fear.

Gut blockages

The gut of the newborn is often found to have some obstruction along its course. When the stoppage is close to the top end, the problem becomes obvious with the very first feed. When it is further down, however, it may take a bit longer for its effects to be felt. Occasionally the blockage is only partial and this gives a more confusing picture, which appears only days or even weeks down the track.

Surgery will be required for most of these babies and although this may sound hazardous and frightening, with the use of modern children's anaesthesia, even the tiniest premature baby is likely to do well. I feel heartened when I see that the advances in surgery have not just been in technique but also in the human approach to it.

Nowadays the smallest child will be given the same high standard of treatment and post-operative pain relief as would be offered to the most demanding adult.

Cleft lip/cleft palate

Cleft lip is where the baby's upper lip is incompletely formed to leave a gap in the centre. Cleft palate is where the roof of the mouth is defective which leaves a small, medium or large gap. It is common for both clefts to occur together and this affects about one in 500 babies.

At birth parents can see nothing but disfigurement for life. However, it is vital that all involved keep an optimistic and positive outlook right from the start. This is justified as the prognosis is extremely good. Most major hospitals reassure the parents with an album of before and after surgery shots which can show convincingly that, though the present may not look any too rosy, the future promises well.

Surgery to repair the lip is performed between two and three months, while the palate is left until six to nine months.

A large cleft will obviously make feeding difficult, but with special teats and other techniques most of the food can be channelled in the right direction. Once surgery is over, speech therapists move in to make sure that the voice develops normally and with a good-quality tone.

Talipes/clubfoot

At birth many completely normal babies hold their feet in a strange posture. This is not due to a foot deformity, but rather as a result of the lack of space to stretch out in the uterus.

Talipes, however, is different. Here the foot is fixed in an in-turned and abnormal position. Unless this is treated, the child would eventually walk on a foot so twisted that it would be the outside of the little toe that touched the ground. This affects about one child in every 1000 born but over half of these will regain a normal foot position without anything more than physiotherapy, home exercises and splints. For the remainder, corrective surgery is needed and is almost always successful.

Hydrocephalus

The human brain is not a solid mass of cells, it has a fluid-filled middle. This inside is made up of a series of connecting lakes called ventricles. The fluid that fills these is manufactured centrally, then flows from chamber to chamber before squeezing through a narrow channel to be absorbed outside the brain.

Hydrocephalus (or water on the brain, as it used to be called) occurs when this narrow exit is obstructed and dams up the fluid flow. When this happens the central lakes overfill, expand and force the soft skull to enlarge. Sometimes hydrocephalus is an isolated finding. It can be associated with the abnormality of the spinal cord, spina bifida. By itself, hydrocephalus is relatively benign, but when associated with spina bifida, the double disability is more serious.

Once the channels are obstructed, they are blocked for good and no surgery can reopen them. To ease the pressure and prevent damage to the developing brain, a small tube is inserted into one of the overfilled ventricles which then drains the fluid outside the brain to be absorbed in another part of the body. This is called a shunt and is remarkably effective. Once the shunt is in place and working, it is usually required for life and keeps the fluid flow under control. Once the pressure is eased, brain growth can once again develop normally. Periodic readjustments of the tubing may be needed as the child grows.

The diagnosis of hydrocephalus is made initially by the simplest of methods—a tape measure. When the baby's head is found to be expanding too quickly, then an ultrasound scan or special head X-ray will be arranged to confirm the diagnosis.

Spina bifida

Spina bifida is a congenital deficiency of the bony arch that protects the spinal cord at the back. If this deficiency is limited to the bony structure then it is called spina bifida occulta and is benign. If, however, both the bony arch and the spinal cord which runs through it are affected then a serious disability may result.

If not seen on the scans, the damaged area on the back will be obvious at birth and comes as a great shock to both the parents and obstetrician. If the baby's legs move well then one hopes that the spinal cord is pretty intact. If the spinal cord is seriously affected then there will be a major paralysis of the legs as well as problems of bladder control and kidney damage. Hydrocephalus will also occur in about 80 per cent of babies born with spina bifida.

Recent research has shown that the naturally occurring vitamin folic acid taken two months before conception and in the first three months of pregnancy greatly reduces the risk of spina bifida.

We do know that spina bifida and hydrocephalus have a definite genetic link. Where parents have had one child born with the condition the risk of a second is greatly increased. For such families an antenatal diagnostic test is now available. A useful, but not entirely reliable, blood-screening test is sometimes offered to parents at the sixteenth week of pregnancy. If the result is suspicious, a high-quality ultrasound scan gives a much more accurate level of diagnosis.

Cerebral palsy

The brain is made up of many different parts, each one of them in charge of a particular function. When the area that controls the movement and body posture of the baby is damaged, then you have what is called cerebral palsy. Though occasionally caused by extreme prematurity, infection or birth complications, this condition usually appears out of the blue for no apparent reason. It is exceptionally rare for it to be caused by breech births, the use of forceps or other obstetric techniques.

The words 'cerebral palsy' used alone tell us little. The condition has many subtypes, each of which can occur with varying grades of severity. There are three major forms of cerebral palsy: the spastic type, the athetoid and the ataxic.

'Spastic' is often seen as a term of abuse but in medical language it means nothing more than the muscles are stiff due to a defect in that part of the brain that controls movement. When this stiffness is isolated to one side of the body it is known as spastic hemiplegia, if only the legs are affected it is called spastic diplegia, and if the whole body is affected, spastic quadriplegia. The most minor cases can often go undetected for the first year, while the most major are devastating right from birth.

Athetosis results in very floppy muscles and many involuntary movements, while ataxia causes unsteadiness, co-ordination problems and poor balance.

Despite these physical difficulties, children with cerebral palsy are generally of normal intelligence. The public need to be constantly reminded that they must never underestimate the intellectual abilities of those with a physical disability.

It is not always easy to diagnose cerebral palsy in the very young baby but there are certain tell-tale signs that worry those of us who work in this area:

- If the muscle tone is too tight or too floppy.
- If the baby doesn't 'feel right' to the experienced mother.
- If motor development seems unacceptably delayed.
- If sucking or spoon-feeding seems to be an unexpected struggle.
- If there is an unusual tightness in the hips or ankles.
- If the head, or any other part of the body, is held in an unusual position.
- If the baby keeps her fists tightly clenched.
- If one side seems to be used more than the other.

Once cerebral palsy has been diagnosed it is important that physiotherapy commences to loosen up the tight muscles and remove unwanted postures. Occupational and speech therapy may also be required at a later stage. How a child with cerebral palsy will progress depends on the severity of the problem, the amount of therapy and the determination of both parents and child to overcome the disability.

Down syndrome

Down syndrome affects almost one in every 600 children conceived and is the result of a chromosome abnormality in the baby. At birth the features can be spotted immediately, although it may take several weeks before the results of the confirming blood tests are available. Initially there may be few obvious differences in the baby other than a characteristic facial appearance and muscles which seem a bit floppy.

Every normal baby is born with 46 chromosomes in each cell which line up in pairs, one half (23) originating from the father, the other half from the mother. These chromosomes carry all our genetic information and are responsible for the uniqueness and family characteristics of every child. In Down syndrome the baby is conceived with a 47th chromosome. This is a genetic mistake which occurred when the egg was being manufactured, which gave it 24 chromosomes rather than the 23 that were expected.

The main concern with Down syndrome is the mental retardation that accompanies it. This is usually of mild or moderate severity. In the old days heart defects coupled with a susceptibility to infection greatly reduced life expectancy of such children, but nowadays with the aid of antibiotics, surgery and good home care, the lifespan will be close to that of any other.

We now believe in getting these babies started on an early intervention program as young as possible. Therapy will get underway soon after diagnosis and many will still have almost normal development at one year with a number now going on to integrate into regular school settings. Treatment should certainly always be optimistic, but kept within the bounds of reality. The most we can do for any child is to help them to achieve the potential within them. This comes mainly from the stimulation of the care of a loving family.

When the dust starts to settle and therapy gets underway, the parents are going to need an awful lot of support. With Down syndrome, as with many disabilities, the important thing is to give your love, try to remain patient and hopeful, and remember that there are other members of your family who deserve equal attention as well.

The risk of a mother conceiving a Down syndrome baby is about one in 600 or 700, but this is much higher when the mother is over 35. This increase is largely offset by the tendency to test older mothers stringently and their frequent choice not to continue with the pregnancy.

PARENTS MATTER—SO DO THEIR FEELINGS!

When a serious illness or disability is diagnosed it is as though the parents have been hit by a thunderbolt. They are left stunned, numb and disbelieving. Gradually this passes, leaving them to weave their way slowly through a grief reaction. It is as though they have lost the child they expected and subconsciously they mourn this loss.

The human brain is not suited to sudden emotional shocks but Nature in its wisdom combats this with a series of protective defences that help keep us on the rails. We defend by denial, activity and even anger. These defences partially protect us from becoming overwhelmed by the stress and unhappiness of the situation.

Denial

This is the most important defence each one of us uses for our day-to-day survival in this worrying world. We know there are famines, fights, nuclear proliferation and terrible injustices, but we cope best when we put these to the back of our minds. Of course, we are aware that the problems exist, but a bit of denial keeps us sane and stops us worrying more than we need to.

Denial is a much-needed defence when we are told our baby has a major disability. At first it is more comfortable to deny the full story than digest it all and consider its implications. It is tempting to deny the opinion you have been given and shop around from doctor to doctor in the vain hope of securing a more favourable diagnosis. It is less painful if we do not accept the harsh reality of the situation, but instead search far and wide for the elusive miracle cure.

Denial is normal, natural and keeps all thinking humans sane. Time eases in the acceptance and then denial becomes unnecessary.

Activity

Keeping minds busy and bodies active lifts the spirits of all worrying adults. When you spend your time alone your problems magnify, as does your sadness. Parents with a disabled child do best when they keep active. They do even better when life goes forward with a purpose and towards a goal. Activity is useful but it must not become overdone, and a large chunk of this energy must be directed towards all our family members.

Anger

This is a strange defence that causes great confusion in those who are looking on. When angry at fate, there's a tendency to direct this at some innocent person close to hand.

Parents who are upset with what has happened to their baby may feel angry at nurses, doctors, neighbours and even those they dearly love. Be warned, many of us may find ourselves at the receiving end of all this. Anger should be handled gently, the flames not fanned but gently deprived of fuel. With this approach, it soon passes.

So what does this mean?
- Parents with a child who is disabled have a right to grieve.
- Parents may deny, be angry and keep unexpectedly busy.
- Defences have a healing role. With time, talk and the help of good friends, soon these defences will no longer be needed.

What friends can do to help

When parents are having a tough time, it helps to have a good friend close by. You are there to provide a shoulder to cry on and an ear to listen.

When the baby is first born you are confused whether to send a card of congratulations, one of sympathy or none at all. Of course, you don't send one of sympathy, but why not a short letter to let them know you are thinking of them. One of my mums got a nice note which said simply, 'Love you—love your baby.' What more could you say?

When you visit, acknowledge that the baby has been born. If you pretend she doesn't exist, it's particularly hurtful. Remember that all parents differ in how much they want to talk. Please be sensitive in how you read the signs. Talk may upset you but it is probably therapeutic for the parents.

As you talk, watch your words and say nothing that could destabilise the situation. You may have your own views but don't use them to create doubts or dispute the diagnosis. Be particularly careful never to undermine the opinion and efforts of the professionals they trust.

Parents are allowed to deny. Friends and relatives must accept this but not collude with them to turn this denial into an immovable blockage to acceptance. When anger is about to blast off, stay cool, stay impartial and use this position of neutrality as a platform from which to gently hose the flames.

When you don't know what to do, get on with something of practical help, such as shopping, some cleaning, providing a meal or looking after the other children. Real friends listen and help.

When it comes to counselling, although you are not trained as a psychologist or social worker, you can still be very powerful. Loosen up, talk, listen, rake gently through the embers and give quiet reassurance.

Attitudes and sadness will change. It is a slow process, but time and good friends can work wonders.

CONCLUSION

Sadly, there will always be babies born with problems. Not only do these disable the child but they cause grief to the parents. Families mourn the perfect child they had hoped for, which is both a normal and a natural thing to do. Time is the great healer, and with good friends and relatives there for support, this will speed the process along.

26

Sudden Infant Death Syndrome (SIDS)

*S*udden *Infant Death Syndrome (SIDS) is a subject that all of us would prefer not to think about. It is a terrifying prospect that a healthy young child can die unexpectedly in his sleep and all without any warning or apparent cause. Unfortunately about one in 2000 of our babies dies in this way. In this chapter we will look at what happens, the theories about SIDS, how parents and siblings are affected, and what we can do to reduce the risk.*

What happens

A perfectly healthy baby is put down to sleep and without any apparent reason is later found to be dead. This is possible anytime in the first two years of life, but 90 per cent will occur in the first six months, with the greatest incidence between two and five months.

When I say 'perfectly healthy', in hindsight about 40 per cent of parents will describe some trivial difference, such as a slightly stuffy nose, but these changes are so minor at the time that they are not thought to be relevant. At later examination no infection, poison, abnormality or other possible cause can be found.

Although night-time is the usual time for death to occur, it can also happen during the day. It can happen after many hours of sleep or within five minutes of going down. There are no warning signs and no sounds of struggle or choking.

Occasionally a baby is discovered in the middle of an attack and is able to be resuscitated. The preferred term is an 'apparent life-threatening event' (ALTE) as its link with SIDS is unclear. Less than ten per cent of SIDS victims had a previous ALTE.

The cause

What causes SIDS? The simple answer is that no-one knows. Death is attributed to SIDS when there is no cause of death found in the child's medical history, autopsy or examination of the death scene. Theories come and theories go, and most of them turn out to be unlikely, however, one theory which has stood up well to the test of time is the apnoea–anoxia theory. Apnoea means stopping breathing, while anoxia refers to lack of oxygen.

The most consistent finding at post-mortems has been evidence of anoxia in the tissues of the body. It seems that in many of these babies, death was due to oxygen starvation and they just stopped breathing. Primitive breathing movements are first detected when the baby is still in the womb at about twenty weeks gestation. By 30 weeks they are regular but prone to periods of forgetfulness and failure. We know this is so with premature babies who often need to be reminded to breathe.

The apnoea theory suggests that the reliable regulation of respiration is slow to mature in certain babies, which will make them more prone to forget to breathe and in certain situations this can cause death. This idea has not been proven, but it certainly sounds most plausible. It would certainly explain the anoxic changes and why death is so quiet. It would also explain why it is slightly more common in premature babies whose regulating systems we know to be immature. It could account for the higher risk in those with colds and infections, as this would be the last straw that tipped the balance.

There are of course many other theories. One of the oldest was the idea of suffocation in a soft pillow or smothering when rolled on in the parents' bed, but this theory has not gained ground.

Starvation at night was another theory which sounded plausible for a while, until it was discovered that most of the babies affected still have milk in their stomachs. Could this milk then have been regurgitated and inhaled? Choking could certainly cause Baby to turn blue, but this is quite different from SIDS. It is a noisy experience anyway, which is quickly resolved by a good splutter.

A defect in the conduction of electrical messages round the heart is another possibility that the medical profession has considered. If the rhythm of the heart were to change dramatically, death by anoxia would follow. This has been well researched but though an interesting possibility, there appears to be little evidence to support it.

We know that these deaths are more common during the winter months. Could they therefore be attributable to cold and hypothermia? The answer again is no, since SIDS can occur in the best-heated houses. It is probably the increase in infections during winter which lifts these figures and overheating appears of greater concern than underheating.

At the time of writing, most researchers believe that an infant is for some reason created to be susceptible to SIDS, then sleep posture and other factors tip the balance.

THE BREAKTHROUGH

In the late eighties the statistics on SIDS were worrying. The risk had not changed over a long period and the progress of knowledge seemed stuck. Researchers were hard at work around the world, and the main breakthrough came when studies showed that incidence was lower when parents changed the popular, tummy-down sleeping posture to lie infants on their backs. This was unexpected as we used to believe that babies slept better tummy down and that it was safer, with less risk of reflux and choking. This was found to be wrong. Overheating also seems to play a part and care is now taken to reduce excessive clothes and wrapping. Reducing exposure to cigarette smoke also makes a difference.

It is uncertain why sleep posture is so important. It is possible that the face-down position reduces air to the nose and also decreases the usual heat loss from the face.

All around the world programs were launched to promote safe sleeping practices and the good news is that SIDS has dropped dramatically.

Safe sleeping recommendations
Sleep baby on his back
Baby can play on his tummy during 'up' time but must settle on his back to sleep. The baby is swaddled carefully and placed on his back for all naps and sleeps. This is the recommendation for all babies unless a medical reason leads your doctor to suggest otherwise.

We now know that reflux is *less* likely in babies who sleep on their back in spite of what we used to believe. This position keeps the airways clearer than face down and this is thought to reduce risk.

Face uncovered

Baby's head must be uncovered, so no hats in bed that might slip down over the nose or mouth. He is positioned at the foot of the cot to prevent him wriggling down under the covers. Swaddle him firmly, including arms and legs, for the first three months and leave his arms free some time after that. Make sure that the wrap does not cover his airways. Fabrics should be breathable (e.g. cotton) and blankets should not be too heavy or hot.

Safe sleep cot

Baby needs a safe cot with a safe mattress and safe bedding to make a safe sleeping place, night and day, when they are sleeping at Nanna's or when they are at day care.

Cots need to meet national safety standards for cots whether they are old or new and should carry a label that says so. Portable cots have a separate standard and should also be labelled. The mattress should be firm and fitted. Remove any quilts, pillows, lambskins and soft toys. In fact keep all toys away from their sleep place when they are small.

Don't smoke

Neither parent should smoke when the mother is pregnant. If one parent smokes, SIDS risk is doubled. If both smoke it is doubled again.

Smoke damages children's health and all children should be kept away from family and friends who smoke. Never allow anyone to smoke in the same room as your baby. No-one should smoke in a car with children of any age.

Sleeping in the same room

Research has shown a reduction of incidence of SIDS where Baby has slept in his own bed in the parents' room. This is recommended for six months or even a year.

Other suggestions

There are other suggestions for practices that may reduce the risk. We know that temperature is important and the room should be comfortable, neither too hot nor too cold. Clothes and blankets should not be too heavy or hot. The risk of SIDS used to be high in winter in cold regions. With sensible heating, good air circulation and appropriate bedclothes, risks have fallen greatly. Some have suggested that a dummy helps to reduce the risk but it is still unclear.

Would it help to have a monitor? There are monitors that register movement of respiration and when there is no movement an alarm goes off. It's not clear that they reduce the risk though and most organisations do not promote their use.

The improvement

Since the launch of the Reduce the Risk campaign in England and Wales in 1991, the incidence of SIDS has fallen by about 70%. Clearly this is much better but there is still much pain and sadness for the terribly unfortunate parents who have to deal with SIDS. This is only the start and research continues so that we can understand more and help parents to avoid ever confronting this awful event.

THE PARENTS

SIDS delivers an incredibly cruel blow to the parents. It is not just that their baby has died, but there is all the uncertainty and soul-searching that surrounds the event and which serves to deepen their grief.

There are some legal formalities that have to be gone through. The police are obliged to interview the parents and the law requires that a post-mortem examination be carried out and the coroner informed. This all happens extremely quickly so that the parents can be reassured that nothing amiss was to blame.

At the end of the enquiries the police, coroner and doctors are very sure that nothing more could have been done, but the parents still find it less easy to convince themselves of this. Their minds are full of 'if onlys'. If only we had gone in to check … If only we had given a midnight feed … If only the cot had been beside our bed … If only I had breast-fed longer … If only … If only …

'How could something like this have happened to us?' they ask. It seems hard to understand how this could strike one so innocent and perfect. Many will question life itself, wondering what there is left to believe in when events like this are allowed to happen.

Anger is always a normal response and this may be directed at family, friends, doctors, God or just life in general. Who wouldn't feel angry in a situation like this?

Grieving goes on for a long time and the parents need a lot of understanding and help. Most large cities have their SIDS support groups who always like to get involved early with every family. In counselling, the parents need the following reassurances:

- This was not caused by any form of inferior parenting.
- This could not have been avoided as babies still die despite following the recommendations.
- This has not been some subtle form of poisoning.
- This is not suffocation.
- This is not starvation.
- This is called SIDS, which descends out of the blue for no known reason and is certainly not the fault of the parents nor anyone else.

Brothers and sisters

I am often asked how to explain to an unhappy little child the idea that his brother or sister has died. Parents tell me that their child is disturbed, insecure and asks endless questions. They believe that the child cannot accept the death.

I am not sure that the parents have always got this quite right though. The child wonders what is going on, so quite innocently he asks copious questions. He is a bit confused and it's not easy to explain the intricacies of life and death to a three-year-old, when we often find them pretty hard to comprehend ourselves.

I feel that little children can accept almost anything as long as their parents are reasonably well adjusted. The questions, behaviours and clinginess are not of the child's making, they are symptoms of living in a stressed environment. Once parents are able to warm up and talk comfortably about it, the questions and clingy behaviour will evaporate.

Subsequent siblings often provoke anxiety in parents. Evidence has suggested that the risk of SIDS is not much higher than for the general population. They are often referred for sleep studies and monitoring may even be suggested.

CAN SIDS BE PREVENTED?

The short answer is yes, but to a limited degree. The trouble is that the onset is so symptom-free and silent that we are given no warning.

As mentioned, home monitors are available, but unless there is some major indication, such as a previous SIDS or ALTE, they are not usually advised. They may give some sense of security, but even they are not 100 per cent reliable and you do get frequent false alarms—and there is no evidence they prevent SIDS.

Some parents keep their little babies close by their bed at night. They then attempt to sleep with one ear switched on, trying to monitor the slightest grunt or change of respiratory rhythm. This can occasionally help prevent a death, but more often than not will only result in excessive wear and tear to nerves. This leaves all focus on the risk-reduction factors.

Minimising the risk of SIDS

These recommendations are currently promoted to reduce the risk of SIDS. Of these, sleep posture appears the most important. It must be emphasised that these are risk factors, they do not cause SIDS. By following these recommendations, we can minimise the risk, but cannot guarantee prevention.

- Sleep your baby on his back, not the tummy or the side, from birth.
- Sleep him with face uncovered (and no quilts, pillows, lamb's wool, bumpers or soft toys in the cot).
- Avoid exposing babies to tobacco smoke before birth and afterwards.
- Provide a safe sleeping environment (safe cot, safe mattress, safe bedding).
- Sleep Baby in his own safe sleeping environment next to the parents' bed for the first six to twelve months.

Working mothers

I ncreasingly, mothers return to the workforce when their children are small. The decision to work is not an easy one, even though it may well be necessary, and parents often feel considerable anxiety as the first day of work approaches. As with all new phases in family life, if we take a positive approach from day one, we can make sure everyone adjusts and thrives.

Can it work?

Studies that have followed the children of working mothers have not been able to show any long-term problems, emotional or otherwise, and my own experience of observing the relationships between working mothers and their children echoes that. There are two important provisions: the quality of day care is good and the quality of care given by parents in the mornings, evenings and weekends is good. By day the child receives nurturing and stimulation and that is then topped up by the parents during family time. This way I can only see that everyone is winning and no-one is missing out.

If Mum decides (and can afford) to stay home with the children that is also a valid decision. These early years flash past in what seems like the blink of an eye and once missed there are no re-runs.

From time to time a childcare pundit will grab headlines with an attack on working parents. While they have their moment in the spotlight the guilt for parents lasts well beyond the moment when they've thrown the newspaper in the recycling. And what good does this do? Guilt is unproductive. Parents need to save their emotional energy for positive and loving parenting.

If at all possible it is desirable to choose the moment you return to work carefully. I do worry when mums return to full-time work in those very early months after birth when she is still in the process of physical recovery. This is a stage of chronic tiredness and befuddled brains where there is already little enough energy for childcare let alone taking on extra work. That said, not everyone has a choice, as we will discuss below.

Often there is no option

Whether we like it or not there are a number of mums who just have to work. There are those who have invested such a large chunk of their lives in establishing a career that they cannot afford to see it lost. Then there are very many who must work out of pure economic necessity.

This is a period of change in how families support themselves and change can be stressful. Once it was straightforward. Men were breadwinners and women stayed at home with the children. Now a woman's financial role in the household is as great or greater than her partner's. Added to this are the higher lifestyle expectations created by this double income. We're used to travel and eating out, and it often takes two pay packets just to service a mortgage.

Then along comes Baby and we're down to half the money. Perhaps less if Mum was the higher earner. And if Dad's income is insecure there's even more pressure for Mum to get back into the workforce. Or it may be that a mother has worked hard to get to the top of her profession and just cannot afford an extended break without losing seniority and earning power. It is all very well to say that parents should plan to have children at the moment when they can afford them, but these days, with parents leaving it until later and later, we run the risk of getting too old to have children at all, and so there is a tension between the right moment financially and career-wise, and the right moment biologically.

The percentage of parents making it on their own is high. For mothers raising children alone there may be absolutely no option about when to return to work.

It's not always about money. Many mothers are simply not cut out to be 24-hour-a-day parents. After a few months at home with a much-loved infant, they feel trapped, isolated and depressingly unstimulated. With the return to work they rediscover their identity and with it their sanity. For them, work is no luxury, it is a necessity that is best for them and best for their children.

Many of these issues are central to a family's decisions. If there is an option to reduce the pressure to get back to work it may be worth a look at the budget. Sometimes temporary adjustments can be made that may buy a few more months at home with Baby, if that's what you feel is important. Perhaps the mortgage will take a bit longer to pay off. It won't matter in the long run and it may reduce pressure at a crucial moment. As well, many firms now offer flexible hours for returning mothers and this may help you to find a balance that suits you.

Full-time dads

Some dads are happy to take the full-time parenting role while Mum works, and this can be a wonderful opportunity for a father to play a greater than usual role in his children's lives while Mum rejoins the workforce.

It is interesting while we are talking about fathers to note that people rarely talk about 'working dads' or expect them to feel guilt about being in the workforce after they had children. That seems to be an anxiety we reserve for mothers.

A fair go for mothers!

I believe few fathers (bar those described above) have any idea of the amount of work and tiredness in motherhood. With working mums, they now have at least three jobs to do, that of mum and house manager as well as paid work, often only for half of a decent wage. If you think of it, there is not a union boss in the country that would accept these conditions for his members.

Relationships change when children arrive and when they do it's time to renegotiate the conditions. If Mum has three jobs then Dad needs to pitch in with the cooking, cleaning, washing and the smelly bits of childcare, not to mention the night shift with the baby. If Dad has managed to maintain his sport and social life through all the changes then Mum should be given a pass to get out and do what she used to enjoy, whether it's playing netball, surfing, painting or having a coffee with friends. This is the sort of stuff that keeps everyone sane.

A fair go for children!

After work you pick up excited little ones from care. Toddlers in particular are all revved up wanting to catch up on some fun, but parents are tired, have a meal to cook, a house to tidy and a bath to run. This split in roles makes working parents feel extremely guilty. What we need to do wherever possible is slow things down. Try to sit with them while they eat (or eat with them) and listen to their babble. Play games in the bath. Notice how they are communicating with you. It's more fun than thinking about the meeting you just left behind and children need this little burst of your attention if they haven't seen you all day. It can be difficult to switch gears, but it's more than worth it.

I learned the hard way how central this attention is to children when I was treating a child for sleep problems. A mother brought a toddler to me who was resisting settling for sleep every evening. By now I found it easy to fix sleep problems but no matter what I tried with this little boy, nothing worked. Eventually I had to take a step back and try to see what was going on in the child's life that made it so difficult for him to sleep properly. His mother was a busy, successful woman bringing up her son alone. After she picked him up from long day care it was a rush to feed, bath and try to put him to bed. I realised eventually that he didn't have a sleep problem; he just needed some more focused attention. Mum moved bedtime a little later and sat down with him in the evenings to eat and read or watch television. It didn't matter what they were doing, as long as they did it together. From then on he was fine at bedtime, and his mother was able to relax and enjoy her time with her little boy.

Childcare

There are a number of options. If available, grandparents, relatives or close friends are usually the best. If extended family are able and willing this is a natural choice. They love your child and traditionally children have always been looked after by a crowd of relatives beyond their parents.

This sort of care is often taken up by grandparents but it's worth noting that grandparents come in different styles. Some will almost bowl you over in their rush to pick up the baby. Others will offer babysitting services with specific provisions and others are still working themselves. Still others have retired but feel they have earned a little quiet time as a couple or simply to rest or travel.

When it comes to choosing childcare many parents don't have any choice; they have to accept anything they can get. If family is not available, the options range from crèches or long day care to family day care or a kind lady across the street. There is a shortage of quality care in some urban areas and quality usually comes with a price tag. This can make the difference to whether you return to work or not as some find it does not add up financially.

Try to choose somewhere that has consistent carers, as little children like to know that the same people will be there every day. When you first enter don't be fooled by the quality of the decor or the number of new Fisher Price toys on the shelf. What is important is how it feels. If you can feel the warmth then sign up, but if all you get is a feeling of cool indifference, keep on looking.

There are concrete things to check too. What is the level of staff training and the ration of staff to children? What are safety and hygiene standards like? There are minimum standards for all kinds of registered childcare including family day care. Make sure you know how payment works, whether there are fines for late pick-up and whether nappies and food are provided (and the quality and nutrition of the food). Make sure too that you know what government subsidies and rebates are available to help with the costs.

When children are sick this really taxes the working mother and unfortunately childcare tends to increase the number of bugs they catch, though it may help build immunity in the long term. Group carers don't want ill infants and, even if they did, mothers often feel guilty about leaving their children when they need them most. Most mothers manage by taking sick leave, but they worry that employers will view them as unhealthy and unreliable. If sick days can be shared between parents with the odd day of back-up from a helpful grandparent you should muddle through. On days when they seem a bit wobbly and you decide to take them to day care you'll need a back-up plan. If you can't get to them if necessary, who is the back-up? Do they have a car seat ready? As long as there's a plan, you can get on with your day without worrying too much.

Separation and anxiety

Be prepared! No matter how good the childcare may be, some children are going to protest wildly when left. This is not a reflection on either you or the centre, nor is it a sign of emotional disturbance in the child. This is a perfectly normal stage of child development.

Babies in the first six months separate well, but soon after that they start to get a real crush on Mum and close family members. When you leave them with someone else they will exhibit separation anxiety which will usually peak at about one year of age and wane gradually over the next two years.

Don't be surprised if you leave for work amid a flood of tears and return at pick-up time to find more tears. It might appear as though the crying has been non-stop, but that is very rarely the case. If you are at all worried, a quick telephone call from work will reassure you.

Make sure that in the first week you allow enough time to help settle your child in. Don't just drop her and run. Remember that all children are different. Some are as independent as Wonder Woman, while others are of the clinging vine variety. The truth of it is that most children are as happy as Larry in childcare once they've got used to it.

Conclusion

Be reassured. Science is on the side of the working mother, who must be encouraged to do what she feels is right for her and her family. These days, it's pretty much the norm. If you choose to be a full-time mother, I'm happy. If you choose to share your time between mothering and work, I commend and support you. If it can be managed, try not to rush back earlier than necessary, but I see no place or time for guilt. This is a balancing act that requires the support of a secure home, good day care and quality top-up time when everyone's back together.

With working parents, it's not the amount of time we spend together, but how we use that time that really matters.

Grandparents—a valuable natural resource

I t is amazing to witness the immense warmth and love that emanates from a grandparent holding their grandchild for the first time. If circumstances allow then the presence of grandparents can give a whole new meaning to family life. The older generation has brought up their own children and now has a chance to relive the joys and take a backseat with the worries and stresses. In this re-run they can love the baby as much as they like all day and then get to hand them back in the evening.

This chapter is about the benefits and joys of being a grandparent and welcoming your parents and in-laws into family life. It is also about keeping the peace when it seems as though things might boil over. With good will on all sides, there is no reason why the involvement of grandparents in a child's life cannot be an overwhelmingly positive experience. Parents can manage without grandparents, but most find life is so much better with them.

THE BENEFITS

If parents are the tightrope performers in the circus of life, then good grandparents must surely be the safety net. We don't expect them to do quite the same acrobatics as we are prepared to do, but they are always there to support us when we most need it.

Families tend to be a bit more scattered than they once were, which can lead to isolation. Or there may just be a lack of involvement in each other's lives that means you don't see each other much. When you are isolated, problems which normally might seem insignificant can be blown out of all proportion and become major hassles. Many of the childcare worries that I have witnessed would never exist if the parents had a sensible granny close by to provide advice and support.

In the case of a newborn baby, grandparents can be of great help. They can provide not just babysitting services for your other children and care for you when you become exhausted, but they are usually available for emergencies. The bugle sounds and the cavalry arrives in seconds flat. They can offer the fruits of a great deal of practical experience if you are willing to listen to them. They can also play a vital part in helping other children in the family adjust to the newcomer, by affording them the time that understandably the mother of a newborn doesn't have.

I believe that many of the older generation have a magic way with little children. Maybe it's because they approach life at a more sensible pace and view today's fashions with an experienced eye, having watched so many come and go. When it comes to making a fuss of the little one, grandparents are certainly top of the first division. They provide an attentive audience for long-winded toddlers, appear ever-interested and rarely pass judgement. Good grandparents are a child's confidantes, counsellors and personal therapists. They boost a child's self-confidence and make the child feel important when the parents are too busy to notice.

Some people may see their parents as being out of touch and old-fashioned, and not all your ideas will be exactly the same, but they do have the benefit of hindsight and perspective and are not so caught up in the daily worries of caring for a new baby. Hear them out, you might pick up something useful.

Not all grandparents are equal. Some do not want a hands–on role, some do but you'd rather they didn't. But leaving these aside, most grandparents are a wonderful help, particularly when a new child is born. They should be encouraged to become involved.

PARENTS AND GRANDPARENTS —KEEPING THE PEACE

It is up to grandparents to use the diplomacy and wisdom that befits their age, and up to parents to exercise restraint and learn not to prickle automatically when advice is given. Let's see how relationships might be improved in the four main areas of potential strife.

Interfering
Goodness knows what comedians would have done for a gag in days gone by if there had never been such a person as the mother-in-law!

Listen to them and the central theme is usually one of interfering. Admittedly it's very hard to stand by and watch your children making all the same mistakes you made 25 years earlier. The skill required is not to tell people what they should do but to influence and advise with great subtlety. I believe that most original ideas attributed to the famous and powerful were in fact seeded subtly into their minds by clever advisers. Everyone likes to think they have had the brainwaves and in this respect parents are no different. Instead of trying to enforce their ideas on someone else, the trick for grandparents is to drop hints that are sooner or later adopted as original thoughts, and pick your battles. Parents will be much more receptive if advice does not become an onslaught.

From the parents' point of view, advice should be taken in the spirit in which it is given. Accept it graciously. It is futile to fight about such things. Accept it with thanks. It's up to you whether you intend to act on it or not.

Taking over

When a new baby is born some grandparents march into the home, set up camp, declare a sort of martial law and start to tell the residents what they can and cannot do. Others arrive with offers of help that are very selective and not always too useful. They monopolise the baby, but are of no help when it comes to sharing the cooking, cleaning, shopping and other chores.

Grandparents must never take over. They may produce a very efficient interim government, but unless the parents are in charge from the start they will never gain the confidence to cope once the occupying forces have left. Grandparents who really want to help should be prepared to help in all areas, not just a few of the choice tasks.

Discipline

There are many ways to bring up children, the best way being the one that feels right and works for you. Little ones are quite capable of coping with different sets of rules in different venues.

What they can't take are squabbles, inconsistencies and disputes between their carers.

Parents and grandparents can spend a lot of time arguing about discipline. Parents, for example, may be strict, allow no food treats and expect impeccable manners. Grandparents, on the other hand, may consider this too tough on a young child and set up a crash course in overindulgence whenever they are in charge. The result? An unwinnable argument that alienates both sides.

Parents often tell me that they find it hard to discipline their children because all their good work is undone when the child goes to Nanna's. This doesn't really wash. As the parent you are the 95 per cent caregiver and as such have the ability to give 95 per cent of the discipline and example. You cannot blame the five per cent of time that the child spends with someone else for your failings.

My recommendation for peace is that when the child is with the grandparents, leave them in charge and accept the way they do things without criticism. The converse should also hold true and the grandparents should never criticise your way of handling the child either. Easy to write, I know, and perhaps not so easy to do, but please give it a try.

Upset relationships

Most family relationships are complex and delicate at the best of times. When a marriage is rock solid it can withstand a lot of outside interference, but when it is a bit shaky and the partners are a little insecure, then sparks can fly far more easily.

Take the visit of Grandma as an example. Dad now has two roles to play, husband to his wife and son to his mother. If Grandma tries to make demands on his time and repossess him without consideration for his other role, this is bound to cause an upset. If Grandma and Dad huddle in a corner and chat cosily together, this can raise the paranoia level in the excluded partner. Where Grandma becomes spokeswoman for her son and issues joint statements on the running of the home, this too is a sure recipe for unrest.

The secret for both parents and grandparents is to be tolerant, gentle and patient in equal doses. Grandparents should be careful to go out of their way to ensure they don't cause any conflict in a marriage. They may be unhappy about the way their daughter-in-law carries on, but should bite their tongues and say nothing. For a start it's none of their business, and secondly they're bound to start protracted conflict.

Parents, on the other hand, should learn to turn a deaf ear to comments that would have been best left unsaid. Be sure that any anger that you may display towards Grandma over her interference isn't your own insecurity and paranoia breaking through.

The rule for both sides is simply this: tread carefully lest you tread on each other.

CONCLUSION

As parents we must use our resources well and the richest and most under-utilised resource of all may be the loving grandparent. Treat them as a blessing and treat them well. Accept their help graciously and show you appreciate it. They love your children almost as much as you do, and what a blessing that can be in our busy lives.

Getting back
into shape

*T*he first thing to come to terms with when you are pregnant is that your body is going to change shape, which is not surprising considering the amazing job it's doing. The ligaments loosen in preparation for delivery, your size increases, and as it does, your insides move out of place to make room for your growing baby. Your body's response to diet and exercise is obviously different at this stage and it's important to listen to how you feel.

What you are going through is a temporary stage and it only takes about six weeks after birth before you can start getting back into exercise. Remember, though, it took nine months to get where you are, and it will take about that long again for everything to return to its position inside. Getting your full strength back is up to you but take it in little steps for safety and sanity.

In this chapter we look at fitness, fatness, stretches and sags, and see how best you can retain and maintain your shape.

WEIGHT AND DIET

Given the choice most mothers would lose all the weight they put on in pregnancy during the birth but it doesn't generally work like that. Putting on weight in pregnancy is normal and healthy within a certain range. The average weight gain during pregnancy is 12.4 kg

Healthy eating

Eat most:	Cereals, bread, vegetables, fruit.
Eat with moderation:	Lean meat, fish, low-fat milk, low-fat cheese, low-fat yoghurt, nuts.
Eat very little:	Raisins, fried foods, butter, margarine, cakes, sweets, honey, sugar, sweet drinks, cordials.

Here are some other useful points about diet which should help you:

- Fatty foods have twice the kilojoules of the sweetest sugary foods (i.e. fat makes you fatter than sugar).
- Breads, cereals and vegetables are all excellent and contain relatively low kilojoules as long as you don't add butter or sugar to them.
- Sweetened drinks can add lots of kilojoules to the diet. So watch out for sweetened cordials, milk and fruit drinks. A glass of orange juice contains about four oranges. Each orange may be low in kilojoules but take the four at one time and it starts to add up.
- Low-fat milk, cutting down (or out) butter and margarine, and changing from fried to steamed food will also make a big difference.
- Watch out for constant snacking as this is an efficient way to heap the weight on.
- All of us have different bodies which metabolise food in a different way. Some people will always stay thin however much they eat, while others have only to smell a chocolate eclair to pile on the kilograms. For those who put on weight easily, then healthy eating is for life. You may take it off but you need to make permanent changes to stay healthy, which is really true for all of us.
- Don't forget your calcium to prevent osteoporosis later in life.

but it varies according to pre-pregnancy weight with weight gains of up to 18 kg considered normal for underweight women.

Weight management is not the be-all and end-all. It's true that it is easier to avoid putting on extra kilos during pregnancy than it is trying to lose them after the event, but if you gain a little more than you thought you would, it's not the end of the world. Healthy eating and exercise will get you back on track when you are ready to get going again after the birth. It is only a temporary stage of your life.

The extreme tiredness most mums feel is due to the big changes in body and lifestyle. This doesn't really put anyone in the mindset for burning off kilojoules. Breast-feeding will cause weight loss in some mums, but for many the weight gain seems to continue. To achieve weight loss after the event, don't go on some spectacular fast, but rather be gentle with yourself, changing the balance of your diet and easing back into exercise after your six-week check-up.

EXERCISE

It's unrealistic to expect that a body that was way out of shape before conception will miraculously fall into shape after birth. In pregnancy the aim is for the fit to retain their fitness and the unfit to try and lift their game a bit. Pregnancy is not an illness; it's a challenging physical role. With a bit of care the post-pregnancy body can be as fit as the pre-pregnancy one.

Motherhood in itself can place great strain on the body. And isn't it ironic that when a woman is recovering from pregnancy and birth, she has to take on her most challenging physical role? There's plenty you can do about this though. The logic and the research are overwhelming: appropriate antenatal and postpartum exercise programs have a significant, positive impact on the wellbeing of mums—and their babies.

Take it easy

Society and the media put all sorts of pressures on women to get back into shape or become a 'yummy mummy'. But there are much better reasons for a little exercise—at a sensible pace. Some mums need to return to work and that requires the energy that comes with a return to fitness. And even if you're not returning to work, you've got a growing child to lug in and out of cars and strollers and you need a strong body to manage the extra strains. Gear your exercise program towards being able to cope with your new tasks, bearing in mind changes in posture and strength and the physical, mental and emotional demands of motherhood.

Your body—the changes and what to expect

When you're pregnant, extra weight on the skeleton, along with special hormones to make you flexible enough for birth, affect the stability of the hips, pelvis and spine. And as the baby grows and you grow bigger to fit her in, postural alignment changes. Late in pregnancy, some women appear to be leaning backwards as they try to offset the forward pull of their belly. Upper-back posture is affected as it compensates for the curve increase in the lower back. When you've had the baby, it takes a little while for all this to settle back down.

Getting started

In most hospitals a physiotherapist will get you started on basic recovery exercises which strengthen the stretched pelvic and abdominal muscles. Try and stick with these even if they're difficult at first. They'll soon get easier. On returning home, tiredness becomes such a part of life that the thought of expending any energy on exercise when it feels like you're running on empty can seem unthinkable. Nevertheless you should try and walk, and even swim when you're up to it, and give some thought to a gentle progressive exercise program. Once you get started you'll feel better for it straightaway, in part because you're out and about, which will give you a nice lift in mood.

- Before exercising—remember it took nine months for your body to stretch out, so don't expect it to snap back into shape as soon as your baby is born. Listen to your body and use the time to bond with your baby. Generally you can start exercising as soon as you feel capable of walking. Don't try too much too soon. Wait until after your six-week check-up and doctor's OK to begin a gentle program. Some women are ready straightaway, others later.

- The first phase of recovery is your body's physical, chemical and emotional return to its pre-pregnancy composition. This is when you can begin pelvic floor strengtheners.
- In the next phase you can begin slowly and increase gradually. Begin your program at a comfortable pace, keeping up the pelvic floor strengtheners. Weight training is valuable, particularly in the upper body, which is often neglected in women but helps with all the lifting, carrying and holding of your baby.
- Prams are great for walking or running.
- Join your local mothers group for peer support and even group exercise.

Breast-feeding and exercise

Research shows that exercise does not have an adverse effect on breast-feeding six to eight weeks postpartum. Breast-feeding straight after exercise though can result in lactic acid build-up in milk and screwed-up little noses. As such breast-feeding is encouraged before exercise—with mum's breasts being less engorged so more comfortable as well.

Breast shape

It is widely believed that breast-feeding damages the shape of your breasts. This is not true. Any damage that may occur takes place during pregnancy, not as a result of breast-feeding. That nine months of enlargement, when the breasts are being bombarded by hormones, stretches and alters the anatomy whether you breast-feed later or not. So be warned—if you've stocked up on canned milk in a bid to save that antenatal model figure, you may be in for a disappointment.

Just how much pregnancy affects the breasts varies in every mum. For most there will be no change whatsoever, while others may find that they waste away or even get bigger. All this is predestined by that great model-maker in the sky; however, with a bit of simple care you can do something to protect your interests.

For a start, stretching can be avoided by using a good supporting bra. A well-fitting one by day and a light one at night. Remember also that excessive fat deposits often land on the breasts so excess weight will cause more stretching.

Stretch marks on the skin of the breasts are another common complaint. Vitamin E cream, a good bra and sensible weight gain are your friends.

Posture

- Feeding—with feeding every few hours in the first months you'll need to find a safe and comfortable way to sit. Good feeding positions include the use of a good chair for back support, a footrest to take the stress off the back and increase circulation, and a nursing pillow to bring Baby up to you when she's tiny rather than you bending over to her.
- Holding—babies like to be held and many mums like to spend a lot of their day carrying their baby. You will have one side that feels more natural than the other but a lot of muscular imbalances can result if they're going to sit on one of your hips for the next one to two years. It is best to try and carry equally on both sides if you can, in the centre with both hands is ideal for posture (though not for freed hands!).
- Baby carrier—slings, backpacks, frontpacks and wraps are all great for soothing Baby and freeing mum's hands but can be tough on backs. Focus on bracing the core with shoulders back and down while you lift and carry. The weight of your baby can be very effective for shoulder blade retractions, lunges and squats (making sure baby is secure first).
- Pushing stroller—one size does not fit all! Make sure your stroller is tall enough so you can walk with good form (without bending to hold handles) with neutral strides (even when running). Try and practise tucking in your chin, retracting shoulders to push and leading with your chest, with wrists as neutral as you can. If there's more than one child in the stroller, swap their positions to even the load.

Stretch marks

Our skin is a flexible cover to our bodies that allows us to move easily and change shape without more than a few wrinkles developing. All this is due to the elastic fibres in the skin which allow the body all this flexibility. Each of us has a genetically predetermined tolerance to stretching of our skin and while some people can take great stretching, others seem to snap the elastic all too easily. When this happens it causes stretch marks, often found over the abdomen or breasts.

There's little more you can do about them than watch your diet and ensure that you wear the proper supporting garments. There are a great many creams and lotions advertised that claim to stop wrinkles and stretch marks. These feel good massaged into the skin and although they leave you all soft and sweet-smelling, I'm afraid they will do absolutely nothing about stopping your elastic snapping.

Skin pigmentation

Our skin contains lots of little pigment cells which turn brown as you lie sizzling on the beach. During pregnancy the body was running high in oestrogens and these stimulated the pigment cells to work overtime in certain places.

The most noticeable pigment occurs on the face, over the cheekbones and around the eyes. This is called 'the mask of pregnancy' and can look a little strange when it is severe. Of course it will fade and totally disappear sometime after the hormone levels go down.

If you wish to avoid this mask, during pregnancy, you should use a wide-brimmed sunhat and lots of suncream. Remember that in a sunny climate you don't have to lie around sunbathing to catch the sun, you can get it as easily out shopping or just going about your daily business.

PARENTS—SHAPING UP FOR THE FUTURE

The birth of a baby is a major landmark in the lives of all good parents. Landmarks such as these are good opportunities to take stock of your lifestyle and see how you can perhaps increase your general fitness, health, purpose and family strength.

Now is a good time for both parents to put the brakes on smoking and excessive drinking. Exercising should become a part of both parents' daily lives and both parties can share in a sensible diet.

Your aim should be to keep up with your children as they grow and become more active, and hopefully there will still be a bit of bounce left when the grandchildren arrive.

Relationships matter—most!

I n many aspects of our modern lives we have lost sight of what really matters. The worries of parenting seem all-encompassing at times. We may spend hours worrying over the big questions: How long should I breast-feed? Should I use Controlled Crying? Is it OK to go back to work now? However, all of our worries, important as they are at the time, pale into insignificance when we consider whether or not we have a stable, conflict-free home environment.

Today's harsh reality is that we live in a community where between one-quarter and one-third of all our children will be part of a single-parent family sometime before they finish school and many more live in unhappy, two-parent homes. Just think of the enormity of all that disruption which we parents have brought to a quarter or more of an entire generation of our children.

It's not separation or single parenthood that does the harm, it's the conflict. Don't fool yourself for a moment. Tension and conflict can never be hidden from children. They may not hear the raised voices but they are painfully aware of the coolness in the atmosphere. Children are ever so sensitive to parents' sulking, quarrels, messy break-ups and disrespect for each other.

I believe that happy families produce the happiest children. I think it is about time that those of us who work in childcare should lift our eyes from the small print and make a strong statement on what really matters. I make no apology for giving over this last and special chapter to relationships. If it's a child's emotional wellbeing you are interested in, this contains the most important message of the entire book.

Be realistic

We live a life of quite unrealistic expectations, forced on us from our earliest years by the media and the misrepresentations of many glossy magazines. We bust ourselves in our quest for the perfection they promote—the perfect whitewash, the perfectly balanced breakfast cereal, perfect sexual fulfilment and of course the perfect marriage.

In the world I inhabit there is little perfection. Life is a compromise where we give our best, try to be flexible and have to accept that nothing is as consistently good as it seems. Those whom we admire for having the perfect lifestyle are generally showing us their perfect public face.

We live in a world of easy outs. It's easy to slip in and out of many situations without any strong commitment to see them through. Easy outs may suit us adults but once we have children there's really no such thing. Everything must be worked out to the benefit of everyone, not just the adults.

In my more reflective moods I often wonder if arranged marriages work just as well as those that have been 'forged in love' because of the in-built commitment that goes with them. Partners in an arranged marriage enter it knowing exactly what the rules and expectations are, and, knowing where they stand, go at it with a strong determination to make it work.

My reflections may be a dream but the word 'commitment' is no dream. It is the mainstay of every successful relationship.

Strong relationships don't just happen

Successful relationships don't just happen. They need a commitment to make them work, not just today or tomorrow, but in the long term. They need to be maintained with care, especially while our children are with us.

The first flush of love fades for all of us as the pressures of day-to-day life edge us towards a more routine existence. We could all benefit from some marriage guidance. Not the sort given when the relationship has hit the rocks and is sinking, but some sound advice before we set out together. Perhaps it's guidelines not guidance that are needed.

Let's look at some sensible expectations of marriage and try to spot a few potential landmines. You will know these, as we all do in our hearts, but it has been useful for myself and the families in my care to remind ourselves every now and then.

Sensible expectations and common stumbling blocks

- No relationship is ever going to be 100 per cent smooth and happy all the time, no matter how good it may appear to those who look on from the outside.
- All relationships have bumpy patches, times of tension and crises. These are normal. Try to minimise these bumps. Stop for a minute. Ask yourself: Is this worth stressing about? If not, let it pass.
- It's the same when hurtful words are on the tip of our tongues. Those little comments that slip out so easily: 'I've just said that', 'You don't do anything', only take a second to say but can wound for a long time. Most of it does not need saying, or can be expressed more thoughtfully and politely.
- All of us who can communicate with our partners will have arguments and disputes. Unresolved conflict tends to fester. The old saying that 'The sun should not be allowed to set on an unresolved quarrel' still holds a lot of wisdom. Let's go for dispute settling, not point scoring. Let's be big enough to apologise when we are wrong and make it easy for others to apologise without loss of face.
- Beware of passive aggression, that poisonous wrecker of any relationship. Not one unpleasant word ever leaves the lips but such is the icy tone and manner that all in your path feel bitter, angry and hurt. Sulking, holding grudges and this non-verbal cold shoulder bring immense unhappiness to many families. Get on with life. It's too short to behave like this.
- Our moods can infect others. At the end of a hard day when the baby hasn't slept properly and Dad's tired from work and the journey home, tempers can flare. Ask your partner about their day. Allow a little space for transition. It can save the evening and the next few days.
- While money should not be allowed to rule our lives, it is important to recognise how financial stress can undermine many a good marriage. Babies are often conceived when parents can ill afford to live on just one income. When the

accounts cease to balance, tension rises and rifts develop. It's hard when things are tight, especially if there's insecurity in the economy, but perspective may help. This is probably as hard as it's going to get in a long, productive working life. This reduced income won't last forever—don't damage a relationship that could last you for life over a temporary dip in fortunes. It's such a waste.

- Having children rattles the equilibrium of the most stable relationship. Having a baby in an attempt to save a faltering marriage is rarely a success.
- Respect and equality are important in any worthwhile relationship. Where one partner behaves as though he or she brings more to the relationship in some way, there will never be warmth and stability.
- Remember that you got here together and the best way through it is together. However hard this sometimes is it will probably be harder alone.

Keeping relationships ALIVE

I was once chatting about life to a mature young teenager when he came out with a great piece of wisdom. 'Love,' he said, 'is something that you don't appreciate or know you have had until you have lost it.' This is so very true for most of us. In our busy lives, we tend to take our greatest possessions such as health and loving relationships for granted, much of the time never realising how important they are until they are going or have gone. The outside world sees our best face, with all our worst behaviour often reserved for those we care for most. It doesn't have to be like this, we can smarten up our act now! It may not be easy to get those we love to change, but if we make the first move, others often follow.

Relationships must not be allowed to get into a rut. They must be worked at to keep them fresh and alive. **Partners must be noticed, encouraged and appreciated.** Kind thoughts, acts and unexpected little gifts all keep richness in a relationship.

Time together is not a luxury, it is a necessity. Some couples find that once the children leave home, they have forgotten how to talk to each other.

Cuddles and all those non-verbal 'I love you's are great. The marriage vows talk of cherishing and we all need to be cherished. It may sound old-fashioned, but gosh, it keeps things alive.

I am not asking for a major change or miracles, just a gentle move to protect and strengthen what matters most to us and our children.

Conclusion

Let's finish this book fired up with a new commitment to those who matter most in our lives and never take them for granted. We should actively work to keep our relationships alive and strong. Let's give, let's forgive, let's notice and appreciate and above all, let's cherish. Love may not pay the bills, cook the meals or wash the nappies, but it sure helps our children.

Peace and happiness at home is the aim. We all have to ask ourselves every now and then: Do I listen? Do I value? Do I thank? How much would it cost us to find a moment to say, 'You put such warmth into my life' or 'I am so very lucky to have you and our babies'?

Appendices

DRUGS, LOTIONS AND POTIONS

A few of the most commonly used remedies

Pain/fever
- Paracetamol (Panadol and other brands)
- Ibuprofen (Nurofen and other brands)
- *Note:* aspirin is not recommended for children

Antibiotics
- Co-trimoxazole (Bactrim, Septrin and other brands)
- Amoxycillin (Amoxil and other brands)

Skin softeners
- Glycerine in sorbolene cream
- Bath oils
- Oatmeal in the bathwater (in a stocking—otherwise it's bathing in porridge)
- Numerous other trade-name products

Nappy area protection
- Zinc and castor-oil cream
- Trade-name products e.g. Amolin
- Vitamin E creams

Nappy rash
- Hydrozole cream (hydrocortisone with the antifungal Clotrimazole) requires prescription

Oral thrush (monilia)
- Nystatin oral drops

Cradle cap
- Olive oil or baby oil following bath—comb and shampoo after some hours
- Trade-name products

Colic preparations
- Infacol-C or other proprietary medicines

Gastro-enteritis
- Clear fluids e.g. diluted (one part to four parts water) lemonade, cola or cordial
- Gastrolyte electrolyte sachets when major
- *Note:* antibiotics and other medicines should not be used

Constipation
- Fruit juices—100 per cent
- Extra water
- Maltogen
- Coloxyl drops
- Glycerine suppositories

Oesophageal reflux
- Brand-name thickeners or cornflour to thicken feeds
- Mylanta (antacid)
- Gaviscon

HOW TO FOLD A NAPPY

The triangle (for small babies)

1. Fold the nappy in half to make a triangle.
2. Fold triangle in half again to make a smaller triangle.
3. Place the baby on the folded nappy and join the three corners with a pin, pinned inside the first fold. This will stop the pin sticking into the baby if it comes undone. Make sure the pin runs across the baby's tummy and not up and down as otherwise it could poke into the tummy.

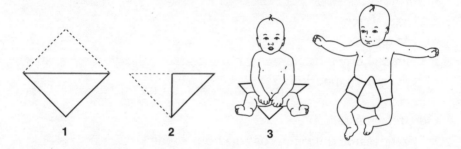

The triangle (for older babies)

1. Fold the nappy in half to make a triangle.
2. Fold down the top edge, adjusting the size to suit your baby.
3. Place the baby on the folded nappy and join the three corners with a pin.

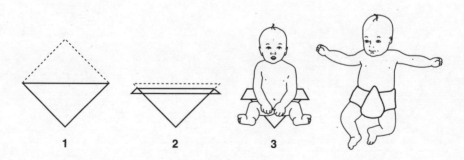

The rectangle (for small babies)

1. Fold the nappy in half to make a rectangle.
2. Fold the top third down for a girl and the bottom third up for a boy.
3. Place the baby on the folded nappy and join the corners on each side with a pin.

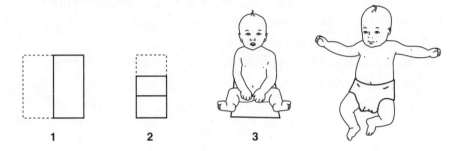

The kite

1. Spread out the nappy in a diamond shape.
2. Fold the left and right-hand corners into the middle.
3. Fold down the top corner and form an elongated triangle.
4. Take the bottom corner up to meet the top corner.
5. Place the baby on the folded nappy and join the corners of each side with a pin.

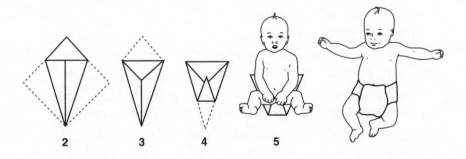

The neat nappy

1. Spread out the nappy in a diamond shape.
2. Fold up the bottom corner so that the corner is level with the other corners of the diamond.
3. Fold down the top corner so that it just crosses over the bottom corner.
4. Fold in the left corner so that the top edge is level with the top fold.
5. Fold the right corner in the same way.
6. Place the baby on the folded nappy and join the corners of each side with a pin.

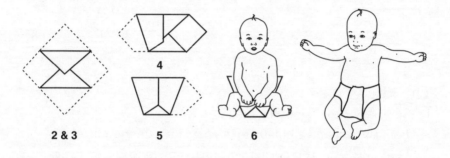

2 & 3   5   6

The Chinese nappy (good for origami experts)

1. Spread out the nappy in a square shape.
2. Fold in half from top to bottom to form a rectangle.
3. Fold in half again from right to left. There should now be two double folds along the top.
4. With your left hand, hold down the bottom three layers of the lower left-hand corner. With your right hand, pick up the fourth lower left-hand corner on the top layer and pull it across to the right as far as it will go. You should now have a square with a triangle attached.
5. Turn the nappy over so that the longest edge of the nappy is at the top.
6. Take the top two layers on the left and fold them over three times from left to right. Leave the triangle underneath. You

should now have a long thick rectangle in the middle and two triangles on either side.

7. Place the baby on the folded nappy with the centre rectangle between his legs. Fold the corners of the two triangles over the rectangle and join with a pin.

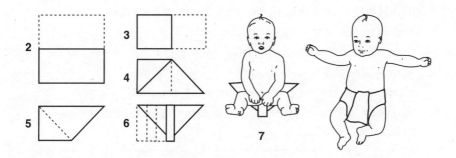

MILESTONES IN DEVELOPMENT

From birth until two years

Please, please remember that these are average levels; the range of normal is very wide.

At birth
- Tends to lie on her tummy with knees drawn up underneath.
- When lifted, her head flops forwards and backwards like a rag doll.
- Hands are usually closed, but not fisted tightly.
- Hands close involuntarily in the grasp reflex. (Place your finger in her palm and her hand clasps tightly onto it.)
- Startles at any loud sound.
- When asleep she is generally oblivious to disturbance around.
- When a face moves slowly across her line of vision, she may briefly focus and follow.
- No other social interaction obvious.
- Almost continuous drowsiness.
- May show a primitive type of walking reflex which soon disappears.

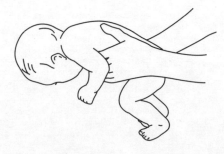

At six weeks
- Lies in a more relaxed, less flexed posture.
- When held in the prone position, her head raises slightly to be on the same plane as the rest of her body. But still has no head control when pulled forward to sit.
- The grasp reflex continues.

- Hands do not voluntarily hold objects.
- When her eyes meet yours, you are rewarded b~~y~~
- Responds to a comforting voice with facial movem~~en~~ altering the rhythm of breathing.
- Sleeps most of the time when not being fed or handled.

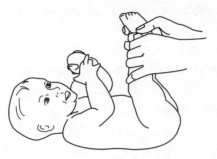

At three months
- Lies on tummy propped up on forearms with head up and looking around.
- When held upright her head has reasonable control.
- When pulled up to sit her head does not flop back.
- Grasp reflex disappears.
- Hands kept open most of the time.
- Will not pick up a toy but waves a rattle put in her hand aimlessly.
- Fascinated to watch and play with her own fingers.
- Quietens when hears an unexpected sound.
- Smiles when hears a friendly voice.
- Excited when sees food coming.
- Eyes are bright and alert.

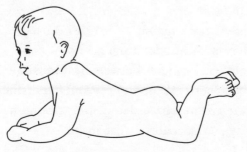

At six months

- Head control complete and strong.
- Just about able to sit alone.
- Can roll easily from front to back, but back to front is more difficult.
- Can take weight briefly when held upon feet.
- Can reach for a toy she wants.
- Toys moved from hand to hand.
- At this stage everything seems to end up in her mouth.
- Turns decisively to the side, to locate a noise.
- Laughs, squeals, chuckles.
- Very interested in everything around—visually insatiable.
- First teeth appear—ouch!
- Still separates easily and is friendly to complete strangers.

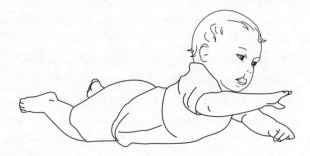

At nine months

- Can sit securely and lean forward to pick up a toy.
- Needs some help to get herself up to sit.
- Can hold onto furniture and pull herself up to stand.
- Makes walking movements when held standing.
- Squirms around floor.
- Some are now crawling, but at first this is backwards.
- Pokes at objects with index finger.
- Starts to hold small objects between thumb and index finger.
- Begins to be able to release things from hand, intentionally. Keenly interested in what is happening around her.
- Babbles away—'Dadadada … babababa …'

- Understands the word 'No!' and obeys it sometimes.
- Plays peekaboo.
- Starts to hold bottle by herself.
- Feeds herself with a biscuit and can now chew lumpy food.
- Less dribbling.
- Likes to be close to the family, fear of strangers usually strong.
- Starts to throw body back in protest— this, I am afraid, is the earliest start of toddlerhood.

At one year

- Walks around the furniture with competence.
- Many can now walk alone (range nine months to eighteen months).
- May walk around the floor on arms and feet—like a bear.
- Drops from walk to sit with a poorly controlled bump.
- Picks up small items with a good pincer grip (between index finger and thumb).
- Gives and takes objects to and from spectator.
- Puts small blocks into a container.
- Turfs toys out of cot to gain attention.
- Now has much tuneful babble.
- Usually says first two meaningful words.
- Turns when own name called.
- Starts to point to things she wants.
- Starts to show an interest in pictures.
- If a toy is hidden under a cup as she watches, she now knows where to look to find it.
- Dribbling usually stops except when teething or with a cold.
- Holds arms up to help dressing.

- Starts to discover that she has great power to wind up Mum.
- A proportion start to be fussy stubborn feeders.

At fifteen months
- Usually walks alone with a broad-based, high-stepping gait.
- Can crawl upstairs.
- Plays with wooden blocks. Enjoys posting them into an open container and may be able to pile two.
- Still enjoys throwing toys.
- Uses two to six words with meaning.
- Babbles away in what sounds like a foreign language.
- Some hold spoon and make a very messy attempt to feed.
- Much less mouthing and chewing of toys.
- Often starts to climb.
- Explores environment with no sense or idea of danger.
- Often frightened by loud noises.
- Usually clingy and likes to be close to familiar family.
- Now eats a cut-up version of the family dinner.
- Some start to show a dislike of wet nappies.
- May be pretty acrobatic when you attempt to change nappy.
- Starts to lose puppy fat, legs lengthen and muscles appear.

At eighteen months

- Walks well, with feet close together and some flow of movement in her arms.
- Runs.
- Throws a ball without overbalancing.
- Builds a tower of three wooden blocks.
- Holds a pen like a dagger and scribbles.
- First signs of hand dominance may start to appear.
- Uses between six and twenty appropriate words.
- Understands many more words than she can say.
- Points to four body parts on demand.
- Points to named items in a picture book.
- Starts to enjoy nursery rhymes.
- Demands what she wants by pointing.
- Extremely impatient.
- Doesn't quite know what she wants but must have it immediately.
- Kicks off shoes and socks.
- Likes to play at moving objects in and out of a container.
- Pushes wheeled toys around.
- Explores, climbs and gets into mischief.
- Usually clingy and likes to be close to family.
- Starts to imitate household tasks like brushing the floor.
- A few start to toilet-train.

At two years

- Holds on and walks upstairs quite reliably.
- Comes down again with difficulty.
- Kicks a ball without overbalancing.
- Rides along on a push car (no pedals).
- Turns the pages of a book.
- Can do a simple three-separate-piece puzzle.
- Builds tower of six to seven blocks.
- Can do circular scribble and copy a vertical line.
- Talks non-stop.
- Constantly asks questions.
- Refers to self by name.
- Uses words 'I', 'me' and 'you'.
- Puts two words together, usually 'me want' or 'don't want'.
- Plays beside, not with, other children.
- No idea of sharing, turns or rules.
- A very little sense is now appearing.
- Start of pretend/imaginative play.
- Toilet-training usually underway by day.
- For half, behaviour is not bad. For the rest—welcome to the terrible twos.

TEETH

Babies have twenty teeth. They appear as follows:

Teeth	Age
Lower central incisors	6-10 months
Upper central incisors	7-10 months
Upper lateral incisors	8-10 months
Lower lateral incisors	12-18 months
First molar	12-18 months
Canine	16-20 months
Second molar	20-30 months

Permanent teeth

The first permanent teeth appear at six years of age and the last by the age of twenty with the arrival of the third molars (wisdom teeth).

The benefits of fluoride

Fluoride is extremely beneficial in the care of teeth. It reduces cavities by about half and is considered safe.

Most of our water supplies contain a small amount of added fluoride. If the water is from a tank or other unfluoridated source, parents may add fluoride, obtained from the dentist. After the age of six months a small amount is dissolved in the fluids for the day. The usual dose is ten drops a litre. Your dentist will advise what's appropriate for your area.

Care of the teeth

It might seem strange, but you should start to think about the care of the teeth before they arrive.

Here are some important points to remember:

• Avoid putting very sweet drinks in the bottle, e.g. some of the high-vitamin C, 'unhealthy-health' drinks.

- Don't allow a toddler to suck on a bottle of milk or juice all night.
- Try to establish a diet with variety—one that is not too sweet.
- Remember 'health foods' such as honey, glucose and sultanas rot teeth just as effectively as chocolate.
- Apples, cheese and such snacks are reasonably kind to teeth, but avoid raw carrot—it's a choking risk.
- Try to introduce a soft, small toothbrush at about one year. It will need to be guided around the mouth for at least another seven years or so. And use flossettes after age two.
- Introduce the toothbrush just after a meal or when playing in the bath. At first, a bit of movement around the mouth is all one can expect.
- At first use no toothpaste, then add a little amount of low-fluoride children's paste.
- It's good to get preschoolers used to visiting the dentist from age two onwards. It may cost you money but it's a good long-term investment.
- I have no objection to thumb-sucking or using a pacifier in the early years, preferably only until two with a limit of three to four years.
- Remember for the future: if a tooth is accidentally knocked out, keep the tooth, soak it in a little milk and go straight to your dentist. Often these can be re-implanted.

IMMUNISATION FOR BABIES

Diphtheria, haemophilus influenzae type B (Hib), hepatitis B, measles, polio, tetanus and whooping cough are unpleasant illnesses that can kill. In recent years new vaccines have been added to reduce deaths and severe illness with pneumococcus and meningococcus (both are bacterial infections) and rotavirus and chickenpox (viral infections). There is no need for deaths from these illnesses if we take the trouble to have our children vaccinated.

Before vaccines were available, a great number of British children died from infectious diseases. Babies continue to die from whooping cough because community vaccination levels are still too low. This means very young babies can be infected before they can be vaccinated themselves. Other vaccine-preventable diseases will return, in large numbers, if vaccination rates are not kept up.

Recommended vaccines are effective, though they occasionally have side effects. These are usually no more than a minor inconvenience. Vaccine-related permanent harm or death is very rare, and thousands of times less likely than death from the actual diseases themselves.

With all the valuable and effective vaccines now used, the immunisation schedule has become quite complex. Variations are also made for particular circumstances—your doctor or early childhood clinic will be up to date with all of it. If you want to read more, go to www.immunise.health.gov.au

Diphtheria

These nasty bacteria set up a focus of infection in the throat which sometimes causes a sudden obstruction to breathing which can be fatal. The infection also releases poisons that can cause paralysis or heart failure. Luckily it has become very rare since immunisation has been widely available. Diphtheria vaccine is given by injection. It is well tried and very safe.

German measles (rubella)

Not as unpleasant or dangerous as ordinary measles, rubella is usually a minor illness. The exception is that when a pregnant woman contracts rubella, the unborn baby is likely to suffer serious, permanent heart, brain or liver disease as well as deafness. The only way to prevent this serious problem is for all children to be immunised against rubella, via the triple vaccine (measles, mumps and rubella).

Haemophilus influenzae type B (Hib)

Hib is a bacteria and, despite its name, has nothing to do with 'flu'— which is a short name for viral influenza.

Before use of the Hib vaccine, Hib infection was widespread in the community, most children becoming immune from mild infection. However, Hib was the most common cause of bacterial meningitis, and caused many other serious, often life-threatening infections. Hib will again become a major cause of disease if all infants are not vaccinated.

Hepatitis B

Hep B is a viral infection, which causes inflammation of the liver, and is very infectious, very common and can also be fatal. Most commonly passed through blood contact, open sores and wounds, the sharing of needles between drug addicts, or even normal sexual activity can transmit this infection. It can also be passed from an infected mother to her baby, usually at the time of birth. However, there is reliable immunisation and it is recommended for all infants. Babies born to an infected mother should, in addition, be given hep B immunoglobin within twelve hours of birth.

Measles

This is just about the most infective of all childhood illnesses. Without vaccination almost everyone will catch it. Measles is more than a rash; it causes children to have high fever, be very sick, have a nasty cough, sore eyes and feel very sorry for themselves. In the Third World, where nutrition is poor, it is a much-feared illness. Children who contract measles often become extremely sick and occasionally there are long-term serious complications.

Babies are born with high antibody levels, which have come across the placenta from Mum. These gradually wane in the first year but give sufficient protection for vaccination not to be advised until after the first birthday. Vaccination is by simple injection and usually without side effects. A few children (ten to fifteen per cent) will suffer with a slight fever about five days after the injection when the vaccine takes hold. Some of these may even have a mild measles-like rash. In these instances, it's best to give paracetamol.

Meningococcus
This bacterial germ can cause meningitis and a rapidly progressive, often fatal bloodstream infection, often incorrectly referred to as 'meningococcal'. The vaccine is not effective against all types of the germ, but will prevent at least 50 per cent of meningococcal disease.

Mumps
For many years there was debate whether to add mumps vaccine to the current immunisation protocol. It was argued that this was a relatively mild condition and not worth the expense of routine vaccination.

Following successful programs in the United States and Canada, it is now believed to be worthwhile and is given at the same time as the measles and rubella vaccination. Also given by injection, it is simple and safe.

Pneumococcus
This is one of the causes of severe pneumonia and meningitis in children. The vaccine protects against only some varieties of the germ but it can prevent serious illness and death in enough infants to make it worthwhile.

Polio

This viral disease often causes permanent paralysis. It is still common in many overseas countries that experience the devastating problems that were seen here before a safe vaccine was available. The 'oral' polio vaccine has been replaced by an injection given at two, four and six months, and four years.

Rotavirus

This is a highly infectious cause of diarrhoea and often also fever. Severe cases requiring hospital treatment are rare in the UK. Children in the UK are not routinely vaccinated against rotavirus.

Tetanus

Tetanus, or lockjaw, comes from an organism that is frequently found in the dirt of our streets, paddocks and gardens. It enters the body through a dirty wound, later to release poisons that cause severe spasms and eventual respiratory failure with a high risk of death. Every child should be vaccinated. A booster injection should be given at fifteen to nineteen years.

Varicella (chickenpox)

This is often thought of as inevitable in childhood, an irritating illness but not too bad. But some children become extremely unwell, and three in 100,000 people with chickenpox die from it. If a mother suffers chickenpox around the time of delivery of a new baby, that baby has a high risk of severe illness and death.

Whooping cough

This illness is very unpleasant although usually not fatal. Those at greatest risk are little babies. Over half of babies under one year of age will need treatment in hospital for whooping cough. It is much less serious in older children.

The Chinese talk of whooping cough as 'the cough of 100 days'. The child gets into a spasm of coughing, loses breath, whoops as he tries to get air into the lungs, spasms again and often ends up by vomiting. It is all extremely distressing for the child, as well as for the parent watching.

In the 1950s there were more than 100,000 reported cases of whooping cough in England and Wales. However, the number of confirmed cases of whooping cough is now very low, due to the introduction of an immunisation programme during the 1950s and, in 2001, the introduction of a pre-school booster jab.

The vaccination can have a mild reaction that causes fever and mild irritability. This is usually nothing to worry about and will be put right with a small dose of paracetamol. Although the number of cases of whooping cough have fallen dramatically since immunisation began, it is still possible for children to get it. Therefore immunisation is vital. Children in the UK are currently vaccinated against whooping cough at two, three and four months, and again before they start school, at between three and five years of age.

Whooping cough is very infectious so if your child is suffering from it keep them away from others until they have completed a course of antibiotics – or, if your GP hasn't prescribed antibiotics, until your child has had the cough for three weeks. Even if the cough continues for longer than three weeks it is unlikely it will still be infectious.

Common questions

Q. What medicine do you give for a child with fever following immunisation?

A. Paracetamol.

Q. If the baby has a cold or flu, with a fever, should he be immunised?

A. No, not until he has recovered.

Q. If you believe there has been a major illness or reaction to a particular vaccine, is further immunisation to be given?

A. Any severe reactions must be reported to your family doctor. If these fit certain criteria, it is possible the doctor may recommend omitting one part of the vaccine.

Q. When do premature babies get their vaccines?
A. If they are healthy, immunisation should start at the same time after birth as it would for any other child.

Q. If I miss one vaccine do I need to start all over again?
A. No! You need no extra shots. Start where you left off and continue at the original spacing.

Q. If the vaccines are commenced at an older age than suggested, do you use the same spacing?
A. Yes.

Q. If a young child has a bad cut or is bitten by a dog, does he need a tetanus shot?
A. Not if he has had a tetanus immunisation in the previous two years. Check with your doctor.

Q. If a child has been sick with measles in his first year of life, does this mean that no measles vaccine should be given?
A. Studies show that most rashes diagnosed as measles in the first year of life are, in fact, misdiagnoses. There is no harm giving the vaccine to a child who has already had measles, so if in doubt, please vaccinate.

Q. What ever happened to smallpox and tuberculosis vaccinations that many of us were given as children?
A. A worldwide vaccination program for smallpox seems to have eradicated the disease and so it is no longer needed. Tuberculosis vaccine is only given in special instances where there is a risk of contracting TB from someone close to your family who is known to have the condition.

Q. If a child is allergic to eggs, should the measles vaccine (which is egg cultured) be given?
A. Most doctors would now say yes, but with care.

NHS ROUTINE IMMUNISATION SCHEDULE
....

For more information visit www.immunisation.nhs.uk

Age	Diseases immunised against
Two months	Diphtheria, tetanus, pertussis, polio and Haemophilus influenzae type b (Hib) Pneumococcal infection
Three months	Diphtheria, tetanus, pertussis, polio and Haemophilus influenzae type b (Hib) Meningitis C (meningococcal group C)
Four months	Diphtheria, tetanus, pertussis, polio and Haemophilus influenzae type b (Hib) Meningitis C (meningococcal group C) Pneumococcal infection
Around 12 months	Haemophilus influenzae type b (Hib) Meningitis C (meningococcal group C)
Around 13 months	Measles, mumps and rubella (German measles) Pneumococcal infection
Three years and four months or soon after	Diphtheria, tetanus, pertussis and polio Measles, mumps and rubella

OLDER MOTHERS—SPECIAL PROBLEMS

Today there is a move towards later pregnancy in many women. Careers seem to take up the twenties then babies arrive in the mid to late thirties. With this trend have come special concerns over birth defects, lack of energy to cope and the difficulty of adapting to such a drastic change in one's life when entrenched in one's ways.

Birth defects—the risks

Probably the ideal time for conception is in the years between eighteen and 26. These will be the times of greatest physical fitness and conceiving health. As the years move on, things start to get more difficult, but having little babies can still be very safe and satisfying right up to the forties.

The great fear of the older mum is having a baby with Down syndrome. The risk of any mother giving birth to a live born Down syndrome baby is about one in 600 or 700. Note the words 'live born'. Most major abnormalities are lost early on through miscarriage, with Nature policing pregnancy and stopping many abnormal foetuses from continuing. Even between sixteen weeks and 40 weeks gestation, there is a natural loss of 30 per cent of all those with Down syndrome.

Figures taken from amniocentesis results at sixteen weeks are therefore 30 per cent greater than live birth figures.

These figures are a bit alarming, but the risks can be removed if prenatal diagnosis is accepted and its recommendations are prepared to be acted on.

Non-invasive first-trimester testing is available to mothers of all ages. This testing is predictive not diagnostic. There are two parts to first-trimester testing. An ultrasound is done between ten and thirteen weeks to measure the amount of fluid beneath the skin at the back of the baby's neck. Increased fluid tends to be present with chromosomal disorders. This testing is called nuchal translucency ultrasound. Then blood is taken to test for levels of proteins produced by the placenta.

The results of the nuchal translucency and the blood tests are combined with maternal age and gestational age and entered into a computer, and the risks of Down syndrome and chromosomal abnormality assessed. If the risk exceeds one in 300 then invasive testing (chorionic villus sampling or amniocentesis) is offered. This combination of testing is about 90 per cent accurate.

Mothers who are 37 years or over (preferably 35 and over) are recommended to have either the chorionic villus sampling test or amniocentesis, either of which will diagnose Down syndrome with accuracy.

Having excluded the possibility of Down syndrome, the risk for these mothers is now equal to that carried by any mother of a younger age.

Remember that medical science is able to exclude some specific defects (e.g. Down syndrome and spina bifida), but no test or investigation can ever guarantee that an unborn baby will be completely normal. Nothing in life is that certain.

Trisomy 21 (Down syndrome) risk by maternal age and gestation (1/n)				
Maternal age (years)	Gestational age (weeks)			
	12	16	20	40
20	1068	1200	1295	1527
25	946	1062	1147	1352
30	626	703	759	895
35	249	280	302	356
40	68	76	82	97

Source: Snijders, RJ, Sundberg, K, Holzgreve, W, Henry, G & Nicolaides, KH, 'Maternal age—and gestation-specific risk for trisomy 21', *Ultrasound in Obstetrics & Gynecology*, 13(3): 167–70, March 1999, 99220401.

Maternal risk for chromosomal disorders					
Maternal age (years)	Risk of Down syndrome	Risk of all chromosome disorders	Maternal age (years)	Risk of Down syndrome	Risk of all chromosome disorders
20	1:1923	1:526	38	1:177	1:105
21	1:1695	1:526	39	1:139	1:80
22	1:1538	1:500	40	1:109	1:63
23	1:1408	1:500	41	1:85	1:48
24	1:1299	1:476	42	1:67	1:39
26	1:1124	1:476	43	1:53	1:31
28	1:990	1:435	44	1:41	1:24
30	1:885	1:384	45	1:32	1:18
32	1:725	1:384	46	1:25	1:15
34	1:465	1:243	47	1:20	1:11
35	1:365	1:178	48	1:16	1:8
36	1:287	1:149	49	1:12	1:7
37	1:225	1:123			

Source: Benzie, RJ, Toronto Hospital, Canada.

WEIGHT FROM BIRTH TO TODDLER

Weight in kg from birth to 2 years—boys (girls)						
Age (months)	Average weight (kg)		Upper average weight (3 % will be heavier) (97 % will be lighter)		Lower average weight (3 % will be lighter) (97 % will be heavier)	
0	3.3	(3.2)	4.2	(3.9)	2.5	(2.3)
1	4.3	(4.0)	5.6	(5.0)	3.0	(2.9)
2	5.2	(4.7)	6.7	(6.0)	3.6	(3.4)
3	6.0	(5.4)	7.7	(6.9)	4.2	(4.0)
4	6.7	(6.0)	8.4	(7.6)	4.8	(4.6)
5	7.3	(6.7)	9.1	(8.3)	5.4	(5.1)
6	7.8	(7.2)	9.7	(8.9)	6.0	(5.6)
7	8.3	(7.7)	10.2	(9.5)	6.5	(6.0)
8	8.8	(8.2)	10.7	(10.0)	7.0	(6.4)
9	9.2	(8.6)	11.1	(10.4)	7.4	(6.7)
10	9.5	(8.9)	11.5	(10.8)	7.7	(7.0)
11	9.9	(9.2)	11.9	(11.2)	8.0	(7.3)
12	10.2	(9.5)	12.2	(11.5)	8.2	(7.6)
13	10.4	(9.8)	12.5	(11.8)	8.5	(7.8)
14	10.7	(10.0)	12.8	(12.0)	8.7	(8.0)
15	10.9	(10.2)	13.1	(12.3)	8.8	(8.1)
16	11.1	(10.4)	13.3	(12.5)	9.0	(8.3)
17	11.3	(10.6)	13.6	(12.7)	9.1	(8.5)
18	11.5	(10.8)	13.8	(13.0)	9.3	(8.6)
19	11.7	(11.0)	14.0	(13.2)	9.4	(8.8)
20	11.8	(11.2)	14.2	(13.4)	9.5	(8.9)
21	12.0	(11.4)	14.4	(13.6)	9.7	(9.1)
22	12.2	(11.5)	14.6	(13.9)	9.8	(9.3)
23	12.4	(11.7)	14.8	(14.1)	9.9	(9.4)
24	12.6	(11.9)	15.0	(14.3)	10.1	(9.6)

Source: World Health Organisation Standards.

Note: The ideal relationship of height and weight is to be in proportion; e.g. if the child is of low average weight, he should also be of low average height.

How to weigh a baby

You will find baby scales at hospitals and baby clinics. Scales can even be hired—see the Yellow Pages telephone book. At home, the easiest but less accurate method is to weigh yourself, then weigh yourself holding the baby. The difference will be the baby's weight.

Note: ★Recent studies show that there is generally a small difference in weight between breast-fed and bottle-fed babies, and this should be taken into account when reading tables.

★See 'Effects of infant feeding practice on weight gain from birth to 3 years', LJ Griffiths et al: http://adc.bmj.com/cgi/content/abstract/94/8/577

LENGTH FROM BIRTH TO TODDLER

Length in cm from birth to 2 years—boys (girls)						
Age (months)	Average length (cm)		Upper average length (3 % will be longer) (97 % will be shorter)		Lower average length (3 % will be shorter) (97 % will be longer)	
0	50.5	(49.9)	54.8	(53.9)	46.2	(45.8)
1	54.6	(53.5)	59.2	(57.9)	49.9	(49.2)
2	58.1	(56.8)	62.9	(61.3)	53.2	(52.2)
3	61.1	(59.5)	66.1	(64.2)	56.1	(54.9)
4	63.7	(62.0)	68.7	(66.8)	58.6	(57.2)
5	65.9	(64.1)	71.0	(69.0)	60.8	(59.2)
6	67.8	(65.9)	72.9	(70.9)	62.8	(61.0)
7	69.5	(67.6)	74.5	(72.6)	64.5	(62.5)
8	71.0	(69.1)	76.0	(74.2)	66.0	(64.0)
9	72.3	(70.4)	77.3	(75.6)	67.4	(65.3)
10	73.6	(71.8)	78.6	(77.0)	68.7	(66.6)
11	74.9	(73.1)	79.9	(78.3)	69.9	(67.8)
12	76.1	(74.3)	81.0	(79.6)	71.0	(69.0)
13	77.2	(75.5)	82.4	(80.9)	72.1	(70.1)
14	78.3	(76.7)	83.6	(82.1)	73.1	(71.2)
15	79.4	(77.8)	84.8	(83.3)	74.1	(72.2)
16	80.4	(78.9)	85.9	(84.5)	75.0	(71.2)
17	81.4	(79.9)	87.0	(85.6)	75.9	(74.2)
18	28.4	(80.9)	88.1	(86.7)	76.7	(75.1)
19	83.3	(81.9)	89.2	(87.8)	77.5	(76.1)
20	84.2	(82.9)	90.2	(88.8)	78.3	(77.0)
21	85.1	(83.8)	91.2	(89.8)	79.1	(77.8)
22	86.0	(84.7)	92.2	(90.8)	79.8	(78.7)
23	86.8	(85.6)	93.1	(91.7)	80.6	(79.5)
24	87.6	(86.5)	94.0	(92.6)	81.3	(80.3)

Source: World Health Organisation Standards.

Note: The ideal relationship of height and weight is to be in proportion; e.g. if the child is of low average height, she should also be of low average weight.

AVERAGE DIMENSIONS OF THE PREMATURE BABY

Length (cm)	Weight (g)
26 weeks (14 weeks early) 34 cm	700 g
28 weeks (12 weeks early) 37 cm	900 g
30 weeks (10 weeks early) 40 cm	1250 g
32 weeks (8 weeks early) 43 cm	1700 g
34 weeks (6 weeks early) 46 cm	2000 g
36 weeks (4 weeks early) 47.5 cm	2500 g
38 weeks (2 weeks early) 49 cm	3000 g
40 weeks (on time) 50 cm	3300 g

Normal pregnancy lasts 40 weeks from the last period. Babies of 26 or 27 weeks may survive.

MEASUREMENT
CONVERSION TABLES

Centimetres to inches—inches to centimetres
(inches expressed as decimals, i.e. inches and tenths of inches)

1 cm = 0.3937 inches   1 inch = 2.54 cm

cm	inches	cm	inches	cm	inches
40	15.75	57	22.4	74	29.1
41	16.15	58	22.8	75	29.5
42	16.5	59	23.2	76	29.9
43	16.9	60	23.6	77	30.3
44	17.3	61	24	78	30.7
45	17.7	62	24.4	79	31.1
46	18.1	63	24.8	80	31.5
47	18.5	64	25.2	81	31.8
48	18.9	65	25.5	82	32.2
49	19.25	66	25.9	83	32.6
50	19.65	67	26.3	84	33
51	20	68	26.7	85	33.4
52	20.4	69	27.1	86	33.8
53	20.8	70	27.5	87	34.2
54	21.2	71	27.9	88	34.6
55	21.6	72	28.2	89	35
56	22	73	28.6	90	35.4

Pounds/ounces to grams—grams to pounds/ounces

1 kg = 2.2 lb   1 lb = 0.45 kg

	5 lb	6 lb	7 lb	8 lb	9 lb	10 lb	11 lb	12 lb	13 lb
0 oz	2270	2720	3175	3630	4080	4535	4990	5445	5895
1 oz	2295	2750	3205	3655	4110	4565	5020	5470	5925
2 oz	2325	2780	3230	3685	4140	4595	5045	5500	5955
3 oz	2355	2805	3260	3715	4165	4620	5075	5530	5980
4 oz	2380	2835	3290	3740	4195	4650	5105	5555	6010
5 oz	2410	2865	3215	3770	4225	4680	5130	5585	6040
6 oz	2440	2890	3245	3800	4250	4705	5160	5515	6065
7 oz	2465	2920	3376	3825	4280	4735	5190	5640	6095
8 oz	2495	2950	3400	3855	4310	4765	5215	5670	6125
9 oz	2525	2975	3430	3885	4340	4790	5245	5700	6150
10 oz	2550	3005	3460	3910	4365	4820	5275	5730	6180
11 oz	2580	3035	3485	3940	4395	4850	5300	5755	6210
12 oz	2610	3060	3515	3970	4425	4875	5330	5790	6240
13 oz	2635	3090	3545	3995	4450	4905	5360	5810	6265
14 oz	2665	3120	3570	4025	4480	4935	5385	5840	6295
15 oz	2695	3145	3600	4055	4510	4960	5415	5870	6320

	14 lb	15 lb	16 lb	17 lb	18 lb	19 lb	20 lb	21 lb	22 lb
0 oz	6350	6805	7255	7710	8165	8620	9070	9525	9980
1 oz	6380	6830	7285	7740	8195	8645	9100	9555	10005
2 oz	6405	6860	7315	7770	8220	8675	9130	9580	10035
3 oz	6435	6890	7340	7795	8256	8705	9155	9610	10065
4 oz	6465	6915	7370	7825	8280	8730	9190	9640	10090
5 oz	6490	6945	7400	7850	8305	8760	9215	9665	10120
6 oz	6520	6975	7430	7880	8335	8790	9240	9695	10150
7 oz	6550	7000	7455	7910	8365	8815	9270	9725	10175
8 oz	6575	7030	7485	7940	8990	8845	9300	9750	10205
9 oz	6605	7060	7510	7965	8420	8875	9330	9780	10235
10 oz	6635	7085	7540	7995	8450	8900	9355	9810	10260
11 oz	6660	7115	7570	8025	8475	8930	9385	9835	10290
12 oz	6690	7145	7595	8056	8505	8960	9410	9865	10320
13 oz	6720	7170	7625	8080	8535	8985	9440	9895	10345
14 oz	6745	7200	7655	8110	8560	9015	9470	9920	10375
15 oz	6775	7230	7680	8135	8590	9045	9495	9950	10405

Temperatures	
°F	°C
96	35.6
97	36.1
98	36.7
99	37.2
100	37.8
101	38.3
102	38.9
103	39.4
104	40.0

Volumes of fluids
1 litre = 1.76 pints
1 pint = 0.57 litres
1000 cc = 1 litre
28.4 cc = 1 oz
20 oz = 1 pint

The normal body temperature is 98.4 °F or 37 °C; 104 °F or 40 °C is extremely high.

Index